LABYRINTH

An International Journal for Philosophy, Value Theory and Sociocultural Hermeneutics

Printed ISSN 2410-4817
Online ISSN 1561-8927

Vol. 24, No. 1, Summer 2022

Hans-Georg Gadamer (1900-2002) and the Impact of Hermeneutics

Editor-in-Chief:
Prof. Dr. Yvanka B. Raynova

Managing **Editor:**
Dr. Susanne Moser

Advisory Board:

Prof. Dr. Seyla Benhabib (Boston), Prof. Dr. Debra Bergoffen (Fairfax), Prof. Dr. Reinhold Esterbauer (Graz), Prof. Dr. Nancy Fraser (New York), Dr. Ludger Hagedorn (Vienna), Prof. Dr. Alison M. Jaggar (Boulder), Prof. Dr. François Laruelle (Paris), Prof. Dr. Hedwig Meyer Wilmes (Nijmegen), Prof. Dr. Herta Nagl-Docekal (Wien), Prof. Dr. Elit Nikolov (Sofia), Prof. Dr. Sonja Rinofner-Kreidl (Graz), Prof. Dr. Markus Riedenauer (Eichstätt), Prof. Dr. Hans-Walter Ruckenbauer (Graz), Prof. Dr. Antonio Russo (Trieste), Prof. Dr. Ronald E. San-toni (Granville), Prof. Dr. Anne-Françoise Schmid (Paris), Prof. Dr. Hans Rainer Sepp (Prague), Prof. Dr. Helmuth Vetter (Wien), Prof. Dr. Andrzej Wiercinski (Warsaw)

Axia Academic Publishers

Bibliographische Information der Deutschen Nationalbibliothek:
Die Deutsche Nationalbibliothek verzeichnet diese Publikation in der Deutschen
Nationalbibliographie, detaillierte bibliographische Daten sind im Internet unter
http://dnb.dnb.de aufrufbar.

*Die wissenschaftliche und redaktionelle Arbeit wurde von der Kulturabteilung
der Stadt Wien – Wissenschafts- und Forschungsförderung unterstützt.*

*Published with the support of the City of Vienna, Cultural Department –
Science and Research Promotion*

*Labyrinth: An International Journal for Philosophy, Value Theory and
Sociocultural Hermeneutics* is a serial publication of the Institut für Axiologische
Forschungen / Institute for Axiological Research, Vienna – www.iaf.ac.at
For more information, please visit the Journal's homepage:
www.labyrinth.axiapublishers.com

ISSN 2410-4817 / ISBN 978-3-903068-36-0

www.axiapublishers.com

LABYRINTH, Vol. 24, No. 1, Summer 2022

HANS-GEORG GADAMER (1900-2002) AND THE IMPACT OF HERMENEUTICS (Part 1)

Table of Contents

READINGS AND INTERPRETATIONS

EDITORIAL

GADAMERS PHILOSOPHISCHE HERMENEUTIK: EINFLÜSSE, WIRKUNGEN, DEBATTEN

Yvanka B. Raynova (Sofia/Wien)

Gadamer's philosophical hermeneutics: influences, effects, debates

(Editorial)

Abstract

At a time when narrow scientific and philosophical specialization dominates our academic landscape and by which respective competence is also measured, a thinking that unfolds in broad ways is always viewed with some suspicion. This, however, is not the case of Gadamer's philosophical hermeneutics. Even though it has triggered various critiques and controversial debates, e.g., on the part of Habermas, Derrida, Ricoeur and others, Gadamer's influence and impact is still present today in the most diverse fields of philosophy and the humanities. The editorial takes up some of these debates and shows their continuing effects on contemporary philosophy and their importance for the sociocultural hermeneutics of any shape.

Keywords: Hans-Georg Gadamer, Hermeneutics, Contemporary Philosophy, Critical Theory, Deconstruction

Man hat schon seit jeher bemängelt, dass die Philosophie keine eindeutigen Resultate liefert, dass die Philosophierenden nur streiten und sich selten einig sind, sodass man schon aus diesem Grund bezweifeln könne, ob die Philosophie eine Wissenschaft sei und überhaupt einen Platz unter den Wissenschaften habe (siehe Brentano 1929, 92; vgl. Raynova 2017, 7-10). Doch im Gegensatz zur wissenschaftlichen Einigkeit bezüglich messbarer eindeutiger Resultate oder gar einer genialen, bahnbrechenden Erfindung, an der man die Größe eines Vertreters der exakten Wissenschaften zu bestimmen vermag, scheint es in der Philosophie gerade das Umgekehrte zu sein: Die Größe eines Philosophen oder einer Philosophin zeigt sich durch die strittigen Fragen und die Diskussionen, die er/sie ausgelöst hat und durch die verschiedenen Wege, die damit eröffnet wurden, sprich gerade durch die Nichteindeutigkeit und Nichtübereinstimmung der diesbezüglichen Meinungen. So zum Beispiel Descartes, dessen angeblich absolut gewisses, "unerschütterliches Fundament" – *cogito, ergo sum* – durch Debatten und Kritik erschüttert und anschließend zu einem "cogito fragile" (Ricoeur1950, 17; vgl. Raynova 2002) erklärt wurde. Und obwohl ich persönlich das Wort "groß" nicht besonders mag, weil es oft mit Zuschreibungen wie "X ist größer als Y" einhergeht, so als ob man alles in Meter und Zentimeter bestimmen könnte, gibt es wohl kaum Zweifel darüber, dass Gadamer zu den bedeutendsten Figuren der Philosophie des 20 Jahrhunderts zählt. In einer Festschrift zu seinem 100. Geburtstag mit Beiträgen von namenhaften Philosophen und Philosophinnen und dem aussagekräftigen Titel *Gadamer's Century* (Malpas, Arnswald, Kertscher 2002) wird Gadamer unter anderem als "einer der einflussreichsten Philosophen der deutschen Gegenwartsphilosophie, vielleicht sogar der einflussreichste von allen", bezeichnet (Albert 2002, 15). In einer fast gleichnamigen Studie, die gerade erschienen ist, erläutert Jens Zimmermann:

> The twentieth century was Gadamer's century in the double sense that its socio-cultural developments shaped his life and thought, and that his hermeneutic philosophy, in turn, shaped that century's academic climate, an influence continuing unabated into the present. For example, Gadamer's influence is the reason that the term "hermeneutics" today refers to the conditions and structures of understanding in general rather than to exegetical methods. (Zimmermann 2022, 9)

An den Veröffentlichungen nach Gadamers Tod gemessen, lassen sich die philosophischen Bereiche seines Einflusses leicht feststellen –

von der Ontologie (Dahlstrom 2010, Chiurazzi 2021), über die Sprachphilosophie und die Ästhetik (Nielsen 2022, Hołda 2021, Sampson 2019) bis hin zur praktischen Philosophie, der Ethik und der Geschichtsphilosophie (Schönherr-Mann 2004, Odenstedt 2017), dient Gadamers Werk als Inspirationsquelle für weitere Untersuchungen und kritische Auseinandersetzungen. Auch außerhalb der Philosophie hat Gadamers Hermeneutik besondere Anerkennung gefunden, schon zu seiner Lebenszeit, und wird weiterhin in der Literaturtheorie, der Soziologie, der Geschichtswissenschaft, der Jurisprudenz und der Theologie rezipiert, um nur einige der sozial- und geisteswissenschaftlichen Disziplinen zu nennen (vgl. Malpas 2022). Dieser weitreichende Einfluss kann als Folge der "Breite" des Gadamersch'en Zugangs, sprich der "Universalität" der philosophischen Hermeneutik angesehen werden und steht in Gegensatz zu den szientistischen Strömungen der Gegenwartsphilosophie, die sich methodologisch nach dem Spezialwissen der schon erwähnten exakten Wissenschaften richten. Nicht, dass dieser Universalitätsanspruch oder auch andere grundlegende Positionen Gadamers von allen angenommen wurden, bzw. werden. Sie lösten diverse Kritiken aus und führten zu grundlegenden Debatten, so z.B. mit Betti, Hirsch, Habermas, Ricœur, Jauss, Derrida, welche die Gegenwartsphilosophie tiefgreifend geprägt haben. Und obwohl manche der Meinung sind, dass diese Debatten der Vergangenheit angehören und vorwiegend von "historischem Interesse" sind (Madison 2000, 463), scheint es, dass sie weiterhin die Philosophen und Philosophinnen beschäftigen, insbesondere die jungen, was aus einigen Beiträgen in den beiden Nummern von *Labyrinth* ersichtlich ist. Dies zeigt wiederum, dass in der Philosophie sowohl bezüglich den Fragestellungen und Lösungsansätzen, als auch deren Auswirkungen und "Wirkungsgeschichte" (Gadamer 1993, 34) kaum je etwas als endgültig abgeschlossen gelten kann. Oder anders gesagt, es zeigt wie (hermeneutische) Traditionen aufgenommen, weiterentwickelt, weitergegeben, weitertransportiert und erneut (um)interpretiert werden in einem quasi unendlichen Prozess.

Inwiefern das Interesse an Gadamers philosophischer Hermeneutik durch den Aufstieg des Poststrukturalismus, der Dekonstruktion, der Postmoderne und ähnlichen intellektuellen Bewegungen nicht in den Hintergrund gedrängt wurde, sondern umgekehrt, die wissenschaftliche Rezeption Gadamers in den letzten Jahrzehnten gestiegen ist, zeigt der soeben erschienene Sammelband *The Gadamerian Mind* (George, Van der Heiden 2022). Dieser Band, der bekannte Gadamerforscherinnen und -forscher zusammengebracht hat, dient nicht nur der Einführung in die Begrifflichkeit und Hauptthemen rund um Gadamers Werk, sondern versucht auch die Weiterentwicklungen der Hermeneutik auf den neuesten Stand hin zu untersuchen. Das Buch ist in dieser Hinsicht ein essentielles und zweifelsohne sehr wertvolles Nachschlagwerk[1].

Bevor ich zu den Beiträgen in den folgenden beiden *Labyrinth*-Nummern, die Gadamer gewidmet sind, komme, möchte ich die Zielsetzung und die Themenwahl genauer erläutern. Oder, besser gesagt, es ist mir ein besonderes Anliegen aufzuzeigen, wieso Hans-Georg Gadamers Hermeneutik für die Arbeit des Instituts für Axiologische Forschungen und insbesondere für *Labyrinth* so wichtig ist.

Als Zeitschrift des Instituts für Axiologische Forschungen, wurde *Labyrinth* 1999, nur ein paar Monate nach dem Institut selbst, gegründet. Die Idee war, die philosophische Werteforschung zu fördern, ohne diese auf die rein kognitiven und/oder emotiven Aspekte zu reduzieren, sondern auch die praktische Ebene miteinzubeziehen und somit eine Brücke zwischen Grundlagenforschung und angewandter Forschung zu schlagen. Dass der Wertbegriff einer der diffusesten ist und deshalb auch zu abstrusen und widersprüchlichen Auffassungen und Definitionen geführt hat, habe ich schon an diversen Stellen gezeigt (siehe Raynova 2015). Was uns am Institut deshalb besonders beschäftigt, ist die Art und

---

[1] Siehe dazu die Buchbesprechung von Vladimir Lazurca in *Phenomenological Review* (Lazurca 2022).

Weise wie Werte "geschmiedet", gedeutet und umgedeutet, bzw. gebraucht und missbraucht werden, wie sie sich in diversen Kontexten verändern, an Bedeutung gewinnen oder verlieren. Werte, verstanden in einem säkularen Kontext ganz allgemein als von Menschen erschaffene (und eben nicht von Gott gestiftete) Prinzipien oder Maßstäbe, entstehen, entwickeln sich und funktionieren in verschiedenen gesellschaftlichen und kulturellen Lebenswelten. Sie prägen sowohl Individuen und Generationen, die sich danach richten, abwenden oder dagegen wenden, wie auch die Gesellschaft selbst mit ihren Sitten und ihrer Kultur und werden von deren Entwicklung wiederum mitgeprägt. Um diese komplexen Interaktionen zu verstehen braucht man eine *soziokulturelle Hermeneutik*. Dies erklärt, zumindest auf eine konzise Weise, warum *Labyrinth* den Untertitel *An International Journal for Philosophy, Value Theory and Sociocultural Hermeneutics* trägt. Damit wird im allgemeinen die Bedeutung der hermeneutischen Denkrichtungen angedeutet. Es geht dabei natürlich nicht nur um die Hermeneutik von Gadamer, aber eben auch um seine Version, unter besonderer Berücksichtigung ihrer praxisbezogenen und axiologischen Aspekte.

Was für die soziokulturelle Hermeneutik, zumindest so wie ich sie verstehe, besonders von Gewicht ist, kann anhand der Gegenüberstellung von Marx und Heidegger verdeutlicht werden. Marx erklärte einst, in seiner berühmten elften These über Feuerbach, dass die Philosophen die Welt nur verschieden interpretiert hätten, es aber drauf ankomme sie zu verändern (MEW 3, 7). Diese These wurde von vielen zurückgewiesen, so z.B. von Heidegger, der den folgenden Einwand erhob:

> Man hat denn auch inzwischen von der Philosophie gefordert, daß sie sich nicht mehr damit begnüge, die Welt zu interpretieren und sich in abstrakten Spekulationen herumzutreiben, sondern daß es darauf ankomme, praktisch die Welt zu verändern. Allein, die so gedachte Weltveränderung verlangt zuvor, daß sich das Denken wandle, wie denn auch hinter der genannten Forderung bereits eine Veränderung des Denkens steht. (GA9, 446).

Auf den ersten Blick erscheinen die Positionen von Marx und Heidegger entgegengesetzt. Wer Marx genauer gelesen hat, weiß jedoch, dass für ihn eine Veränderung der Welt nicht ohne eine Veränderung des Bewusstseins möglich ist, da Herrschaft durch Religion und Ideologie legitimiert wird und wir deshalb auch die "Waffe der Kritik" brauchen. Noch mehr, die Revolution beginnt im Kopf des Philosophen, oder anders gesagt, die theoretische Emanzipation geht der sozialen, d.h. der politischen und ökonomischen, voraus und macht sie erst möglich (MEW 1, 385)[2].

Diese Gegenüberstellung hat eine gewisse Ähnlichkeit mit der Habermas-Gadamer Debatte. Habermas wirft Gadamer unter anderem einen linguistischen Idealismus vor, da das Sein und insbesondere Prozesse des gesellschaftlichen Seins uns nicht ausschließlich durch die Metainstitution der Sprache gegeben sind, daher auch nicht auf linguistische Strukturen reduziert werden können.

> Es hat einen guten Sinn, Sprache als eine Art Metainstitution aufzufassen, von der alle gesellschaftlichen Institutionen abhängen; denn soziales Handeln konstituiert sich allein in umgangssprachlicher Kommunikation. Aber diese Metainstitution der Sprache als Tradition ist offenbar ihrerseits abhängig von gesellschaftlichen Prozessen, die nicht in normativen Zusammenhängen aufgehen. Sprache ist auch ein Medium von Herrschaft und sozialer Macht. Sie dient der Legitimation von Beziehungen organisierter Gewalt. […] Dabei handelt es sich nicht um Täuschungen in einer Sprache, sondern um Täuschung mit Sprache als solcher. Die hermeneutische Erfahrung, die auf eine solche Abhängigkeit des symbolischen Zusammenhangs von faktischen Verhältnissen stößt, geht in Ideologiekritik über. (Habermas 1971, 52-53)

Die Auswirkungen dieser Diskussion haben sich bald als sehr produktiv erwiesen, insofern sich beide Proponenten gegenseitig beeinflusst haben. Gadamer stellte rückblickend fest:

---

[2] Erwähnenswert in diesem Zusammenhang ist das neulich erschienene Buch von Peter Trawny *Der frühe Marx und die Revolution* (Trawny 2018).

My studies since *Truth and Method* have [...] taken me in another quite different direction: into practical philosophy and the problems of the social sciences. The critical interest that Jürgen Habermas showed in my work during the 1960s itself gained critical significance for me and drew my interest into these areas. (Gadamer 1977, 55)[3]

Ich würde an dieser Stelle hinzufügen, dass die Habermas-Gadamer Debatte, auch wenn darüber schon viel geschrieben wurde, nicht nur von "historischem" Interesse ist. Sie spricht gerade diese komplexen Beziehungen von Denken, Sprache und Praxis an, die zentral für jede soziokulturelle Hermeneutik sind, unabhängig davon ob letztere sich als "kritisch", "radikal", "realistisch" oder wie auch immer bezeichnet.

*

In den folgenden beiden Nummern von *Labyrinth* werden Neulektüren von Gadamers Werk hinsichtlich seiner Wirkung, Rezeption und Anwendung vorgestellt.

In der ersten Nummer werden neben zentralen Themen der Gadamer'schen Hermeneutik und deren Verwendung zur Auslegung philosophischer Schriften die wenig bekannte Debatte zwischen Gadamer und Blumenberg, der kaum berücksichtigte zweite Teil der Auseinandersetzung zwischen Gadamer und Derrida sowie die dialogischen Modelle der Interpretation bei Gadamer und Davidson diskutiert.

Die zweite Nummer versucht die Aktualität von Gadamers philosophischer Hermeneutik und ihren Anwendungsmöglichkeiten konkreter zu

---

[3] An Gadamers Würdigung von Habermas sieht man, dass es bedeutenden Philosophen um die Sache selbst geht und nicht darum, um jeden Preis recht zu behalten. Deshalb muss ich hier anmerken, dass sich die Größe eines Philosophen oder einer Philosophin, die ich anfangs angesprochen habe, auch an Eigenschaften wie Bescheidenheit, wertschätzender Umgang und Anerkennung der Leistungen der Anderen messen lässt. Dass dies auf Gadamer zutrifft, sieht man aus dem Bericht von Riccardo Dottori: "I was most impressed by the figure of Gadamer himself, by his friendliness and his attentiveness in the discussions, [...] by his ability to follow other people's ideas as if he were always ready to learn something from them" (Dottori 2003, 3).

aufzuzeigen. In diesem Kontext werden auch die Versuche die Hermeneutik zu naturalisieren debattiert sowie die Relevanz der Hermeneutik für die politische Philosophie, die feministische Kritik und die Werteforschung untersucht.

Als Herausgeberin möchte ich mich bei allen Teilnehmerinnen und Teilnehmer für ihre Mitarbeit an dieser zweiteiligen Nummer zu Ehren von Hans-Georg Gadamer herzlich bedanken.

Prof. Dr. Yvanka B. Raynova,
Institute of Philosophy and Sociology - Bulgarian Academy of Sciences,
Institut für Axiologische Forschungen, Wien, raynova [at]iaf.ac.at

Literaturangaben

Brentano, Franz. 1929. "Über die Gründe der Entmutigung auf philosophischem Gebiete." In *Über die Zukunft der Philosophie*. Leipzig: Meiner.

Chiurazzi, Gaetano. 2021. "Incrase or Kenosis: Hermeneutic Ontology between Hans-Georg Gadamer and Gianni Vattimo". In *Open Borders. Encounters between Italian Philosophy and Continental Thought*. New York: SUNY Press, 65-82. Edited by Silvia Benso & Antonio Calcagno (eds.)

Dahlstrom, Danel. 2010. "Hermeneutic Ontology." In *Theory and Applications of Ontology: Philosophical Perspectives*, edited by Roberto Poli and Johanna Seibt. Dordrecht: Springer. https://doi.org/10.1007/978-90-481-8845-1_17

Dottori, Riccardo. 2003. "Introduction." In *A Century of Philosophy. Hans-Georg Gadamer in Conversation with Riccardo Dottori*, 1-17. New York: Continuum.

Gadamer, Hans-Georg. 1993. "Das Problem der Geschichte in der neueren deutschen Philosophie". (1943). In Hans-Georg Gadamer, *Hermeneutik II. Wahrheit und Methode, Ergänzungen, Register (Gesammelte Werke*, Bd. 2), 27-36. Tübingen: Mohr.

Gadamer, Hans-Georg. 1977. "Reflections on My Philosophical Journey." In *The Philosophy of Hans-Georg Gadamer* (The Library of Living Philosophers, vol. 24), Chicago: Open Court, 1977),

George, Theodore and Gert-Jan van der Heiden. 2022. *The Gadamerian Mind*. New York: Routledge.

Guimarães, Hiago Mendes. 2022. *Hermenêutica Filosófica e Retórica: con-vergências a partir do conceito de phronesis em Hans-Georg Gadamer*. Porto Alegre: Editora Fi.

Habermas, Jürgen. 1971. "Zu Gadamers Wahrheit und Methode". In *Herme-neutik und Ideologiekritik*, hg. von Karl-Otto Apel, Frankfurt: Suhrkamp.

Heidegger, Martin. 1976. *Wegmarken* (Gesamtasugabe = GA, Bd. 9), Frank-furt am Main: Vittorio Klostermann.

Hołda, Małgorzata. 2021. *On Beauty and Being: Hans-Georg Gadamer's and Virginia Woolf's Hermeneutics of the Beautiful*. Berlin, Germany: Peter Lang Verlag. DOI 10.3726/b18300

Lazurca, Vladimir. 2022. "Theodore George, Gert-Jan van der Heiden (Eds.): The Gadamerian Mind", book review. In *Phenomenological Reviews*, Thursday, April 21st. https://reviews.ophen.org/2022/04/21/theodore-george-gert-jan-van-der-heiden-the-gadamerian-mind-2/

Madison, Gary B. 2000. "Critical Theory and Henneneutics: Some Outstand-ing Issues in the Debate". In *Perspectives on Habermas*, edited by Chicago and La Salle, Illinois: Open Court. 463-486.

Malpas, Jeff. 2022. "Hans-Georg Gadamer." In *Stanford Encyclopedia of Phi-losophy*, First published Mon Mar 3, 2003, substantive revision Mon Aug 22, 2022. https://plato.stanford.edu/entries/gadamer/

Marx, Karl. 1958. Zur Kritik der Hegelschen Philosophie (Karl Marx/Fried-rich Engels, *Werke* = MEW, Band 1), Berlin, Dietz Verlag.

Marx, Karl. 1969. *Thesen über Feuerbach* (Karl Marx/Friedrich Engels Werke = MEW, Band 3), Berlin: Dietz Verlag.

Nielsen, Cynthia R. 2022. *Gadamer's Hermeneutical Aesthetics* (Routledge Research in Aesthetics). New York: Routledge.

Odenstedt, Anders. 2017. *Gadamer on Tradition - Historical Context and the Limits of Reflection*. New York: Cham, Springer.

Raynova, Yvanka B. 2002. "Sein und Cogito. Zu Paul Ricœurs Heidegger-Lektüre". In *Nach Heidegger*, hg von Helmut Vetter, 207-219, Frankfurt am Main: Peter Lang, 207-219.

Raynova, Yvanka B. ". *Sein, Sinn und Werte. Phänomenologische und her-meneutische Perspektiven des europäischen Denkens*. Frankfurt am Main: Peter

Lang.

Raynova, Yvanka B. 2015. "The European Values: A 'Dicatatorship' or a Chance for Union?" In *Community, Praxis, and Values in a Postmetaphysical Age*. 333-50. Vienna: Axia Academic Publishers.

Ricœur, Paul. 1950. *Le Volontaire et l'Involontaire*. Paris : Aubier.

Sampson, Jeremy. 2019. *Being Played: Gadamer and Philosophy's Hidden Dynamic*. Delaware: Vernon Press.

Schönherr-Mann, Hans-Martin. 2004. *Hermeneutik als Ethik*. München: Fink.

Trawny Peter. 2018. *Der frühe Marx und die Revolution. Eine Vorlesung*. Frankfurt Am Main: Vittorio Klostermann.

Zimmermann, Jens. 2022. "Gadamer's century: life, times, and works". In *The Gadamerian Mind*. New York: Routledge.

GADAMER IN DEBATE

MARCELLO RUTA (Zürich)

Wirkungsgeschichte and Background Metaphorics:
A Reading of the Gadamer-Blumenberg Debate about Secularization

Abstract

The purpose of this paper is twofold: firstly, it aims to analyze the philosophical debate between Gadamer and Blumenberg concerning the notion of secularization, which, in the author's view, has received less attention than it deserves; secondly, it intends thereby to shed light on an ontological ambiguity in Gadamer's hermeneutics, unintentionally detected by Blumenberg in his reply to Gadamer's review of The Legitimacy of the Modern Age. *The importance of the paper is both historical-philosophical and theoretical: it spells out different aspects of a philosophical discussion whose relevance concern not only the secularization debate, but more generally the philosophy of history and the role of metaphors in understanding. The most relevant original contribution consists in the usage of Blumenberg's notion of background metaphorics as a tool for interpreting the role of the notion of history of effects in Gadamer's hermeneutics.*

Keywords: Hans-Georg Gadamer, Hans Blumenberg, history of effects, metaphor, secularization

In his article on Blumenberg's notion of *Umbesetzung* (in French *réinvestissement*, in English *reoccupation*), Jean Greisch formulates two considerations, both related to Part I of the second edition of *The Legitimacy of the Modern Age* (henceforth LMA in the main text), the monograph in which that notion has been most extensively employed.

The first of the two considerations, according to which a French (or more generally a non-German) reader of LMA has the impression of witnessing a "fam-ily discussion" (Greisch 2004, 279), is easily defensible, and indirectly confirmed by Robert Wallace in his introductory note to his English translation of LMA:

> *Die Legitimität der Neuzeit* was published in 1966, the first major work of a younger German philosopher who, without being identified with anyone of the dominant philosophical schools in Germany, had clearly assimilated all of them, together with the historiography of philosophy, science, and theol-ogy. The book soon became the center of a widespread discussion, and it continues to be one of the recent works most frequently cited in German philosophical discourse. A second edition, substantially revised in order to respond to criticisms and dispel misunderstandings evident in the reviews,

appeared in three paperback volumes in 1973, 1974, and 1976. (Wallace 1983, xi)

In fact, a full understanding of the main topics broached by Blumenberg in the first part of his main work, and particularly in its second edition, presupposes acquaintance with a series of authors and notions related not only to the secularization debate, but also to other connected philosophical discussions that characterized the German philosophical landscape in those years.[1] Some of the main actors of that landscape are thinkers like Karl Löwith, Carl Schmitt, Odo Marquard, Rudolf Bultmann and Hans-Georg Gadamer.

Much less defensible is the opening statement of the second section of Greisch's article, dedicated to the second chapter of Part I of LMA, according to which, on the one hand, the title of that chapter ("A Dimension of Hidden Meaning?") is "enigmatic", and, on the other, this same chapter contains a "disguised critique of Gadamer's hermeneutics" (Greisch 2004, 284). Actually, the title of the chapter is an explicit reference to the first lines of Gadamer's review of LMA, where he defends the "legitimate hermeneutic function" of the notion of secularization, on the grounds that it "contributes a whole dimension of hidden meaning to the self-comprehension of what has come to be and presently exists, and shows in this way that what presently exists is and means far more than it knows of itself" (Gadamer 1968, 201–202, translated in Blumenberg 1983, 16–17. And in fact, Blumenberg thereby embarks in this same chapter on a critique of Gadamer's hermeneutics that is not at all disguised, being on the contrary based on an explicit reference to Gadamer's own review of his main work.

The importance of this second chapter of LMA consists, *inter alia*, in the fact that it does not formulate a critique of the notion of secularization *per se*, but rather of its supposed "hermeneutic function", as explicitly stated by Gadamer and implicitly assumed by other representatives of the secularization discourse (Löwith and Schmitt *in primis*), and as criticized by Blumenberg in the subsequent chapters. In other words, this answer moves within a *meta-discourse*, which to some extent underlies the following chapters of LMA, where more content-related criticisms of secularization are formulated. Besides, it is Blumenberg's answer to Gadamer's criticism which furnishes the elements based on which the very notion

---

[1] This point is stressed, among others, by Daniel Weidner (2014, 245), who also provides a synthetic and informative account of that philosophical landscape (ibid., 246–7). Robert Wallace, on the other hand, locates Blumenberg's argument within the wider theoretical framework of the criticism of modernity, paradigmatically beginning in 1755 with Rousseau's Discourse on the Arts and Sciences, and developed, in different ways and in different contexts, throughout the 19th and 20th centuries. See Wallace 1983, xii–xiv.

of "reoccupation", appearing for the first time in Chapter 4, acquires its argumentative role in LMA. Conversely, Blumenberg's analyses of the notion of "reoccupation", formulated in different parts of LMA,[2] furnish an implicit critique of Gadamer's hermeneutics, and more specifically of the conception of human history that, according to Blumenberg, is entailed in Gadamer's main philosophical work *Truth and Method* (henceforth TM in the main text).

The main thesis of this essay is that Blumenberg's answer to Gadamer inadvertently reveals a sort of hidden ambiguity in Gadamer's conception of history. Accordingly, the essay will be developed in three main sections: in the first, I spell out the part of Blumenberg's criticism of secularization, as formulated in LMA, which constitutes the main object of Gadamer's criticism, as well of Blumenberg's subsequent answer. I base my analysis also on an important article, published in 1964 and recently translated into English (Blumenberg 2020), which constitutes one of the foundation stones in the construction of LMA, namely "'Secularization': Critique of a Category of Historical Illegitimacy" (henceforth SEC in the main text). In the second section, I refer to both Gadamer's criticism and Blumenberg's answer in order to detect in the latter some elements that *essentially pertain to* Gadamer's hermeneutics and that, nevertheless, are used *against* Gadamer's conception of human history, which, in Blumenberg's reading, should be characterized as *substantialist*. This point leads me to formulate the diagnostic hypothesis that TM contains a sort of ontological ambiguity: namely the fact of adopting a dialogical characterization of history (in line therefore with Blumenberg's approach) which is incompatible, however, with the historical substantialism it implicitly endorses. In the third and last section, I verify the tenability of this hypothesis, while also trying to provide a plausible explanation of the reasons for such ontological ambiguity based on Blumenberg's notion of *background metaphorics*.

1. *Umsetzung* versus *Umbesetzung*: The Ontological Front of Blumenberg's Criticism of Secularization

At the beginning of LMA, Hans Blumenberg furnishes a more or less accepted definition of secularization,[3] rather as if it were something that needs no explanation, as follows:

---

[2] For an identification of the main passages of LMA, where the notion of "reoccupation" plays a relevant role, see Kopp-Oberstebrink 2014, 355–356. The page numbers refer to the German edition.

[3] Two things: First, in this essay I won't tackle the question of whether Blumenberg's definition is right or wrong. The key thing is that such a definition was in any case the

> What the term "secularization" signifies should, it seems, be readily deter-
> minable. Whether as an observation, a reproach, or an endorsement, every-
> one is familiar with this designation for a long-term process by which a dis-
> appearance of religious ties, attitudes to transcendence, expectations of an
> afterlife, ritual performances, and firmly established turns of speech is driv-
> en onward in both private and daily public life. [...] In this descriptive
> sense one can cite almost anything as consequence of secularization, in-
> cluding specific losses, as, for instance, when someone says that the crisis
> of all authority is a phenomenon or a result of secularization. Something is
> absent, which is supposed to have been present before. (Blumenberg 1983,
> 3–4)

The *first step* to understanding Blumenberg's approach to the question of
secularization consists in realizing that, in his view, such a *descriptive usage* of
the term "secularization" may indeed be shortly criticized as *indeterminate* and
as thereby allowing as an indefinite number of statements which are barely
falsifiable: however, this first criticism does *not* constitute the main focus of
LMA and SEC.

The second, much more extensive, criticism differs from the first one in
two aspects: First, it concerns not the *descriptive* usage of this category, as quoted above, but rather its *explicative* usage:

> Expressions of such a generous character, of such a degree of generality
> and intransitive indeterminacy, are allowed to pass, in our overrich supply
> of terminology, until almost without arousing notice or suspicion they pre-
> sent themselves in a more precise function. The world that became ever
> more worldly was a subject whose extension was about as obscure as that
> of the impersonal "it" in the proposition "It's raining." But in the more pre-
> cise function, propositions of an entirely different form appear, propositions
> of the form 'B is the secularized A.' For example: The modern work ethic is
> secularized monastic asceticism; The world revolution is the secularized
> expectation of the end of the world [...] I am not proposing a linguistic
> prohibition here. [...] Only the claim to render intelligible by this terminol-
> ogy something that would otherwise not be intelligible, or would be less so,
> will be contradicted here. [...] The question how the term "secularization"
> [Säkularisierung] is used in texts of contemporary historical theory is di-
> rected, above all, at the difference between descriptive and explanatory us-
> es. (Blumenberg 1983, 4–5, 9)

---

object of Gadamer's review, and this is what counts in this context. Secondly, Robert
Wallace uses the word secularization to translate both the German terms Verweltlichung
and Säkularisierung. Whether or not these two terms in Blumenberg's text are truly syno-
nyms, as Wallace states (see the translator's notes in Blumenberg 1983, 11), plays no role
in my argument.

Secondly, the criticism of the explanatory use is not that it is vague or indeterminate, but rather that it is simply *wrong*, as it misses its mark:

> What emerges here is a precise usage of the term secularization, one that goes back to its original legal meaning and content, that is, the expropriation of ecclesiastical possessions as it has been practiced and referred to since the Peace of Westphalia. It is easy to see that there is an analogy between the usages of the term secularization recounted here and these processes of expropriation—an analogy that makes the idea of secularization liable to be used as a basic concept of historical understanding.[...] For the time being, it should be quite coolly noted that a historical interpretation seeking to avail itself of the expression secularization bears, from a methodical perspective, the burden of proving that the features of the seizure are in evidence in the thematic process. Failing that, what emerges may well be a statement that sounds profound and creates the illusion of having understood something, but its grasp for a historical structure misses the mark. (Blumenberg 2020, 54–6)

The *second step* consists in understanding *why* Blumenberg considers such a usage hermeneutically inadequate. From the second chapter of LMA onwards, his argument is developed, in a parallel way, on two levels or *fronts* of criticism.[4]

A *first front* concerns a *specific content issue*, as consisting in the implied attributions in such an explanatory usage, and thereby in the (falsely) presupposed correctness of the analogy instituted between the literal (juridical) notion of secularization, referring to "the expropriation of church property," "so practiced and so named from the Peace of Westphalia onward" (Blumenberg 1983, 19), and its historical (explanatory) usage. The decisive point entailed here concerns the attribute of *illegitimacy* that is transposed, in the exercise of this analogy, from the literal to the historical (explanatory) usage of secularization, thereby delegitimizing *a priori* all the concepts or notions, which are claimed to be secularizations of something else:

> [T]he example of the 'Final Resolution of the Reichstag's Special Commission' [*Reichsdeputatwnshauptschluss*] of 1803 established the term "as a concept of the usurpation of ecclesiastical rights, as a concept of the illegitimate emancipation of property from ecclesiastical care and custody." These defining elements make "the attribute of illegitimacy into a characteristic mark of the concept of secularization." (Blumenberg 1983, 20)

---

[4] There is in fact a third level, related to the question of how it happened that we, "without arousing notice or suspicion" (see Blumenberg's excerpt previously quoted), passed from a descriptive to an explicative usage of this notion. This point will be developed in the last section of the essay as playing a decisive role in my interpretation of Gadamer's hermeneutics as ontologically ambiguous.

While this point is evidently of primary importance in LMA, as indeed seen in its title, it does not play a central role in the question with which this essay is concerned, so it won't be further treated.

A *second front* of Blumenberg's criticism concerns a *general, formal and ontological issue*, as the *legitimacy of the modern age* is treated as a sort of case study for a more comprehensive question, thereby constituting a *meta-level* compared to the first one, related to the understanding of historical processes (Kopp-Oberstebrink 2014, 351)[5] The formal aspect of the issue concerns the *morphology* of historical processes; the ontological aspect concerns the question whether such processes have to be understood in *substantialist* or *functionalist* terms. Accordingly, Blumenberg defines the "secularization theorem as a special case of historical substantialism" (Blumenberg 1983, 29). It can be plausibly stated, together with Robert Wallace, that this second point constitutes the very center of Blumenberg's criticism of secularization, as "[t]he contrast of content with function is what ultimately distinguishes Blumenberg's model from the secularization theory" (Wallace 1983, xxvi). In any case, this ontological issue, in my reading, constitutes the focus of the Blumenberg–Gadamer debate, and will be therefore extensively treated in the rest of this section and the next.

Both these two fronts are activated in Blumenberg's diagnosis of the ontological implications of the explanatory usage of the notion of secularization. The main point in this regard is constituted by what Blumenberg calls a substantialist account of historical processes, which interprets some apparently radical changes in terms of transformation or metamorphosis of one single substance:

> So simple is it, apparently, to identify the substance in its metamorphoses, and to line up the metastases relative to their one origin, once one has found the formula. Naturally its easy applicability and the consequent frivolous multiplication of instances do not speak against the procedure itself, they only make the examination of its admissibility, of its rational presuppositions and methical requirements, all the more urgent. [...] For a usage defined in this way, what is called for is [...] evidence of transformation, metamorphosis, conversion to new functions, along with the identity of a substance that endures throughout the process. Without such a substantial identity, no recoverable sense could be attached to the talk of conversion and transformation. (Blumenberg 1983, 15–6)

We should now ask why Blumenberg criticizes such explanatory usage of the notion of secularization and the entailed historical substantialism. The

---

[5] A double level for Blumenberg's discourse is also stressed by Robert Pippin in his critical review of LMA, although through a different argument (See Pippin 1987, 536).

answer consists in the model of expropriation implicitly adopted in such usage, as stressed in the excerpt previously quoted, and further articulated as follows:

> The transference taking place here draws its assumptions from the *features* of the process of expropriation, which are:
> a) the ability of the expropriated goods to be identified;
> b) the legitimacy of primary ownership;
> c) the seizure being unilateral. (Blumenberg 2020, 55).

All these three features are criticized by Blumenberg, both in SEC and in the first chapters of LMA, particularly in relation to the notion of modern progress as a secularization of Christian eschatology, formulated by Karl Löwith in *Meaning and History* (Löwith 1949), which constitutes a sort of *casus belli* of a conflict related to the "substantialist ontology of history" (Blumenberg 2020, 79) whose consequences reach far beyond the specific question of legitimacy of modernity. We can, simplifying, say that while the second and third features concern the question of *legitimacy* versus *illegitimacy* (the first front of Blumenberg's criticism, as previously formulated), the first one concerns the question of *substantialism* versus *functionalism* (the second front), which is the key issue of this section.

For reasons of clarity and space, I will articulate the Blumenberg's criticism of the first feature in four summarized points:

1. As already formulated in SEC and thereafter re-stated in LMA, Christian eschatology and the modern notion of progress show "a manifest difference", as the first one depends on "an event breaking into history" which "transcends and is heterogeneous to it", while the second one "extrapolates from a structure present in every moment to a future that is immanent in history" (Blumenberg 1983, 30).

2. The modern notion of progress finds its immediate sources in two main events which shaped the beginning of modernity: the idea of "the unity of methodically regulated theory as a coherent entity developing independently of individuals and generations" (Blumenberg 1983, 31), and the *Querelle des Anciens et des Modernes*, which developed in the specific context of aesthetics, but which Blumenberg, together with Hans Robert Jauss, sees as the "aesthetic analogue of the detachment of theory from the authority of Aristotelianism" (Blumenberg 1983, 33).

3. This modern source of the notion of progress, however, *does not* yet explain its application to history as a whole, which produces a sort of "overstretching" of the notion of progress "to the generality of a philosophy of history" (Blumenberg 2020, 63), in a way which is morphologically analogous

to the eschatological model, and which therefore generated the idea of progress as being a secularization of its (supposed) theological source. In this respect, "the formation of the idea of progress and its taking the place of the historical totality that was bounded by Creation and Judgment are two distinct events" (Blumenberg 1983, 49).

4. This overstretching of the notion of progress to the totality of history is explained, both in SEC and LMA; by Blumenberg through the key notion of reoccupation (*Umbesetzung*), which is Blumenberg's alternative to the notion of transposition (*Umsetzung*) implied in the very idea of secularization:

> What mainly occurred in the process that is interpreted as secularization [...] should be described not as the *transposition* of authentically theological contents into secularized alienation from their origin but rather as the *reoccupation* of answer positions that had become vacant and whose corresponding questions could not be eliminated. (Blumenberg 1983, 65)

Blumenberg's analysis yields two results: on the one side, the notion of historical progress *cannot* be identified as the expropriated (secularized) notion of Christian eschatology: they are rather to be considered as two distinct conceptual entities. On the other side, the notion of reoccupation, together with the related functionalist account of history, allows Blumenberg to provide an explanation of the morphological similarity between those two entities. In this respect, Löwith, in Blumenberg's view, provided a *wrong ontological* explanation to a *morphological* similarity that had been *rightly* detected:

> The idea of progress [...] is viewed neither as a secularized Christian idea nor as a modern idea unaffected by Christianity; in Blumenberg's account, it is essentially modern in its content (the initial idea of possible progress) but heavily affected by Christianity in the function that the content is forced to perform (the function of explaining the meaning and pattern of history as a whole) [Wallace 1983, xxvi].

This articulated argument would be criticized by Hans Georg Gadamer in a review published in 1968 in the *Philosophische Rundschau*, to which Blumenberg answered in the second chapter of the revised version of LMA, published in 1974, which is nowadays the one usually read and translated. For the purposes of the present essay, the main interest of Gadamer's critique and Blumenberg's answer consists in the fact that Blumenberg uses Gadamerian notions and arguments to answer Gadamer's own critique; this will be the topic of the next section. On this basis, I will formulate the hypothesis of there being an *essential ambiguity* lying at the core of Gadamer's ontology of history, which Blumenberg involuntarily detected in answering his criticism.

2. "That was what I was afraid of": Blumenberg's Answer
to Gadamer's Criticism and the Debate about Ontology of History

Gadamer's review of LMA is by no means a negative one: in several parts, Gadamer expresses deep respect for the originality and erudition on display in LMA, whose qualities exceed the expectations created by his already-published essays, which, in part, anticipated the themes treated in his main work. In three points of his review, however, Gadamer formulates concise yet penetrating criticisms, touching upon three different aspects of LMA:

1. The first criticism, formulated at the very beginning (Gadamer 1968, 201–2), concerns the very main topic of LMA, namely the critique of the notion of secularization, and contains the expression "hidden meaning" to which Blumenberg refers in the title of the second chapter of LMA (see above).

2. The second criticism, formulated a page later (Gadamer 1968, 203–4), concerns the usage of the notion of *reoccupation* (*Umbesetzung*) in Blumenberg's work, which, in Gadamer's view, recalls (without mentioning it) the methodology pursued by Cassirer in his historical-philosophical work (which configures the history of philosophy as history of problems).

3. The third criticism, formulated at the end of the review (Gadamer 1968, 208–9), concerns Blumenberg's reading of Nicholas of Cusa, to whom Gadamer had dedicated some significant pages of TM (see Gadamer 2004, 432–6).

Blumenberg addresses *all the critiques* formulated by Gadamer, although in *different parts* of LMA: the first critique is explicitly addressed in the second chapter of Part I (Blumenberg 1983, 16–19), and implicitly in other passages of LMA, which will be quoted in the remaining part of this section. The second critique is implicitly addressed in Chapter 6 of Part I (Blumenberg 1983, 65–6). The third critique is addressed in Chapter 1 of Part III (Blumenberg 1983, 476–80). While all three points raised by Gadamer, and Blumenberg's respective answers, are of high theoretical interest, in this section (and in this essay) I will mainly treat the first issue.

The main point made by Gadamer at the beginning of his review is explicitly quoted by Blumenberg in the following excerpt:

> Against my critique of the concept of secularization, Hans-Georg Gadamer has asserted that this concept performs "a legitimate hermeneutic function." He describes this function of the secularization concept as follows: "It contributes a whole dimension of hidden meaning to the self-comprehension of what has come to be and presently exists, and shows in this way that what presently exists is and means far more than it knows of itself" (Gadamer 1968, 201–202). And he adds a sentence that is significant for his convic-

tion of the epochal range of this category: "This holds also and especially for the modern age." (Blumenberg 1983, 16–7)

The first aspect to be noticed is that Gadamer, in a concise yet pregnant formulation, stresses three different points: first, by rhetorically using the same category as Blumenberg against him, he states that "secularization" should be considered as a notion which exercises a *legitimate* hermeneutic function, namely consisting in discovering a dimension of hidden meaning of historical events or epochs; secondly, this shows that the meaning of historical periods *exceeds*, so to speak, their self-understanding; and thirdly, that these two points are particularly relevant for the epoch of the modern age.

In his answer, Blumenberg also stresses three different points, which need to be separately expounded:

1. The first point Blumenberg makes is that Gadamer's criticism, and particularly the reference to a *hidden meaning*, activates a series of notions which essentially pertain to the tradition of hermeneutics, as a discipline concerning the interpretation of texts which "in general has only to do with a surplus of meaning over and above what is granted and understood as self-evident"; and, more specifically, it activates a model of understanding which recalls the Heideggerian notion of *philosophical hermeneutics*, according to which the notion of interpretation is extended from mere textual objects to the process of self-uncovering of *Dasein*. According to all this, self-consciousness is a "consciousness that is not transparent to itself in its substantial relations, a consciousness to which hermeneutics discloses its background" (Blumenberg 1983, 17). While Blumenberg in his text explicitly refers only to Heidegger, such considerations also essentially concern Gadamer's hermeneutics, as the following excerpt related to the notion of *wirkungsgeschichtliches Bewusstsein* (more on that in the last section) makes evident:

> Consciousness of being affected by history (*wirkungsgeschichtliches Bewusstsein*) is primarily consciousness of the hermeneutical *situation*. To acquire an awareness of a situation is, however, always a task of peculiar difficulty. [...] This is also true of the hermeneutic situation—i.e., the situation in which we find ourselves with regard to the tradition that we are trying to understand. [...] *To be historically means that knowledge of oneself can never be complete.* All self-knowledge arises from what is historically pregiven, what with Hegel we call "substance," because it underlies all subjective intentions and actions, and hence both prescribes and limits every possibility for understanding any tradition whatsoever in its historical alterity. This almost defines the aim of philosophical hermeneutics. (Gadamer 2004, 301)

2. The second point is condensed in the seven words quoted in the subtitle of this section: "that was what I was afraid of." With these words Blumenberg stresses that Gadamer's criticism is in fact a re-instantiation of the thesis that Blumenberg had already criticized in the first edition of LMA. The point at issue specifically concerns the relation between the "hermeneutic process of uncovering" (Brient 2002, 22) and the explicative usage of the notion of secularization. In Blumenberg's eyes, Gadamer's criticism is a re-statement of the historic substantialism implicit in such usage, because, to take the example of the notion of *progress as mark of modernity*, its hidden meaning is exactly what makes it *illegitimate*; this means that, in spite of appearing as a discontinuity with the notion of tradition and authority which characterized pre-modern ages, modern progress actually re-proposes theological notions (specifically: Christian eschatology) under so to speak non-immediately-recognizable appearances.[6] This point is very well stressed in this excerpt from Elizabeth Brient:

> The thesis that fundamental concepts, institutions and attitudes of the modern age are really just secularized versions of medieval correlates presupposes the identity of an originally sacred content or substance that is preserved (though transformed) in the transition to the modern world. It thus depends on an understanding of history dominated by the category of substance [...] The task of the historical theorist would then become that of identifying the core content, to unmask layers of "hidden meaning" or a series of "alienated forms". [...] The secularized idea is then understood in a deeper way or rather, truly understood for the first time, once its essential connection to its theological origin is made explicit. (Brient 2002, 21–2)

3. The third point made by Blumenberg consists in radically questioning such historical substantialism, the historical ontology implied by the notion of secularization, which is the reason why Gadamer's point is what Blumenberg was *afraid of*:

> The alienation of a historical substance from its origin, which it carries with it only as a hidden dimension of meaning, unavoidably raises the question whether this is a process of self-alienation or externally induced deformation. (Blumenberg 1983, 18)

---

[6] The question of whether Blumenberg's reading of secularization as implying historical substantialism is correct here remains open, and I won't take a position on the notion of secularization itself. I will simply mention that Blumenberg supports his reading by a series of quotes that are, in my view, and at least in the first instance, quite convincing (see particularly the quote from Delekat 1958 in Blumenberg 1983, 24).

Here Wallace translates as "self-alienation" and "externally induced deformation" the German words *Selbstentfremdung* and *Fremdverformung* respectively. The common root *fremd* ("alien" or "foreign"), included in both words, makes lexically evident the two opposite configurations: while in the second case we are concerned with the interaction of *two* distinct individuals that are foreign to themselves, in the first case we are concerned with the movement of *one* individual in a foreign territory or element (the typical movement of alienation, related to the notion of secularization).

The conceptual articulation of the process of *Fremdverformung* is one of the main theoretical achievements of LMA and constitutes Blumenberg's alternative to the historical substantialism, implicit in the explicative usage of the notion of secularization and re-affirmed by Gadamer's endorsement of its hermeneutic legitimacy, as uncovering a hidden meaning of historical epochs.

For reasons of both clarity and synthesis, I will, further, articulate and condense Blumenberg's theoretical approach in three main points, based on some key passages of LMA:

1. The first step consists in passing from historical substantialism to historical functionalism: different conceptual *contents* can have identical *functions*, and so appear to be two instances of the same type (while in the case of secularization the second, secularized instance is regarded as a disguised copy of the first, original one):

> The only reason why 'secularization' could ever have become so plausible as a mode of explanation of historical processes is that supposedly secularized ideas can in fact mostly be traced back to an identity in the historical process. Of course this identity, according to the thesis advocated here, is not one of contents but one of functions. (Blumenberg 1983, 64)

2. Such historical functionalism entails the notion of *reoccupation* (*Umbesetzung*), which Blumenberg opposes to the notion of *transposition* (*Umsetzung*), this latter being the one entailed by historical substantialism: while in the latter case, we have an *identical content* which is transposed into *another (secularized) context*, in the first case we have an *identical function*, left empty, we can provocatively say, by a delegitimation of an existing notion (Christian eschatology), and *reoccupied* by a new one (modern progress), whose content is different from the first one:

> It is in fact possible for totally heterogeneous contents to take on identical functions in specific positions in the system of man's interpretation of the world and of himself. In our history this system has been decisively determined by Christian theology, and specifically, above all, in the direction of its expansion. Theology created new 'positions' in the framework of the

statements about the world and man that are possible and are expected, 'positions' that cannot simply be 'set aside' again or left unoccupied in the interest of theoretical economy. [...] What mainly occurred in the process that is interpreted as secularization, at least (so far) in all but a few recognizable and specific instances, should be described not as the *transposition* [Umsetzung] of authentically theological contents into secularized alienation from their origin but rather as the *reoccupation* [*Umbesetzung*] of answer positions that had become vacant and whose corresponding questions could not be eliminated. (Blumenberg 1983, 64–5)

3. Such a theoretical framework is activated by a *dialogical attitude* adopted with respect to historical contents and functions: the identification of a function left empty and to be reoccupied is made possible by a sort of *dialogical glance at the past*, whereas delegitimated notions are read as inadequate answers to historical questions which remain open, as a sort of residuum of the process of critique, thereby needing a new, more adequate answer (the new content occupying the empty function):

The insight that all logic, both historically and systematically, is based on structures of dialogue has not yet been brought to bear in the construction of historical categories. If the modern age was not the monologue, beginning at point zero, of the absolute subject—as it pictures itself—but rather the system of efforts to answer in a new context questions that were posed to man in the Middle Ages, then this would entail new standards for interpreting what does in fact function as an answer to a question but does not represent itself as such an answer and may even conceal the fact that that is what it is. Every occurrence [*Ereignis*], in the widest sense of the term, is characterized by 'correspondence'; it responds to a question, a challenge, a discomfort; it bridges over an inconsistency, relaxes a tension, or occupies a vacant position. (Blumenberg 1983, 379)

Now the question I intend to stress at the end of this second section, and as an introduction to the next and final one, is the following: the notion of dialogue is, with no doubt, part of the theoretical backbone of Gadamer's hermeneutical and historical approach. Not only is the last sub-chapter of the second part of TM, which introduces to the last and conclusive part, dedicated to "The hermeneutic priority of the question", but it can be stated that the notion of dialogue is central to the whole of Gadamer's hermeneutical approach, and constitutes one of the elements of novelty compared to his predecessor Heidegger, to whom he is nevertheless in debt in many other respects. In Gadamer, understanding is always *presupposing intersubjectivity*, not in the Heideggerian deceived form of the "they" (Man), but rather in the authentic form of the Socratic dialogue, as testified by the closing sentence of the second section of TM:

> To reach an understanding in a dialogue is not merely a matter of putting
> oneself forward and successfully asserting one's own point of view, but be-
> ing transformed into a communion in which we do not remain what we
> were. (Gadamer 2004, 371)

Accordingly, in order to criticize Gadamer's review of LMA, a review which, as previously stressed, activates some central notions of his hermeneutics, Blumenberg employs a series of *other* notions that *also* essentially pertain to Gadamer's hermeneutical approach. What we want to investigate in the next and final section is whether such a paradoxical situation can be interpreted as a symptom of a sort of *ontological ambiguity* implicit in the whole approach of TM, and which Blumenberg's answer to Gadamer has, involuntarily, made explicit.

3. Dialogical Understanding and *Wirkungsgeschichte*:
An Ontological Ambiguity at the Core of Gadamer's Hermeneutics
as an Effect of Background Metaphorics

While Kant's *Critique of Judgment* and Gadamer's *Truth and Method* evidently have different structures and contents, they share however an important and not negligible trait: the fact of treating in the same work the domain of aesthetics on the one hand, and on the other a domain which cannot be reduced to simple causal relations, and which thus in some sense transcends the notion of mechanism: the domain of biology, in the case of Kant; that of history, in the case of Gadamer. The notion which allows them to treat such heterogeneous domains within the same argument is, in the case of Kant, that of reflective judgment, and in the case of Gadamer that of understanding.

Accordingly, when Gadamer affirms in the last part of the second section of TM that "the hermeneutic phenomenon [...] implies the primacy of dialogue and the structure of question and answer" and that "the logic of the human sciences is a logic of the question" (Gadamer 2004, 363), he refers not only to the understanding of texts, but also to the understanding of history. The dialogical structure of understanding goes beyond the domain of interpretation of texts, the original domain of hermeneutics, to potentially inform all the domains of human knowledge, and eminently that of human history.

This point becomes evident when, in that same section, Gadamer criticizes Collingwood's philosophy of history:

> It is like understanding works of art. A work of art can be understood only
> if we assume its adequacy as an expression of the artistic idea. Here too we
> have to discover the question which it answers, if we are to understand it as
> an answer. This is, in fact, an axiom of all hermeneutics: we described it
> above as the "fore-conception of completeness." For Collingwood, this is

the nerve of all historical knowledge. The historical method requires that the logic of question and answer be applied to historical tradition. We will understand historical events only if we reconstruct the question to which the historical actions of the persons involved were the answer. (Gadamer 2004, 364)

Gadamer's criticism concerns both the artistic and the historical domain, and is a radical denial of Collingwood's intentionalism:

Collingwood's use of the logic of question and answer in hermeneutical theory is made ambiguous by this extrapolation. Our understanding of written tradition per se is not such that we can simply presuppose that the meaning we discover in it agrees with what its author intended. Just as the events of history do not in general manifest any agreement with the subjective ideas of the person who stands and acts within history, so the sense of a text in general reaches far beyond what its author originally intended. The task of understanding is concerned above all with the meaning of the text itself. (Gadamer 2004, 365)

The hermeneutic value of historical distance is in fact more evident in the understanding of historical facts than in that of artworks: it is only when historical facts lie at a certain distance that we are able to detect their meaning independently from the *intentions* of the respective *actors*. This process, according to Gadamer, articulates also the constitution of historical traditions, as "preservation" which is also an "act of reason" (Gadamer 2004, 282).

As one can easily see, Gadamer's approach is fully compatible with his endorsement of the secularization thesis: on the one side, the understanding that modernity has of itself, i.e. as breaking with the principle of authority and thereby building anew, does not have to coincide with what *in fact* modernity is, and which can be detected possibly only when we start to see modernity from a certain historical distance; on the other side, the notion of modern progress as secularized Christian eschatology constitutes a paradigmatic example of how a tradition maintains itself, in spite of the different stages of the process which actualize different elements of it.

So, the question to be asked is why, despite sharing the same understanding of history in terms of dialogical process, Blumenberg and Gadamer can arrive at opposite conclusions. In the case of Gadamer, what is at stake with this question is something which goes beyond the specific topic of secularization and which concerns rather his *conservatism*—the term used by Habermas in order to characterize Gadamer's hermeneutic position, in a notorious exchange between the two thinkers (Apel et al., ed. 1971). The different aspects of this philosophical debate, whose theoretical relevance seems to me increasingly evident even though more than half a century has now gone by, has been widely commented upon and cannot be broached here, not even in very general terms (see Warnke 1987, and Harrington 2001). One point, however, stressed by Georgia Warnke in the following excerpt, is important for the argument I intend to develop:

> Gadamer's thesis here is the fundamentally conservative one that since we are historically finite, since we have no concept of rationality that is independent of the tradition to which we belong and hence no universal norms and principles to which we can appeal, we ought not even to attempt to overthrow the authority of that tradition. This thesis goes beyond his hermeneutic claim that in any attempt to overthrow tradition (whether artistic, epistemological or political) we accept more than we deny and more, perhaps, than we are willing to admit. Here his position is that since we cannot justify revolutionary practice absolutely, through recourse to transhistorically valid principles, we ought to dispense with it entirely. Even if one rejects Habermas's attempt to found a modern correlate to the Enlightenment's appeal to reason in the universal pragmatics of language, Gadamer's position does not seem to follow. Failure to find axiomatic grounds for our criticism of authority does not mean that we must submit dogmatically to it. (Warnke 1987, 136)

In the following pages of her study, Warnke shows how such a dogmatic reading of Gadamer's hermeneutic approach does not take into consideration some non-dogmatic implications of his dialogical notion of consensus, according to which consensus is not conceived simply as reaching an agreement, but rather as taking into account other points of view, which will lead in any case to an enrichment of its own position. Thereby, according to Warnke, "it follows that we are not limited to the premises of our tradition but rather continually revise them in the encounters with and discussions we have of them. In confronting other cultures, other prejudices and, indeed, the implications that others draw from our own traditions we learn to reflect on both our assumptions and our ideas of reason and to amend them in the direction of a *better* account" (Warnke 1987, 170). According to such a reading, it seems to me, Gadamer's approach is *reformist* rather than *dogmatic*, as traditions are *both constituted and renovated* through the same dialogic process.

The point that I intend to make in the last part of this essay is the following: while *reformism* is not *dogmatism*, it remains in any case a form of *conservatism*. In my view, while endorsing Warnke's reading of Gadamer's account of dialogical agreement as not entailing authoritarianism or dogmatism, it is not so evident that the result of such agreement should be the renovation or amendment of a tradition rather than a break with it. In fact, this is the very point made by Blumenberg when he criticizes the explicative usage of the notion of secularization, by opposing historical functionalism to substantialism. The risk implicitly stressed by Blumenberg, it seems to me, is that of *ontological stipulation*: when we consider, for example, the notion of progress as the secularization of providence, we *stipulate* that an existing tradition is being amended and renovated through the secularization of one of its key concepts—whether for better or for worse is not my point here. In the same vein, to assume that in the dialogical exercise the comprehension of the reason of the other should produce a sort of common revision and agreement, is also, to be fair, a stipulation (see Habermas's later account of this point): many dialogues (including the one between Gadamer and Blumenberg) have as their legitimate result the *clarification of the incompatibility* of the different points of view. In some cases, the dialogical process is exactly the opposite of the one envisaged by Gadamer. We start a dialogue assuming that our points of view are in principle compatible, and in the end, *thanks to (and not in spite of) the dialogical exercise*, we arrive at the conclusion that our positions are not compatible, and that we have to break, for example, with a position that we assumed could have been amended.

So now the question should be cast in the following terms: what made Gadamer implicitly assume that the good dialogue should produce agreement and not disagreement, thereby enabling, so to say, *a priori* the maintenance of a tradition by its internal amendments? The answer I intend to propose will consist in a Blumenbergian reading of one of Gadamer's key concepts, namely the "history of effects" (*Wirkungsgeschichte*).

The notion of "history of effects" is generally considered an essential element of the theoretical backbone of Gadamer's hermeneutical approach: it has been defined as "a notion unsurpassable in importance in *Truth and Method*" constituting "the true speculative summit of the work" (Grondin 2003, 90), "core constituent of Gadamer's theory of hermeneutic experience" (Gander 2011, 93), as well as "the central point around which the theoretical part of *Truth and Method* turns" (Di Cesare 2013, 93).

As is well known, the notion of *Wirkungsgeschichte* was not devised by Gadamer, and indeed "was already widespread in the literary criticism of the nineteenth century. It refers to the auxiliary discipline that deals with the reception of a work and, above all, with the interpretations that have arisen in the reception" (Di Cesare 2013, 93). What Gadamer did was to extend the usage of this notion to a potentially universal domain: somehow, "The Hermeneutic Claim to Universality" (Habermas 1980) is also a claim to universality for the history of effects. What all this can signify, particularly in the domain of historical knowledge, is very well illustrated by Jean Grondin:

> Along the thread of reception, every work and every event (the French revolution, the discovery of America, etc.) is enriched with new meanings and

new relevances that are determined by the attempts of their historical context of reception, and also by the previous interpretations to which they react. For example, in 1992, in the quincentennial celebrations of the discovery of America, we no longer always saw, as had been the case in previous commemorations, the glories of European civilization being spread to barbarians, but instead, in reaction to this history of conquest, the discovery of America was interpreted as the beginning of the annihilation of non-European civilizations. (Grondin 2003, 91)

Gadamer's next step consists in further extending such a notion from the understanding of historical facts to, so to speak, our *congenitally historical forms of life*, as the way in which we all stand within historical tradition. The history of effects is thereby the process by which the historical traditions renovate themselves, remaining alive in the process of history:

Historical tradition can be understood only as something always in the process of being defined by the course of events. Similarly, the philologist dealing with poetic or philosophical texts knows that they are inexhaustible. In both cases it is the course of events that brings out new aspects of meaning in historical material. [...] This is what we described as the history of effect as an element in hermeneutical experience. Every actualization in understanding can be regarded as a historical potential of what is understood. It is part of the historical finitude of our being that we are aware that others after us will understand in a different way. And yet it is equally indubitable that it remains the same work whose fullness of meaning is realized in the changing process of understanding, just as it is the same history whose meaning is constantly in the process of being defined. (Gadamer 2004, 366)

It is at this point that I intend to provide a reading of such a notion, and particularly its universal usage in Gadamer's hermeneutic approach. The first point to be stressed is what, in my view, proves most problematic in the last quoted excerpt. The usage of the notion of *Wirkungsgeschichte* in order to explain our way of dealing with historical facts can be plausibly be seen as implicitly adopting the metaphor of the *world as text to be understood*: while Gadamer's conception of reading and understanding (which here cannot be spelled out, not even summarily, for reasons of space) can be rightly considered as highly innovative, the adoption of such metaphor is nothing new, as Blumenberg has shown in *The Readability of the World* (Blumenberg 2022) and is not problematic per se.

What in my view is much less endorsable is the implicit assumption, contained in the previous excerpt, that in history, or even in a single tradition, we can talk of *one* single book, or *one* single text, differently interpreted in different ways. It is this assumption which is at stake in the debate between functionalism and substantialism, as well as in the very notion of secularization. Even if we consider it legitimate to treat historical events and epochs as texts to be interpreted, and even if we consider that in such interpretation we are always situated in a finite historical situation, never transparent to itself, which determines our interpretative acts, it remains totally undecided whether such a history of effects, metaphorically applied to history, is the history of *one* text interpreted in *different ways*, or of *different texts*. In other words, it is still undecided whether or not the historical process has to be considered as the process of one single entity, which passes through different transformations (interpretations), or of different entities, which have impact on each other while remaining clearly identifiable as distinct entities. This is the point lying at the core of Blumenberg's answer to Gadamer's review: and it is in this point where, in my reading, the notion of *Wirkungsgeschichte* becomes, *nolens volens*, also a theory of historical conservatism (and historical substantialism).

I do not intend here to take a position about *who is right*: the idea of this essay is not to provide a theory of historical understanding, or even less an ontology of history. Rather, I would like to provide an interpretation of the assumption implied in the previously quoted passage, which, in my reading, constitutes the *hidden core of conservatism* of Gadamer's hermeneutics. In this reading I intend to activate Blumenberg's notion of *background metaphorics*,[7] as defined in his *Paradigms for a Metaphorology*:

> Metaphorics can also be in play where exclusively terminological propositions appear, but where these cannot be understood in their higher-order semantic unity without taking into account the guiding idea from which they are induced and 'read off'. Statements referring to data of observation presuppose that what is intended can, in each case, be brought to mind only within the parameters of a descriptive typology [...] In undertaking an interpretive reconstruction, we will succeed in reviving such translations, which we propose to call 'background metaphorics'. (Blumenberg 2010, 62–3)

The notion of background metaphorics plays an important role in the second edition of LMA, as it is involved in the criticism of what above has been described as the explicative use of the notion of secularization. Such use, as already stressed, goes far beyond its descriptive use as detection of the loss of theological reference points, as it provides a much more specific statement about single events: but this specificity, according to Blumenberg, is only ap-

---

[7] For this notion and its role in Blumenberg's histories of metaphors as a heuristic tool for the Begriffsgeschichte see Betzler 1995, 461.

parently exactitude, as it is rather, the effect of the *translation* of the notion of secularization as *illegitimate* appropriation of a good, as *typology* applicable to different historical events. In its explicative usage, the term "secularization" provides thereby a *pattern* (typology) that plays a heuristic role while at the same time remaining hidden, and this is what leads Blumenberg to consider it as an instance of background metaphorics. It is precisely this positioning in the background that creates the appearance of going without saying: the *illegitimacy* is *implied* precisely by the hidden presence of the metaphoric pattern within our interpretative frame. And this leads Blumenberg to propose the additional formula *implicative metaphorics*:

> [I]t is not the usage that is metaphorical but rather the orientation of the process of concept formation. A tightening up from a vague exhortative and lamenting usage to the definition of a typical process form makes the 'recollection' of the historical legal proceedings appear almost inevitable. This is an instance of what I have tried to describe as "background metaphorics," a process of reference to a model that is operative in the genesis of a concept but is no longer present in the concept itself, or may even have to be sacrificed to the need for definition, which according to firm tradition does not permit inclusion of metaphorical elements. One could also speak of implicative metaphorics. (Blumenberg 1983, 22–3)

The thesis endorsed herewith is that in the notion of *Wirkungsgeschichte*, as employed by Gadamer in his theory of understanding, a background metaphorics is in action. More specifically, the history of effects is implicitly understood as the effect of the reception of *one* single entity in different historical and cultural contexts, as it happens in the original domain of the notion of *Wirkungsgeschichte*, namely the interpretation of texts. Such a *background* metaphorics is, so to speak, inadvertently brought in the *foreground* in the previously quoted passage, where, in order to clarify our being involved in traditions, Gadamer argues that "Similarly, the philologist dealing with poetic or philosophical texts knows that they are inexhaustible." The supposed continuity of tradition, and continuity between traditions, is thereby understandable as an effect of the background metaphorics, where in the history of effects a single text is always recognizable as an *identifiable single entity* beyond its different interpretations.

There is a last point I would like to make: in *The Theory of Communicative Action*, originally published by Habermas in 1981, we can find the following remark relating to Gadamer's notion of understanding:

> Gadamer gives the interpretive model of *Verstehen* a peculiarly *one-sided twist*. If in the performative attitude of virtual participants in conversation we start with the idea that an author's utterance has the presumption of rationality, we not only admit the possibility that the interpretandum may be

exemplary *for us*, that we may learn something from it; we *also* take into account the possibility that the author could learn *from us*. Gadamer remains bound to the experience of the philologist who deals with classical texts [...]. The knowledge embodied in the text is, Gadamer believes, fundamentally superior to the interpreter's. (Habermas, 1984, 134)

In this excerpt, Habermas does not make use of Blumenberg's notion of background metaphorics: but to state that Gadamer "remains bound to the experience of the philologist" suggests a similar diagnosis. In this essay it will remain open whether the transmission of a single text, as the original domain of the notion of *Wirkungsgeschichte*, not only plays a role in the characterization of our being inscribed in traditions, but more generally of the notion of understanding, thereby becoming a sort of encompassing metaphorical background of Gadamer's hermeneutics. What I intend rather to stress is that, even if in this case, such a role won't reduce Gadamer's hermeneutics to a conservative or reactionary one, as it *coexists* with other elements, starting for the dialogical characterization of the act of understanding, which goes *against* such conservative trait: not only as it *explicitly enables* amendments of traditions, as rightly stressed by Warnke, but also as it *implicitly makes space* for historical discontinuities. In this respect, we could say that the notion of the "classical", as the ultimate background metaphorics of Gadamer's hermeneutics, constitutes *both its progressive and conservative nucleus*. On the one side, exemplifying a radically open notion of interpretation consisting in a dialogical process between interpreter and text; on the other side, implicitly making our relation with the past, whether textual, cultural or historical, a question of inscription in a continuous (as referring to one single entity, always recognizable beyond and behind the multiplicity of its interpretations) process of reception, thereby risking an a priori delegitimation of any effort to detect discontinuities in it. Which is, it seems to me, the very core of Blumenberg's critique of the notion of secularization, including his critique of the defense mounted by Hans-Georg Gadamer.

Dr. Phil. Marcello Ruta, Zurich University of The Arts,
Department of Cultural Analysis, marcello.ruta@zhdk.ch

References

Apel et al., ed. 1971. *Hermeneutik und Ideologiekritik.* Frankfurt am Main: Suhrkamp.

Betzler, Monika. 1995. "Formen der Wirklichkeitsbewältigung. Hans Blumenbergs Phänomenologie der 'Umbesetzungen': Ein Porträt." *Zeitschrift für philosophische Forschung*, 49 (3): 456–71.

Blumenberg, Hans. 1983. *The Legitimacy of the Modern Age.* Translated by Robert M. Wallace. Cambridge: MIT Press.

Blumenberg, Hans. 2010. *Paradigms for a Metaphorology.* Translated by Robert Savage. Ithaca, New York: Cornell University Press.

Blumenberg, Hans. 2020. "'Secularization': Critique of a Category of Historical Illegitimacy." In *History, Metaphors, Fables: A Hans Blumenberg Reader,* edited by Hannes Bajohr, Florian Fuchs, and Joe Paul Kroll, 53–82. Ithaca and London: Cornell University Press.

Blumenberg, Hans. 2022. *The Readability of the World.* Translated by Robert Savage. Ithaca: Cornell University Press.

Brient, Elizabeth. 2002. *The Immanence of the Infinite: Hans Blumenberg and the Threshold to Modernity.* Washington: CUA Press.

Delekat, Friedrich. 1958. *Über den Begriff der Säkularisation.* Heidelberg: Quelle and Meyer.

Di Cesare, Donatella. 2013. *Gadamer: A Philosophical Portrait.* Translated by Niall Keane. Bloomington and Indianapolis: Indiana University Press

Gadamer, Hans-Georg. 1968. "Die Legitimität der Neuzeit by Hans Blumenberg." *Philosophische Rundschau* 15 (3): 201–9

Gadamer, Hans-Georg. 2004. *Truth and Method.* Translation revised by Joel Weinsheimer and Donald G. Marshall. London and New York: Continuum.

Gander, Hans-Helmuth. 2011. „Erhebung der Geschichtlichkeit des Verstehens zum hermeneutischen Prinzip." In *Wahrheit und Methode,* edited by Günter Figal, 93–111. Berlin: Akademie Verlag.

Greisch, Jean. 2004. "Umbesetzung Versus Umsetzung: Les ambiguïtés du théorème de la sécularisation d'après Hans Blumenberg." *Archives de Philosophie* 67 (2): 279–97.

Grondin, Jean. 2003. *The Philosophy of Gadamer.* Translated by Kathryn Plant. Chesham: Acumen.

Habermas, Jürgen. 1980. "The Hermeneutic Claim to Universality." In *Contemporary Hermeneutics,* edited by Josef Bleicher. London: Routledge, 181–211.

Habermas, Jürgen. 1984. *The Theory of Communicative Action: Volume One: Reason and the Rationalization of Society.* Translated by Thomas A. McCarthy. Boston: Beacon Press.

Harrington, Austin. 2001. *Hermeneutic Dialogue and Social Science: A Critique of Gadamer and Habermas.* London: Routledge.

Kopp-Oberstebrink, Herbert. 2014. "Umbesetzung." In *Blumenberg Lesen,* edited by Robert Buch and Daniel Weidner, 350–62. Berlin: Suhrkamp.

Löwith, Karl. 1949. *Meaning in History: The Theological Presuppositions of the Philosophy of History.* Chicago: University of Chicago Press.

Lübbe, Hermann. 1965. *Säkularisierung.* Freiburg: Karl Alber.

Pippin, Robert. 1987. "Blumenberg and the Modernity Problem." *The Review of Metaphysics* 40 (3): 535–57

Wallace. Robert. 1983. "Translator's Introduction." In Blumenberg 1983, xi–xxxi.

Warnke, Georgia. 1986. *Gadamer: Hermeneutics, Tradition and Reason.* Cambridge: Polity Press.

Weidner, Daniel. 2014. "Säkularisierung." In *Blumenberg Lesen,* edited by Robert Buch and Daniel Weidner, 245–59. Berlin: Suhrkamp.

MAYA SHIRATORI (Tokyo)

Aus-einander-setzung zwischen Hermeneutik und Dekonstruktion und Gadamers Solidaritätsverständnis

Aus-einander-setzung between Hermeneutics and Deconstruction
and Gadamer's Concept of Solidarity

Abstract

This paper will analyze the debate between Gadamer and Derrida and Gadamer's concept of solidarity. The previous research literature focused only on their first debate, which could only lead to limited results, even though the exchange between these two philosophers continued after the first debate. In addition, Gadamer revised a large part of his speech, which caused the first debate with Derrida, for publication. In this way, the accentuation of concepts and themes that Derrida found problematic in the published version differs considerably from that in Gadamer's real speech. For this reason, this paper will consider Gadamer's original manuscript, which is preserved in Deutsches Literatur Archiv in Marbach. My point is that in Derrida's funeral oration for Gadamer, Uninterrupted Dialogue, can be found some shared points of view between both philosophers, namely their interpretation of Paul Celan's poems. By means of their Celan interpretations, I will demonstrate that it is not good will that unites all human beings, but their existential fate to find death. Here we encounter the problem of solidarity in Gadamer's work, since in his interpretation of Celan he considers death (or mortality) to be the "ultimate solidarity" of human beings, whereas in his other texts he defines solidarity as a kind of friendship. Hence, Gadamer's understanding of solidarity is discussed in the last part of this paper. My argument is that the concept of solidarity and that of belonging are interconnected in Gadamer's texts and that in this point the concept of openness shows its fundamental role.

Keywords: Gadamer, Derrida, Celan, good will, solidarity, finitude

I. Tod als Solidarität? (*Aus-einander-setzung* zwischen Gadamer und Derrida über Celans Gedicht)

1. Ein anderer Blickwinkel auf die "Gadamer-Derrida-Debatte"

Im Jahr 1981 trafen sich Hans-Georg Gadamer und Jacques Derrida zum ersten Mal in Paris. Dieses Treffen wurde später als sogenannte Gadamer-Derrida-Debatte bekannt, die aus dem folgenden Austausch besteht:

- "Text und Interpretation" – Gadamers Beitrag basierend auf seinen Vortrag in Paris, der Ausgangspunkt der "Debatte"
- "Guter Wille zur Macht (I)" – Derridas drei Fragen an Gadamer mit kurzem Kommentar zum oben genannten Vortrag
- "Und dennoch: Macht des guten Willens" – Gadamers Antwort auf Derridas Fragen

Diese Beiträge sind 1984 zuerst auf Französisch erschienen, gefolgt von der deutschen, erweiterten Version *Text und Interpretation* (Forget, 1984), die im selben Jahr von Philippe Forget herausgegeben wurde. Dieses Treffen müsste jedenfalls eine Begegnung der Vertreter der zwei verschiedenen Strömungen der kontinentalen Philosophie des 20. Jahrhunderts gewesen sein. Sind die Bezeichnungen "Debatte" und "Konfrontation" (ebd., 10), wie sie in der meisten Forschungsliteratur genutzt werden, tatsächlich adäquat für diese Begegnung? Forget betitelt zum Beispiel seinen einleitenden Beitrag in *Text und Interpretation* "Leitfäden einer *unwahrscheinlichen* Debatte". Darin schreibt er, dass die "Debatte" der beiden Philosophen "nicht recht gelingen will" und Derridas Fragen an Gadamer "weitgehend ‚ungerecht' sein" mögen (ebd., 7-9). Er ist aber nicht der Einzige, der die Auseinandersetzung zwischen Gadamer und Derrida als "Debatte" oder "Konfrontation" betitelt und diese für eine misslungene oder eine nicht-entstandene hält. Auch Diane Michelfelder und Richard Palmer, die die englische Übersetzung der Gadamer-Derrida-Debatte herausgaben, schreiben das Scheitern des Gesprächs Derrida zu: "The failure of a conversation to materialize in Paris would consequently be attributable to Derrida's having seized upon the concept of the sign as the gateway to an understanding of language" (Michelfelder 1989, 8). Beim Rückblick auf diese "Debatte" ist es zu beachten, dass ein Großteil der bisherigen Forschungsliteratur nur die publizierte Version der Pariser Debatte in den Fokus nahm. Ist es ausreichend, nur diese publizierte Version als Quelle heranzuziehen? Gadamer hat für die Veröffentlichung von *Text und Interpretation* große Teile seines Vortrags umgeschrieben. Dadurch unterscheidet sich die Akzentuierung der von Derrida problematisierten Begriffe und Themen in der veröffentlichten Version beachtlich von der im Vortrag. So ist zum Beispiel aus den oben genannten Titeln der Debatte ersichtlich, dass es sich dabei um den *guten Willen* handeln soll, allerdings taucht dieser Begriff nur einmal in Gadamers veröffentlichten "Text und Interpretation" auf. Außerdem erwähnt Gadamer die Psychoanalyse in der publizierten Version kaum, während Derrida hingegen in "Guter Wille zur Macht (I)", Gadamers Ansicht in Frage stellt, ob die Psychoanalyse in die allgemeine Hermeneutik integriert werden soll. Einige Hintergründe von Derridas Fragen sind somit unklar geworden. Aus diesen Gründen soll im vorliegenden Artikel das originale Vortragsmanuskript Gadamers, das sich im Deutschen Literatur Archiv in Marbach befindet[1], zu Grunde gelegt werden. Dabei liegt der Schwerpunkt vor allem auf der Analyse, wie die Begriffe vom guten Willen und der Psychoanalyse, die Derrida scharf kritisiert, im Vortragsmanuskript behandelt wurden.

Das Ziel des vorliegenden Aufsatzes ist, sich der "Gadamer-Derrida-Debatte" unter einem anderen Aspekt zu nähern: anstelle von "Debatte" oder "Konfrontation" ist es meines Erachtens treffender, Ausdruck von *Aus-einander-setzung* im Heideggerschen Sinne zu benutzen und entsprechend zu analysieren. Es soll zudem angemerkt werden, dass dieser Artikel weder eine umfassende Analyse von Gadamers Texten rund um das Thema Dekonstruktion bereitstellt, noch das Auflisten der Unterschiede der beiden Philosophen, was die Interpretation von Heidegger oder Themen wie die Metaphysik und Psychoanalyse betreffen.

Meine Hypothese lautet, dass es zwischen Gadamer und Derrida trotz des Unterschieds ihrer Standpunkte eine gewisse Resonanz zu finden ist. Was fungiert in ihrer Auseinandersetzung als "gemeinsame Sache"? Das ist weder Gadamers *gute Wille* noch Derridas *responsabilité*, sondern es geht um Celans Gedichte. Ihre – exemplarische – Auseinandersetzung um diese Sache widerspricht weder Gadamers philosophischer Hermeneutik noch Derridas Dekonstruktion, wie es im Folgenden erläutert werden soll. Ihre Begegnung wird oft nur im Kontext der Konfrontation von Hermeneutik und Dekonstruktion thematisiert. Wie die Begegnung selbst, so muss der weitere Verlauf ihres Austausches nach der Pariser Begegnung genauer erforscht werden, um den Gehalt der "Gadamer-Derrida-Debatte" zu bergen.

2. 1981: erste Begegnung in Paris

Eine Analyse der Auseinandersetzung zwischen Gadamer und Derrida muss zunächst mit der Klärung der Gründe angefangen werden, weshalb ihre Begegnung überhaupt als "Debatte" oder "Konfrontation" bezeichnet worden ist. Wie bereits erwähnt, stellte Derrida nach Gadamers Vortrag in Paris drei Fragen, die alle auf das Konzept des *guten Willens* gerichtet sind, den Gadamer in seinem Vortrag betont hatte. Da der gute Wille in der publizierten Version von "Text und Interpretation" jedoch nur einmal auftaucht, wird in einigen Interpretationen behauptet, dass Derrida wegen eines Begriffs, den Gadamer nur ein einziges Mal verwendet habe und dem er somit keinen großen Wert beimaß, Haarspalterei betreibt (Di Cesare 2004, 74; Dasenbrock 1994, 267). Im Marbacher-Manuskript wird dieser Begriff aller-

---

[1] Das Vortragsmanuskript von "Text und Interpretation" (Gadamer 1982) besteht aus den 23 maschinengeschriebenen Blättern (Seite 13 fehlt).

dings sechs Mal verwendet, deswegen darf die Bedeutsamkeit des *guten Willens* nicht unterschätzt werden. Es ist daher angezeigt zu klären, an welcher Stelle dieses Konzept im Marbach-Manuskript Verwendung findet.

Im Redetext erläutert Gadamer zunächst, was er unter den Begriffen "Verstehen" und "Interpretation" als Verständigung und Gespräch mit einem anderen fasst: "Verstehen ist nur in Verständigung. Verständigung, das schliesst [sic] natürlich ein, und alles allererstes, die Partnerschaft des einen und des anderen. Es gibt keine Rede ohne Anrede" (Gadamer 1982, 6). In diesem Sinne sieht er in dem *guten Willen* die erste Bedingung, die die Verständigungsmöglichkeit bestimmt:

> Die erste Bedingung ist: guter Wille. Es gibt keine Verständigung, wo nicht sowohl der Sprechende mit gutem Willen das zu sagen sucht, was er meint, und wo der Zuhörende oder Antwortende nicht mit gutem Willen das, was der andere sagen wollte, herauszuhören und auf es einzugehen versucht. (Ebd., 7)

An dieser Stelle wird die Voraussetzung deutlich, dass beide Gesprächspartner, also sowohl der Sprechende als auch der Zuhörende, einen *guten Willen* haben sollen. Auch als Gadamer anschließend die zweite Bedingung erläutert, unterstreicht er erneut die Bedeutung des *guten Willens* in seinen Augen: "Also, meine These ist: erste Bedingung – dieses füreinander mit *gutem Willen* Geöffnetsein und das zweite ist selbstverständlich, dass wir etwas sagen, dass wir über etwas Verständigung suchen und nur in dieser Abzweckung[sic] überhaupt aufeinander hören". Im Konkreten beschreibt dieser *gute Wille* die "Bereitschaft, den anderen in seinem sachlichen Rechten geltend zu machen" und ohne diesen gelinge die "Verständigung *mit* jemandem *über* etwas" (ebd., 8) nicht. Nach der publizierten Version von *Text und Interpretation* wird dieser *gute Wille*, "einander zu verstehen", sowohl "im schriftlichen Gespräch" als auch im "mündlichen Austausch" "in Anspruch genommen" (Gadamer 1984, 38). Dieser *gute Wille* wurde von Derrida in dessen ersten Frage stark kritisiert, weil er sich als "Axiom" für "die absolute Verbindlichkeit im Bestreben nach Verständigung" (Derrida 1984, 56-57) darstellt. Darüber hinaus bezieht Derrida Gadamers Konzept des *guten Willens* auf die Metaphysik und weist darauf hin, dass dieser "einer vergangenen Epoche", die eigentlich Heidegger zu überwinden versuchte, "nämlich jener der Metaphysik des Willens" (ebd., 57) angehören soll. Auch in seiner dritten Frage greift Derrida diesen *guten Willen* an und stellt die Frage, ob "die Bedingung des Verstehens" *nicht* "ein sich kontinuierlich entfaltender Bezug" wie Gadamer behauptet, sein soll, sondern vielmehr einen "Bruch des Bezugs", "eine Aufhebung aller Vermittlung" (ebd., 58) sein soll. Derrida beendet seine dritte Frage mit einem Zweifel an Gadamers These wie folgt: "Ich bin nun meinerseits auch nicht sicher, ob wir eben diese Erfahrung überhaupt machen,

die Professor Gadamer meint, nämlich daß im Dialog "Einvernehmen" oder erfolgs-
bestätigende Zustimmung zustandekommt." (ebd., 58) Was Derrida Gadamer gegenüber stellt, ist die Kritik am *guten Willen* und skeptische Fragen nach der vor-
programmierten Kontinuität und dem sich an Konsens richtenden Verstehensprozess
à la Gadamer.

Über die Pariser Begegnung veröffentlicht Richard Bernstein, einen Aufsatz
mit dem Titel "The Conversation that Never Happened". Darin weist er auf die
Gemeinsamkeiten zwischen den beiden Philosophen hin, wie zum Beispiel, dass der
Begriff "play" zwar in unterschiedlicher Weise aber in den jeweiligen Theorien der
beiden eine bedeutsame Rolle spielt und sowohl Gadamer als auch Derrida Verstehen und Interpretation nicht für Kunst (techne), sondern für die Verantwortung für
die Sache halten (Bernstein 2008, 591). Dennoch geht Bernstein nicht über die Konsequenz hinaus, die in den bisherigen Forschungen wiederholt wird, und kommt
zum folgenden Schluss: "The so-called encounter of Gadamer and Derrida strikes
one as a classic instance of non-communication, of two philosophers speaking past
each other; neither really making substantial contact" (ebd., 578). Ist das tatsächlich
der Fall? Bernstein versucht die Gemeinsamkeiten und die Unterschiede von Gadamer und Derrida zu extrahieren und beschreibt ihren Kontrast folgendermaßen:

> Gadamer's "conversation," "dialogue," "understanding," and "fusion
> of horizons" are shaped by a metaphorics of overcoming barriers,
> achieving agreement, commonality, and reconciliation. But Derrida
> constantly speaks of rupture, of abysses, of "possible impossibles"
> and "impossible possibles." Derrida, in his deconstructive practices,
> seems to delight in locating discontinuities, breaks, obstaclest "con-
> tradictory logics" and unstable undecidables. (Ebd., 588)

Die Formulierung "unstable decidable", stellt ein gemeinsamer Bezugspunkt von
Gadamer und Derrida dar, wie im Folgenden erläutert wird. Bernstein sieht einerseits "a productive tension" (ebd., 597) zwischen den beiden Philosophen, aber
andererseits lautet seine Konsequenz "there is no evidence that they ever really had a
real dialogue" (ebd., 579). Dass dabei die Texte nach der Pariser Begegnung gar
nicht thematisiert werden, lässt den Vergleich als zu kurzatmig erscheinen.

Jedenfalls sollte das Pariser Treffen nicht einfach für fehlgeschlagen und
misslungen oder für Nichtzustandekommen gehalten werden, denn aus dieser "Debatte" ist mindestens ein Widerspruch Gadamers Hermeneutik ersichtlich geworden,
der bislang ungeachtet wird. Als Voraussetzung der Verständigung *guten Willen* zu
haben, den Wahrheitsanspruch des anderen anzunehmen, und dann das Verstehen als
Gespräch zu beginnen. All dies scheint auf den ersten Blick plausibel und harmlos,
jedoch verbirgt darin aber auch die Gewalt des Willens – das was Nietzsche nämlich

als "Wille zur Macht" benannt hat und was die Pointe von Derridas Fragen formte. Für Derrida bedeutet Gadamers *gute Wille* nichts anders als ein Erbe der Metaphysik, das sich von Plato bis Kant erstreckt und eigentlich der Vergangenheit angehören soll.

3. Die Celan-Lektüre von Gadamer und Derrida

Die bisherige Erläuterung in den vorigen Abschnitten evoziert womöglich den Eindruck, dass sich Gadamer und Derrida in den mehreren Hinsichten nicht miteinander verständigen können: Während Gadamer den *guten Willen* beim Verstehen als eine Gegebenheit für jeden ansieht, betont Derrida die Bedeutsamkeit des Bruchs und der Ruptur im Verstehen. Somit scheint es, dass die beiden von den völlig anderen Voraussetzungen fürs Verstehen ausgehen und daher ihre "Debatte" sich nicht ineinandergreifen lässt. In diesem Abschnitt soll es aufgezeigt werden, – wie Donatella Di Cesare auch darauf hinwies – dass sich der Verbindungsknoten zwischen Gadamer und Derrida doch in ihren Celan-Lektüren finden lässt. Interessanterweise publizierten die beiden Philosophen im selben Jahr jeweils ihre Celan-Interpretation (Derrida 1986 / Gadamer 1986). Allerdings thematisieren sie darin verschiedene Gedichte Celans, was den Vergleich ihrer Lektüre schwermacht. Aus diesem Grund wird an dieser Stelle beabsichtigt, anhand ihrer Celan-Interpretationen, die vor allem in zweiten und dritten Teilen Derridas Trauerrede gezeigt werden, den Berührungspunkt von Gadamer und Derrida aufzuzeigen. In seiner Trauerrede versucht Derrida durch seine erneute Celan-Lektüre anhand Gadamer den Bruch bzw. die Ruptur, die er bei der Begegnung in Paris behauptete, mit Gadamers *gutem Willen* zu verbinden. Beispielsweise zieht er Gadamers Deutung von Celans "Wege im Schatten-Gebräch" heran und erläutert:

> Mehr noch als die Unentschiedenheit an sich bewundere ich Gadamers ausgesprochenen Respekt gegenüber einer solchen Unentschiedenheit. Sie scheint zwar die Entzifferung der Lektüre zu unterbrechen oder aufzuheben, sichert jedoch tatsächlich deren Zukunft. Die Unentschiedenheit hält die Aufmerksamkeit immerzu in Atem, d.h. am Leben, wach und wachsam, bereit zu neuem Engagement auf ganz anderen Wegen, bereit, jenes andere Wort mit gespitztem Ohr und genauem Hinhören kommen zu lassen, im Atem des andren Wortes und des Wortes des anderen gehalten – selbst dort, wo es noch unverständlich, unhörbar und unübersetzbar scheinen mag. *Die Unterbrechung ist unentschieden, sie unentscheidet* [indécide]. Sie haucht der Frage ihren Atem ein, der nicht etwa lähmend wirkt, sondern sie in Bewegung bringt. Die Unterbrechung setzt sogar eine

unendliche Bewegung frei. (Derrida 2004, 23; die Kursivierung ist von mir).

Durch die Aussage "Die Unterbrechung ist unentschieden, sie unentscheidet" zeigt Derrida die Berührungsmöglichkeit zwischen ihm und Gadamer auf, denn was er obigen als "Unentschiedenheit" beschreibt, erinnert einen an Gadamers Beschreibung der Offenheit in *Wahrheit und Methode* (Gadamer 1990, 369) und inhaltlich überlappt sich in hohem Maßen mit ihr. Hinzu kommt der Satz "Die Unterbrechung setzt sogar eine neue unendliche Bewegung frei", der die potenzielle Verbindungsmöglichkeit zwischen der Unterbrechung, die Derrida betont, und Gadamers "unendlichem Gespräch" darstellt. Darüber hinaus teilen sich die beiden Philosophen die Ansicht über Gedicht, vor allem die abstrusen und mehrdeutigen Gedichte Celans, dass es bei solchen Gedichten keine einzige entscheidende Interpretation zu geben ist. In Derridas Trauerrede lassen sich außerdem mehrere Passagen finden, in denen er die Fragen von Gadamer annahm und sich damit beschäftigte. Dies ist vor allem dort ersichtlich, wo Derrida Interpretation des letzten Verses "Die Welt ist fort, ich muss dich tragen" von Celans "Grosse, Glühende Wölbung" unternommen hat. Diesen kurzen, einfach aussehenden Vers versucht Derrida subtil und vielschichtig – er würde bestimmt "disséminal" beschreiben – auszulegen. Denn Derrida hält den Tod für das Ende einer Welt (Derrida 2007, 11) und dies trifft genau seine damalige Situation, d.h., Gadamers Tod ist auch das Ende einer Welt, die nunmehr "fort" ist und trotzdem Derrida tragen muss. In dieser Hinsicht drückt die folgende Passage genau Derridas damalige Situation aus:

> Ich bin allein auf der Welt, dort wo es keine Welt mehr gibt. Oder gar: Ich bin allein auf der Welt, sobald ich dir verpflichtet bin, sobald du von mir abhängst, sobald ich, unter vier Augen, von Angesicht zu Angesicht, ohne einen Dritten, Vermittler oder Schlichter, ohne auf Erden oder in der Welt einen eigenen Platz zu haben, die Verantwortung trage und übernehmen muß. Eine Verantwortung, der ich entsprechen muß, vor dir und für dich. (Derrida 2004, 43)

Dieser Passus legt offenkundig dar, dass Derrida "Verantwortung (responsabilité)" vor und für Gadamer trägt und sie übernehmen muss, "wo es keine Welt mehr gibt" und "ohne einen Dritten, Vermittler oder Schlichter". Nach Derrida stellt die "Erklärung" dieser Verantwortung auch "ein Engagement" (Derrida 2004, 43) dar, welches auf Französisch sowohl Beteiligung als auch *Versprechen*[2] bedeutet.

---

[2] Auch in seiner Gedenkschrift für Gadamer, die nach 10 Tagen nach Gadamers Tod in FAZ veröffentlicht wurde, nennt Derrida Versprechen als ein Licht, das "so viele Augenblicke unserer Freundschaft erhellt" hat. (Derrida 2002, 41)

Weil die Celan-Interpretation von Derrida in seiner Trauerrede sehr weitläufig und verwickelt ist, soll die Analyse an dieser Stelle nur auf Derridas Interpretation des Verses "Welt ist fort, ich muss dich tragen" konzentriert werden. Bei der Interpretation dieses einen Satzes fokussiert Derrida mehrfach auf die zwei Wörter, nämlich *tragen* und *fort*. *Tragen* bedeutet als Verb etwas (hoch-)heben, irgendwohin bringen oder etwas auf sich nehmen. Was Derridas Aufmerksamkeit jedoch besonders erweckt und auf sich zieht, ist die Zweideutigkeit von *tragen*. Das deutsche Wort *tragen* – wie Derrida auch mit einem französischen Wort *porter* darlegt – hat die Bedeutung, trächtig zu sein, aber auch, um jemanden Trauer zu tragen. In dieser Hinsicht erläutert Derrida:

> Wenn jedoch andererseits Tragen die Sprache der Geburt spricht, wenn es sich an ein anwesendes oder noch kommendes Lebewesen wenden muß, kann es sich doch auch an ein Totes wenden, an das Überlebende oder an deren Gespenster, und dies in einer Erfahrung, die darin besteht, den anderen in sich zu tragen, wie man Trauer trägt – und Melancholie trägt. (Ebd., 45)

Nach Derrida bedeuten sowohl Trächtig-zu-sein als auch Trauer-Tragen, *einen anderen in sich zu tragen*. Bedeutet das nicht, dass Derrida in diesem Vers "Die Welt ist fort, ich muss dich tragen" etwas ansieht, was den Lebenden und den Toten miteinander verbindet, d.h., den Tod, der sich zwischen Derrida und dem verstorbenen Gadamer befindet, als Bruch, aber gleichzeitig auch als Solidarität? Mit anderen Worten: Im Wort *tragen* sieht Derrida das Bild von Trauer, das es zwischen dem Leben und dem Tod, zwischen dem Lebenden und dem Toten gibt. Dennoch darf Derridas Celan-Interpretation in seiner Trauerrede nicht auf den Akt der Trauer im Freud'schen Sinne, d.h., die "normale" und "normative" Verinnerlichung des anderen reduziert werden:

> Nach Freud besteht die Trauer darin, den anderen in sich zu tragen. Es gibt keine Welt mehr, es ist das Weltende für den anderen bei seinem Tode, und ich nehme dieses Ende der Welt in mich auf, ich muß den anderen und seine Welt, die Welt in mir tragen: Introjektion, Verinnerlichung der Erinnerung, Idealisierung. Die Melancholie würde das Scheitern und die Pathologie dieser Trauer aufnehmen. Doch wenn *ich* den anderen in mir tragen *muß* (darin besteht Ethik), um ihm treu zu sein, um seine einzigartige Alterität zu respektieren, dann muß sich noch eine gewisse Melancholie gegen die übliche Trauer auflehnen. Sie darf sich niemals mit der idealisierenden Introjektion abfinden. Sie muß aufbegehren gegen das, was Freud mit einer gelassenen Sicherheit über sie sagt, als wolle er die Norm der

Normalität bestätigen. Die »Norm« ist gar nichts anderes als das gute Gewissen eines Gedächtnisschwunds. Sie erlaubt uns zu *vergessen*, daß wir, wenn wir den anderen in uns bewahren, ihn *wie uns* bewahren, wie ihn dann bereits *vergessen*. Das Vergessen beginnt hier. Also bedarf es der Melancholie. An diesem Ort diktiert das Leiden einer gewissen Pathologie das Gesetz – und das Gedicht, das dem anderen gewidmet ist. (Ebd., 46)

Ist diese Aussage nichts anderes als Derridas Treue und responsabilité gegenüber seinem verstorbenen Freund, Gadamer? Nachdem man Derridas diese energische Beschreibung über Trauer und Melancholie liest, ist es zudem einleuchtend, warum Derrida seine Trauerrede mit einem folgenden Geständnis beginnt:

Kann ich hier vor Ihnen meine Bewunderung für Hans-Georg Gadamer überhaupt angemessen und wahrheitsgetreu wiedergeben? Sie ist vor so langer Zeit aus Respekt und Zuneigung zu ihm entstanden, und in sie mischt sich dunkel eine uralte *Melancholie*. (Derrida 2004, 7; die Kursivierung ist von mir)

Darauffolgend fügt er gleich hinzu: "Diese Melancholie hat, so würde ich sagen, nicht nur historische Gründe". Die Melancholie, die Derrida an dieser Stelle erläutert, ist also weder die wehmütige Erinnerung an den Toten noch das Scheitern des pathologischen Trauerakts im freudianischen Sinne, sondern Widerstreben und Rebellion gegen das Vergessen und zugleich responsabilité, um Versprechen nicht zu vergessen.

Bisher stand Derridas Trauerrede im Fokus der Analyse und anschließend werde ich im Folgenden darauf hinweisen, dass die beiden Philosophen in ihren Celan-Interpretationen resonieren, wo sich ihre *Aus-einander-setzung* gestaltet, und sie beide jeweils in ihren eigenen Art und Weise das Erbe Heideggers Denkens antreten. Nach Gadamer sei Heideggers Versuch die Sprache des Denkens "mit der Sprache des Dichters" zu verbinden (Gadamer 1987, 227). Ist das nicht eben die Aufgabe, mit der sich Gadamer und Derrida jeweils in ihren Celan-Interpretationen befassen? Im Jahr 1975, d.h. vor der Begegnung mit Derrida, veröffentlicht Gadamer zwei Abhandlungen über Celans Gedicht *Tenebrae* und darin erwähnt er bereits Tod als *Solidarität*. Währenddessen schreibt Derrida im Vorwort von *Jedes Mal einzigartig, das Ende der Welt*, dass seine Trauerrede für Gadamer als die echte Einleitung dieses Buches angesehen werden soll und ihm der mehrmals genannte Vers von Celans "seit Jahren nicht mehr aus dem Sinn geht" (Derrida 2007, 13). Für eine genaue vergleichende Analyse ihrer Celan-Interpretationen ist hier kein Raum. Was aber aus den kleinen Auszügen ihrer Celan-Interpretationen herauslesbar ist, dass ihre Celan-Interpretationen Nachdenken über den Tod und den Leben fordern und darauf hinweisen, um das Verhältnis von Menschen, Welt und Gott zu überdenken.

In der Pariser "Debatte" betont Derrida den Bruch und die Ruptur, während Gadamer den jedem gemeinsamen *guten Willen* unterstricht. In der Tat aber lässt sich aus Gadamers Celan-Interpretation herauslesen – auch wenn Derrida interessanterweise diese Stelle in seiner Trauerrede nicht zitiert hat –, was Gadamer für die "letzte" Gemeinsamkeit des Menschen hält, ist nicht den *guten Willen* zur Verständigung oder zum Einverständnis, sondern, die Tatsache, dass jeder sterben muss:

> Da die Menschen den Tod kennen, unter dem Gesetz des Todes stehen, sind sie mit dem, der stirbt, *auf einzigartige Weise solidarisch.* Dessen soll der Sterbende sich im Beten zu uns vergewissern, *dieser letzten Gemeinsamkeit.* (Gadamer 1993, 455; die Kursivierung ist von mir)

Auch in "Die Erfahrung des Todes" hält Gadamer den Tod für "eine wahre Solidarität des Menschen" (Gadamer 1983, 293). Als eine "letzte Gemeinsamkeit" verbindet die Mortalität die Menschen, die Lebenden und sogar die Toten auch miteinander. Der Tod scheidet die beiden (Derrida von Gadamer, dem Lebenden vom Toten) aber stellt gleichzeitig Solidarität dar. Diese Doppeldeutigkeit des Todes bringt meines Erachtens Gadamers bislang unbeachtete Radikalität ans Licht. Diese Radikalität ist vor allem in "Sinn und Sinnverhüllung bei Paul Celan" ersichtlich, wo Gadamer seine Interpretation von Celans *Tenebrae* darlegt. In diesem Text fokussiert Gadamer vor allem auf das Moment des Sterbens Jesu Christi:

> 'Mein Gott, mein Gott, warum hast du mich verlassen?' Ist das überhaupt ein Gebet? *Gewiß ist es ein Anruf an Gott.* Und vielleicht muß man wirklich sagen, daß *eben darin der einzig mögliche Inhalt eines Gebetes überhaupt besteht,* solchen Anruf zu tun. Denn 'wir wissen nicht, was wir beten sollen'. (Gadamer 1993, 454; die Kursivierung ist von mir).

Besonders interessant im gerade zitierten Passus ist, dass Gadamer jene letzten Worte Jesu Christi, die üblicherweise als verzweifelter Schrei des Gekreuzigten verstanden werden, als ein Gebet und eine Anrufung von Gott auslegt. Dennoch taucht seine Radikalität nicht in der genannten Stelle auf, sondern in seiner Interpretation von Gott anhand Celans Gedichts, d.h. sogar für Gott gibt es Unkenntnis:

> Weil Gott den Tod nicht kennt, ist er in der Todesstunde nicht erreichbar. Wir dagegen kennen den Tod, wissen um ihn und seine Unausweichlichkeit und verstehen deshalb diesen letzten Seufzer der Verlassenheit zutiefst. Offenkundig wollten diese letzten Worte Jesu

nicht Zweifel an seinem Gott ausdrücken, sondern die Übergewalt des Leidens und des Todes besiegeln. (Ebd., 454)

Unkenntnis Gottes ist der Tod des Menschen und eben darin besteht die Gemeinsamkeit und Solidarität des Menschen. Was dieser Celan-Interpretation Gadamers eigen ist, läuft darauf hinaus, dass der "absolute Herr", den Gadamer in diesem Gedicht anspricht, nicht Gott, sondern doch der Tod ist: "Das, wovon wir ergriffen sind, kann nur der 'absolute Herr' sein, der Tod, dem die Menschen gehören" (ebd., 455).

Aufgrund der oben vorgenommen Analyse stellt sich nun meine These: der Austausch von Gadamer und Derrida lässt sich als *Aus-einander-setzung* auffassen, die weder der Hermeneutik noch der Dekonstruktion widerspricht. Gadamer und Derrida sind ihrer unterschiedlichen Positionen und des daraus entstandenen Bruchs zwischen ihnen inne, halten Abstand, hören trotzdem nicht auf, einander zu fragen und zu antworten. Wird die sogenannte "Gadamer-Derrida-Debatte" aus derartigem Standpunkt erneut berücksichtigt, lässt sich nicht sagen, dass ihre Auseinandersetzung "zwischen der Vertrautheit und der Fremdheit", wo Gadamer eben als den "wahre(n) Ort der Hermeneutik" (Gadamer 1990, 300) ansieht, entstanden ist? Ihre "Debatte" 1981 schien zwar zerstritten zu sein, stellt jedoch Derridas Trauer um Gadamer durch seine Celan-Deutung den Gestus dar, dass Derrida eben an der "gemeinsame(n) Sache" (ebd., 391) teilnimmt, was sich Gadamer zum Grundprinzip für Verstehen und Gespräch macht. Derridas Beschäftigung mit Celans Gedichten legt gleichzeitig seine Verantwortung gegenüber Gadamer dar. Zudem, was ihre Auseinandersetzung ermöglicht, ist Celans Gedicht als *Sache*. Wird ihr Austausch in derartigen Weisen gelesen, lässt sich sagen, dass Gadamer und Derrida jeweils im Sinne von "Tod als Solidarität" und "Trauer" Heideggers Ansicht "verstehendes Sein zum Ende, d.h. als Vorlaufen in den Tod" (Heidegger 1927/1967, 305) nachfolgen. Wie sich beiden jeweils mit der Aufgabe von Heidegger, nämlich "die Sprache des Denkens (…) mit der Sprache des Dichters" (Gadamer 1987, 227) zu verbinden, und mit dem Thema "Sein zum Ende" beschäftigen, muss weiterhin erforscht werden.

II. Freundschaft und Solidarität bei Gadamer – Über ihre Probleme und Bezugspunkte zum Begriff der *Endlichkeit*

1.   Einen Platz für Solidaritätsbegriff in Gadamers Hermeneutik?

Im vorigen Kapitel wurde die These dargelegt, dass es sich in der sogenannten Gadamer-Derrida-Debatte weder um eine aggressiv geführte Debatte noch eine feindliche Konfrontation handelt, sondern um eine *Aus-einander-setzung* im Heideggerschen Sinne. Bei der Analyse von Gadamers Celan-Lektüre wurde herausgearbeitet, dass die Idee vom Tod als Solidarität in Gadamers Celan-Deutung wurzelt und dieser den Tod für eine "letzte Gemeinsamkeit" der Menschen hält. Jedoch gibt es bei ihm auch eine andere Konzeption der Solidarität. Dieses Kapitel fokussiert daher auf die Analyse dieses bislang wenig beachteten Begriffs der Solidarität bei Gadamer. Dabei soll geklärt werden, in welcher Konstellation von Gadamers Hermeneutik der Solidaritätsbegriff steht und welche Problematik dieser Begriff in sich trägt.

Gadamers Ausführungen über Solidarität sind relativ begrenzt, was auf den ersten Blick den Eindruck erweckt, dass der Begriff Solidarität in Gadamers Theorie keinen großen Stellenwert besitzt. Zudem gilt die Solidarität – anders als *sensus communis* oder Horizontverschmelzung – nicht unbedingt als ein für Gadamer typischer Begriff. Allerdings zeigt eine nähere Analyse wie er einerseits vom verbreiteten Solidaritätsverständnis, sich beim Einsatz ein gemeinsames Ziel oder beim Widerstand gegen einen gemeinsamen Feind zu verbinden, abweicht. Andererseits ist der Begriff in ein grundlegendes Konzept von Gadamer eingebettet. Neben "Sinn und Sinnverhüllung bei Paul Celan" und "Die Erfahrung des Todes" behandelt Gadamer Solidarität in "Freundschaft und Solidarität". In letzteren Text wird die Solidarität mit den Freundschaftsbegriffen bei Plato und Aristoteles assoziiert, was deren Sinngehalt von der Solidarität als Tod unterscheidet. Eine umfassende Analyse hinsichtlich Gadamers Beschreibung des Solidaritätsbegriffs wird zeigen, dass hinter beiden Solidaritätsbegriffen eine gemeinsame Voraussetzung, die *Endlichkeit des Menschen* steht.

2.   Freundschaft und Solidarität bei Gadamer

2.1. Gadamers *vage* Begriffe: Freundschaft und Solidarität

Die Solidarität wurde je nach dem Zeitalter oder Fachbereich unterschiedlich begriffen. Gadamers Solidaritätsbegriff hebt sich jedoch davon ab. Zum Beispiel verbindet er seinen Solidaritätsbegriff im Abschnitt über *sensus communis* in *Wahrheit und Methode*, in dem er eigentlich den Einfluss von Shaftesbury auf den Humanismus im 18. Jahrhundert erläutert, mit dem Begriff der Freundschaft. Dabei sieht er *wit* und *humour*, die Shaftesbury "auf den geselligen Umgang unter Freunden" beschränkt, dergestalt an, dass beide eben von "einer tieferen Solidarität mit seinem Gegenüber" (Gadamer 1990, 30) ermöglicht werden. An dieser Stelle setzt Gadamer die Solidarität unter den Freunden voraus, damit Witze und Humor überhaupt funktionieren können. Die Idee dieser auf Freundschaft basierenden Solidarität kommt nicht nur in *Wahrheit und Methode* vor, sondern wird in Gadamers späterer Schrift "Freundschaft und Solidarität" unter Bezugnahme auf den Solidaritätsbegriff der griechischen Antike weiterentwickelt. Die Diskussion über Freundschaft und Solidarität, die Gadmer in dieser kleinen Schrift und in "Freundschaft und Selbsterkenntnis" führt, steht im Folgenden im Fokus.

"Freundschaft und Solidarität" gilt als nahezu einziger Text, in dem sich Gadamer dem Solidaritätsbegriff als Hauptthema widmet. Er betont: "Wir müssen erkennen, wie im Leben unserer Gesellschaft die Gruppierung zu Solidaritäten führt und uns damit anderen gegenüber verpflichtet" (Gadamer 2000, 57). Hier ist die Verpflichtung für die gegenseitige Hilfe, die ursprüngliche Bedeutung der Solidarität, die am Anfang erwähnt wurde, zu sehen. Obwohl in "Freundschaft und Solidarität" ein Großteil des Texts nicht der Beschreibung von Solidarität, sondern von Freundschaft gewidmet ist, meint er, dass man Freundschaft "nur leben aber nicht definieren kann" (ebd., 57).

2.2. Gadamer Analyse des antiken Freundschaftsbegriff

Darüber hinaus zieht Gadamer die Freundschaftsbegriffe der griechischen Antike heran. Dabei wird vor allem die Freundschaftskonzeption in Platons *Lysis* thematisiert[3]. In diesen wird die Frage gestellt, ob eine wahre bzw. echte Freundschaft auf Gleichartigkeit oder auf Ungleichartigkeit basieren soll:

> So ist es wohl kein Wunder, daß die erste sokratische Frage lautet, ob Freundschaft darauf beruht, daß Gleiches sich zu Gleichem findet. Das kann den Jungen einleuchten und auch, daß das nicht standhält. Sie sehen schnell, daß das nicht stimmt. Vielleicht ist eher das Umgekehrte wahr: Freundeswahl bildet sich oft durch das Ungleiche, indem man in dem Anderen etwas Bewundernswertes und Liebenswertes entdeckt. (Gadamer 2000, 58)

An dieser Stelle stimmt Gadamer einerseits der auf Ungleichem beruhenden Freundschaftskonzeption zu, in der man "etwas Bewundernswertes und Liebenswertes" an einem Anderen, was man selber nicht hat, findet, andererseits zieht er Platons Begriff von *Oikos* und *Oikéion* heran, was der oben genannten Stellen zu widersprechen scheint. Oikos bedeutet in der griechischen Sprache "Haus" und daraus stammt z.B. das Wort Ökonomie, die ursprünglich "Hauswirtschaft" bedeutet. Mit Oikos ist Oikéion eng verbunden und bedeutet die "in einem Haus Wohnende[n]", d.h. Familie, Verwandte oder Vertraute (Inazu 2009, 36). Daraus resultierte Gadamers folgende Stellungnahme, dass er Solidarität auf die gemeinsame Heimat oder Herkunft basieren lässt und die Freundschaft aus dem gemeinsamen Heim und Haus stammt:

---

[3] Eine andere Variante Gadamers Analyse über *Lysis*, die in der vorliegenden Arbeit gelegentlich erwähnt werden soll, findet sich: (Gadamer 1985, 171-186)

Dann gibt es aber die wahre, die vollkommene Freundschaft. Die wirkliche Freundschaft. Was ist sie, was heißt das, daß sie das *Oikéion* sei? Das Zuhause, das, wovon wir nicht sagen kann, was es ist. (…) Das wissen wir alle, daß Heimat etwas Unvordenkliches ist. Etwas wovon wir nicht sagen können, warum es so die Seele rührt und warum es so die Menschen verbindet. *Aber daß Heimat und Herkunft eine Bindung darstellt, eine Art Gemeinsamkeit, eine Art Solidarität echter Art ist, da braucht es das nicht erst, daß man sich solidarisch erklärt.* Man ist es und will gar nicht wissen, was da eigentlich im Spiele ist. (Gadamer 2000, 60; nur die letztere Kursivierung sind von mir).

Im Gegensatz zu der vorhin erwähnten Freundschaft, die sich durch das Ungleiche bildet, verbindet Gadamer hier die Freundschaft mit der Heimat und Herkunft als "eine Art Gemeinsamkeit". Als Oikéion, also unter den aus der gemeinsamen Heimat und Herkunft Stammenden muss man sich nicht solidarisch erklären[4]. Bedeutet das aber nicht, dass man sich mit jemandem aus der gemeinsamen Herkunft, d.h. in einer "Wir"-Beziehung miteinander verständigen kann, ohne sich solidarisch zu erklären? Wenn ja, lässt sich das nicht als Gadamers Wiederkehr zu jenem eine bestimmte Gemeinsamkeit voraussetzenden Verstehen lesen, wie er bei seinem Pariser Vortrag von 1981 den guten Willen zum miteinander Verstehen betonte und von Derrida stark kritisiert wurde?

Gadamer schränkt jedoch Heim und Haus nicht auf den Platz für Familie und Blutsverwandtschaft ein, sondern er sieht Oikos als "die Stätte des Zusammenlebens" mit den Anderen an und behauptet: "Nun, eins ist jedenfalls sicher: Heim und Haus, das ist die Stätte des Zusammenlebens. Das heisst [sic] nicht gemeinsame Überzeugungen haben, das ist also deswegen auch nicht die Übereinstimmung in Neigung und Interessen" (Gadamer 2000, 61). Eben diese Stelle ist, woran sich die Wissenschaftler:innen aus dem englischsprachigen Raum, wie Darren Wahlhof und Georgia Warnke in ihren Aufsätzen zu Gadamers Solidaritätsbegriff, die unten in Betracht gezogen werden, anlehnen. Auf Grundlage dieses Gedankens betonen sie den Aspekt von Zusammenleben mit dem Anderen bei Gadamer besonders stark.

Ob "Freundschaft darauf beruht, daß Gleiches sich zu Gleichem findet" oder im Gegenteil, diese Frage gerät in Platons *Lysis* schließlich zur Aporie. So ähnlich ergeht es auch Gadamers Auffassung von Freundschaft. Diese auf den ersten Blick

---

[4] Statt mit Heimat und Herkunft verbindet Gadamer Oikeion allerdings in "Logos und Ergon im platonischen 'Lysis'" mit Zugehörigkeit, die später in diesem Kapitel im Mittelpunkt steht (Gadamer, 1985, 184). Selbstredend erinnert dies an Heideggers Formel "Sprache ist ein Haus der Seienden".

etwas widersprüchlich wirkende Unentschiedenheit, ob Freundschaft auf die Gemeinsamkeit oder Andersheit beruht, deute ich als *Gadamers Offenheit für den Begriff der Freundschaft*. Beachtenswert ist auf jeden Fall, dass er ausdrücklich betont, dass *nicht* die Einmütigkeit vom Ich und dem Anderen die wahre Freundschaft ausmacht (Gadamer 2000, 61). In "Freundschaft und Solidarität" findet sich zwar keine Erwähnung mehr, aber Gadamer beschreibt in "Logos und Ergon im platonischen 'Lysis'" die andere Möglichkeit der Freundschaft:

> *Zu einem Gegensatz kann es immer auch noch die dritte Möglichkeit des Weder-Noch geben.* Und so scheint es mit der Freundschaft wirklich zu sein. Wer zu jemandem Freundschaft empfindet, meint in dem anderen etwas, das er selber nicht ist. Aber was er so nicht ist, *ist wie eine Unentschiedenheit – und damit Möglichkeit – in ihm selbst,* die einen in anderen das Vorbild suchen läßt. Alle frühen Freundschaften, die das Niveau der Knabenfreundschaft hinter sich lassen, sind so etwas wie Vorbildwahlen, und alle dauernden Freundschaften behalten etwas davon, wenn auch in einer Gegenseitigkeit, die einen neuen Grund legt. (Gadamer 1985, 180; die Kursivierung ist von mir).

Diese andere Möglichkeit hält Gadamer für einen Grund der Freundschaft und sieht sogar darin die Offenheit bzw. Möglichkeit, über sich hinauszugehen: "Wenn einer, der weder gut noch schlecht ist, das Gute zu lieben vermag, so heißt das nicht nur, daß er selber trotz der Anwesenheit von etwas Fehlendem, und d. h. von etwas Schlechtem, nicht selber schlecht ist, sondern heißt auch positiv, *daß er über sich selbst hinausgeht*; das eben ist das Verlangen." (Ebd., 181)

Ferner kommt seine These: "Freundschaft braucht man erst einmal mit sich selbst. Dessen bedarf es, damit man für den Anderen und mit ihm wirklich verbunden ist." [5] (Gadamer 2000, 61) Diese Einigung mit sich selbst setzt Gadamer deshalb als "den wahren Grund und die Bedingung für alle mögliche Verbindung mit anderen" (ebd., 60) voraus, weil er vom altgriechischen Spruch "Erkenne dich selbst" ausgeht:

> 'Erkenne dich selbst'. Das heißt, erkenne, daß du *nur ein Mensch bist* und *nicht* ein von göttlicher Vorsehung Bestellter oder von einem besonderen Charisma Gesalbter, dem sozusagen diesseits und jenseits aller menschlichen Verbindlichkeiten Vorrecht, Sieg und Erfolg, verliehen ist. Das alles nicht. Das ist nun offenbar Freundschaft, was Aristoteles hinzufügt: *daß man sich am Anderen erkennt und daß auch*

---

[5] Die ähnliche Behauptung findet sich auch in "Was ist Praxis?" (Gadamer 1976).

der Andere sich an uns erkennt. Nicht allein im Sinne des: So ist er. Vielmehr auch in dem Sinne, daß *wir einander das Anderssein zubilligen* und daß es geradezu – mit Droysen zu reden gilt: 'So mußt du sein, denn so liebe ich dich'. Kurz, das ist wahre Freundschaft. (Ebd., 62; die Kursivierung ist von mir)

Wie oben erwähnt, hält Gadamer Freundschaft eigentlich für undefinierbar. Aus den bisherigen Ausführungen werde ich dennoch folgende Definition herleiten: Die "wahre Freundschaft" bei Gadamer bedeutet, dass man den Anderen so liebt, wie er ist, ohne ihn ändern zu wollen, und sie wird von der Offenheit für Anders- und Fremdheit und der Reziprozität, was als gegenseitige Anerkennung der Unterschiede zwischen dem Ich und dem Anderen konkretisiert wird, gestützt und im Zusammenleben mit dem Anderen entwickelt.

2.3. Freundschaftsbegriff in "Freundschaft und Selbsterkenntnis"

Während Gadamer in "Freundschaft und Solidarität" die Freundschaft mit sich selbst betont, stellt er jedoch in seiner 1985 veröffentlichten Schrift "Freundschaft und Selbsterkenntnis. Zur Rolle der Freundschaft in der griechischen Ethik" auch eine kritische Einsicht über die Freundschaft mit sich selbst dar.

Selbst wenn die Sympathie oder das Wohlwollen tatsächlich auf beiden Seiten vorläge und insofern Gegenseitigkeit bestünde, wären sie, solange sie einander nicht wirklich offenbar und miteinander verbunden sind, bloße Freundlichkeit. Die *gemeinsame* Bedingung aller 'Freundschaft' ist eben mehr: *echte 'Verbundenheit', die* – in verschiedenen Graden – *ein 'Zusammenleben' bedeutet.* (Gadamer 1991, 401 / außer dem ersten Kursiven sind es von mir)

An dieser Stelle scheint Gadamer mehr Gewicht auf die Verbundenheit, die im Zusammenleben mit dem Anderen kultiviert wird, als auf die Freundschaft mit sich selbst zu legen. Im darauffolgenden Abschnitt schreibt er sogar, dass sich Aristoteles wohl der *Paradoxie* bewusst sei, "die in der platonischen Lehre liegt, daß einer mit sich selbst Freund sein muß, wenn er der Freund von anderen soll sein können. Dem natürlichen Vorverständnis von Freundschaft und von Selbstliebe entspricht das durch aus nicht" (ebd., 401-402). Hieraus lässt sich herauslesen, dass Gadamer auf eine Widerspruchsmöglichkeit an Platonischer Freundschaft mit sich selbst, die er selber in seinem 2000 veröffentlichten Text zum Vorbild nimmt, hinweist. Der Widerspruch im Platonischen Freundschaftsbegriff lässt sich so zusammenfassen: Die Freundschaft, in der "zwei unzertrennliche Freunde" wie eine Seele wären, soll es nur bei den guten bzw. großartigen (spoudaíos) Menschen geben. Allerdings, wer in

Wahrheit gut oder großartig ist, braucht eigentlich keine Freunde, weil er alleine sich selbst genügt und vollendet. Diese klare Kritik an Freundschaft mit sich selbst in "Freundschaft und Selbsterkenntnis" findet sich in "Freundschaft und Solidarität" nicht mehr. Das könnte möglicherweise als ein Mangel an Kohärenz von Gadamers Freundschaftsbegriff betrachtet werden. Zugleich kann diese Auffassung von Freundschaft meines Erachtens als eine Synthese von den zwei möglicherweise zum Gegensatz neigenden Elementen, nämlich von der Freundschaft mit sich selbst und dem Zusammenleben mit den Anderen, betrachtet werden. Beide findet Gadamer unentbehrlich für die wahre Freundschaft. Zudem muss darauf geachtet werden, dass der Sinngehalt der Freundschaft mit sich selbst in "Freundschaft und Selbsterkenntnis" und derjenigen in "Freundschaft und Solidarität" anders sind. Während in "Freundschaft und Selbsterkenntnis" die Freundschaft mit sich selbst als solche nur bei den Guten und Großartigen, die fast Gott nah sind, möglich ist, wird die Freundschaft mit sich selbst in "Freundschaft und Solidarität" als Erkennung davon geschildert, dass man "nur ein Mensch" und nicht ein von Gott ausgewähltes besonderes Wesen ist. Das bedeutet zu erkennen, *dass man als Mensch anders als Gott ein endliches Wesen ist.* Anders als Gott braucht der Mensch als endliches Wesen Freund. Hier lässt sich bestätigen, dass hinter dem Freundschaftsbegriff Gadamers auch die Endlichkeit des Menschen steckt.

2.4. Die Endlichkeit des Menschen als Hintergrund von Freundschaft und Solidarität

Aufgrund der oben geführten Analyse von Gadamers Freundschaftsbegriff wird im Weiteren Gadamers Solidaritätsbegriff in den Vordergrund gerückt. Auch wenn Gadamer beide Begriffe für untrennbar hält, gibt es an seinem Solidaritätsbegriff eine Besonderheit, die sein Freundschaftsbegriff nicht hat. Darren Walhof behauptet, dass Solidarität und Freundschaft weder dasselbe Phänomen noch parallel sind, sondern er definiert die Solidarität als "partial and temporary manifestations of bounds that reflect a civic life together of reciprocal co-perception" (Walhof 2006, 571). Oben haben wir gesehen, dass sich die "wahre Freundschaft" bei Gadamer im Zusammenleben entwickeln, das von der Offenheit, der Reziprozität als die Anerkennung der Andersheit zwischen dem Ich und dem Anderen, und dem Vertrauen unterstützt wird. Dennoch lässt sich aus der folgenden Stelle in "Freundschaft und Solidarität" herauslesen, dass die Solidarität auch von einer gemeinsamen Bedrohung bzw. der Betroffenheit erweckt wird:

> Man erklärt sich in etwas solidarisch oder auch man fühlt sich solidarisch. Ich erinnere mich im Augenblick an Dinge, die in meine eigene Lebenserfahrung hineinleuchten, und ich bin gewiß, daß die

Älteren unter Ihnen auch Ähnliches erlebt haben. Ich meine, wie der Bombenkrieg Solidarität geweckt hat. Plötzlich war der Nachbar, dieser in den städtischen Lebensverhältnissen ganz unbekannte Fremde, zum Leben erwacht. So wirkt Not, und *insbesondere Not, die alle betrifft, sodaß ungeahnte Möglichkeiten des sich solidarisch Fühlens und des solidarisch Handelns zustandekommen.* (Gadamer 2000, 63; die Kursivierung ist von mir).

Zu beachten sind die letzten Zeilen: Dass "insbesondere Not, die alle betrifft," "ungeahnte Möglichkeiten des sich solidarisch Fühlens und des solidarisch Handelns" erweckt, erinnert uns an den Tod als Solidarität. Die Solidarität, die durch Not und Betroffenheit gebracht wird, habe keine Bedeutung mehr, – so Gadamer – "wie uns das Wort solidarisch es allerdings nahelegt" (ebd., 63). Dies drückt aus, dass die Solidarität bei Gadamer weder gegenseitige Entschädigung noch Bund meint, wie die ursprüngliche Wortbedeutung nahelegt, sondern, sie bedeutet, bei der gleichen Not zu sein, d.h. *Not gemeinsam zu tragen.* Außerdem lässt sich auch der Tod als die Not, "die alle betrifft" begreifen. Hinzu kommt die folgende Beschreibung in "Freundschaft und Solidarität": "Bis in die Wortbedeutung hinein müssen wir auch im militärischen Bereich an Soldatentreue denken, die im Kriegsfalle die Solidarität auf Leben und Tod von uns fordert" (ebd., 64). Auch daraus lässt sich ableiten, dass die Solidarität, die in enger Verbindung mit dem Freundschaftsbegriff steht, auch mit dem Tod als Solidarität zu tun hat. Zum Thema Tod und Solidarität schreibt Gadamer zudem in "Was ist Praxis? Die Bedingungen gesellschaftlicher Vernunft":

Der Mensch ist ein Wesen, dessen Lebensinstinkt so verdreht worden ist, daß er gegen über allem, was wir aus dem Tierreich kennen, eine unbestrittene Besonderheit besitzt, die auch nicht durch das Studium von Tiergesellschaften und ihre Kommunikationsformen, Solidaritätsformen und Aggressionsformen auch nur im geringsten gemindert wird. *Das ist das Hinausdenken des Menschen über sein eigenes Leben auf der Welt, d.h. das Denken des Todes.* Das ist die Bestattung der Toten, vielleicht das Grundphänomen der Menschwerdung. (Gadamer 1976, 61; die Kursivierung ist von mir).

Ebenso wie bei der Beschreibung des Freundschaftsbegriffs stellt Gadamer hier den Menschen den Tieren gegenüber und hält das Denken des Todes für eine Charakteristik, die den Menschen vom Tier abhebt. Zusammenfassend: Sowohl Freundschaft als auch Tod und Bestattung des Toten als Solidarität bzw. Tragen des Todes hält Gadamer für etwas, was dem Menschen eigen ist. Dabei stellt er den Menschen Gott und Tieren gegenüber und hebt dabei die Endlichkeit des Menschen besonders heraus.

3. Solidarität, der Andere und Politik

Durch die oben geführte Analyse von Gadamers Texte bezüglich der Solidarität lässt sich nun festlegen: Freundschaft und Solidarität bei Gadamer setzten wie Tod als Solidarität *die Endlichkeit des Menschen* voraus. Wie am Anfang erwähnt, wird Solidarität gemeinhin nicht als ein Gadamer typischer Begriff angesehen und entsprechend seinen nicht umfassenden Darlegungen diesbezüglich existiert wenig Forschungsliteratur darüber[6]. Die bestehenden Arbeiten stammen vor allem von Wissenschaftler:innen aus de, englischsprachigen Raum. Die Aufsätze von Darren Walhof, Gerogia Warnke und John Caputo werden in den nächsten Abschnitten näher in Betracht gezogen. Das Ziel in diesem Abschnitt lautet, aufgrund der kritischen Lektüre der genannten Forschungsliteratur folgende Thesen zu veranschaulichen: Wenn auch kein Wort "Solidarität" verwendet wird, findet sich schon in *Wahrheit und Methode* ein *struktureller Prototyp* dessen, was Gadamer in seinen späteren Werken Solidarität nennt, und auch in seinem anscheinend inkonsequenten Solidaritätsbegriff ist der Anhaltspunkt für Offenheit, auf die die vorliegende Arbeit ein Schlaglicht wirft, zu finden.

3.1. Gadamers "political turn"?

Zunächst soll auf Walhofs Aufsatz "Friendship, Otherness, and Gadamer's Politics of Solidarity" von 2006 und Warnkes "Solidarity and Tradition in Gadamer's Hermeneutics" von 2012 eingegangen werden. Der Grund dieser Auswahl ist, dass Warnke in ihrer Analyse auf Walhofs genannten Aufsatz verweist und beide Gadamers Solidaritätsbegriff demjenigen von Richard Rorty gegenüberstellen. Zudem bringen beide einen Einwand gegen Rortys Einsicht vor, dass Gadamers Aufmerksamkeit auf den Solidaritätsbegriff in seinen späten Texten als ein Wendepunkt von ontologischen Interessen zu ethischen und politischen Interessen anzusehen sei (Bernstein 1982, 335). Diesbezüglich entgegnet Warnke, dass sowohl in Gadamers Früh- und Spätwerken als auch in *Wahrheit und Methode* ständig Gadamers Interesse an ethischen und politischen Problemen zu sehen sei und bestreitet damit die von Rorty postulierte Kehrtwende Gadamers (Warnke 2012, 6). Auch Wahlhof rückt die politi-

---

[6] Warum die Gadamer-Derrida-Auseinandersetzung und Gadamers Solidaritätsbegriff mehr Aufmerksamkeiten im englischsprachigen Raum, vor allem in den USA als in der deutschen akademischen Welt gesammelt haben, beruht darauf, dass Gadamers Hermeneutik im englischsprachigen Raum häufig zusammen mit Derrida oder Emmanuel Levinas, die sogenannte French Theory vertreten, als Philosophie des Anderen bzw. der Alterität vorgestellt wird (Figal 2011, 5).

sche Dimension von Gadamers Diskussion über Solidarität in den Vordergrund[7] und bezieht sie auf den Begriff von "Citizenship", auch wenn er gleichzeitig Gadamers folgende Aussage bei einem Interview von 1986 zitiert: "My argument has not become more political than it was, but it is more direct (…)" (Misgeld 1992, 150). Auch wenn sich hinsichtlich Gadamers Kehre nach *Wahrheit und Methode* die Geister scheiden, ist es beachtenswert, dass Warnke und Walhof, die Gadamers Kehre verneinen, Solidarität als entscheidenden Grund in ihrer Argumentation verwenden. Es scheint insofern lohnenswert bei Gadamers Solidaritätsbegriff zu verweilen.

3.2. Rortys "erweiternde Solidarität"
und Gadamers "selbst-erfindende Solidarität"

Walhof und Warnke teilen darüber hinaus die Ansicht, dass sie bei Gadamer eine "politics of solidarity" anerkennen. Aufgrund dessen nennt Wahlhof "solidarity", "friendship" und "otherness" als drei politischen Konzepte, die bei der Forschung zu Gadamer bislamg unbeachtet geblieben sind, und behandelt ihre Zusammenhänge (Walhof 2006, 571). Wahlhof sieht Freundschaft als "a life together with reciprocal co-perception" und Andersheit als ein notwendiges Moment für Gadamers Verstehen und Freundschaft an. Er definiert Gadamers Solidarität als "bounds [that] go beyond conscious recognition of observable similarities and differences and emerge from encounters among those who are, and remain, in important ways other to each other" (ebd., 569). Ferner hält er Gadamers Solidaritätsbegriff für "bounds that may include the bonds of friendship but also *extend beyond our friends to fellow citizens*" (ebd., 571). Diese Ansicht resultiert aus dem Vergleich zwischen Gadamers Solidaritätsbegriff mit demjenigen Rortys. Dabei weist Wahlhof darauf hin, dass Rorty die Konzeption einer auf "recognition of one anothe's common humanity" (Rorty 1989, 189-91) basierenden Solidarität ablehnt und vielmehr die Verbindlichkeit der Solidarität betont, die die anderen mit "uns" gleichsetzt. Dabei zieht er Rortys folgenden Satz heran: "[O]ur attachment to and concern for others are strongest when they are seen "as 'one of us,' where 'us' means something smaller and more local than the human race" (ebd., 189-91). So fokussiert Walhof auf die verbindende Funktion der Solidarität, den anderen mit "uns" gleichzusetzen und diese Hinsicht hält er für den Scheidepunkt zwischen Gadamer und Rorty. Aus dem Vergleich der beiden Philosophen zieht Walhof folgende Schlussfolgerung:

---

[7] Hierbei muss jedoch beachtet werden, dass Walhof vorwiegend die Interview-Texte heranzieht, in denen Gadamer nach der Rolle Europas bei der Universitätsreform oder während des Kalten Kriegs gefragt wurde, und somit Gadamers Aussage schwer vermeiden konnte, politische Töne beizumischen.

> For Rorty solidarity is the *consequence* of identification; it proceeds
> from a knowledge that those included in the "us" have something in
> common. On Gadamer's terms, in contrast, we cannot *create* solidari-
> ties because they are not the consequence of a consciousness of simi-
> larities. (Walhof 2006, 575)

Hinsichtlich dieser Identifikation des anderen mit "uns" teilt auch Warnke eine ähnliche Ansicht. Auch sie fokussiert auf Rortys vorigen Satz und betont, dass es sich
bei Rortys "one of us" nicht um die Gleichsetzung im Sinne von "wir sind alle Menschen", sondern um "wir" in einem noch engeren, mehr beschränkten Sinne handelt.
Warnke kompariert: "Thus, whereas Rorty links solidarity to the recognition of
similarities and advocates a future of expanding solidarities based on imaginatively
seeking out additional similarities, Gadamer links solidarity to the recognition of
distinct others whose distinctness for us has always been there but has been ob-
scured by the conditions of modern mass society." (Warnke 2012, 12) Wie oben
gesehen, während Rorty auf Identifizierung und Ähnlichkeiten zwischen sich selbst
und dem anderen Gewicht legt, wird von Gadamer auf die gegenseitige Anerkennung der Unterschiede großen Wert gelegt, weshalb bei letzterem die Andersheit und
Reziprozität unentbehrlich ist, so lautet: die gemeinsame Ansicht von Walhof und
Warnke.

3.3. Das "Wir"-Problem: Solidarität als Aneignung oder Inklusion?

Wie oben bei der Analyse Gadamers Freundschaftsbegriffs erwähnt, war es seit
Platon ein großes Problem, ob Freundschaft auf die Identifikation zwischen dem
Selbst und dem anderen oder auf die Anerkennung von deren Unterschieden basiert.
Wir haben gerade gesehen, dass sowohl Walhof als auch Warnke die auf die Anerkennung der Unterschiede basierende Freundschaft präferieren und damit großen
Wert auf das Zusammenleben mit dem Anderen legen, das Gadamer betont. Allerdings möchte ich darauf hinweisen, dass hinter der Freundschaft oder Solidarität,
welche auf die Anerkennung der Unterschiede fußen soll und Walhof und Warnke so
befürworten, auch die Gefahr von Aneignung versteckt.

    Warnke begreift Gadamers Freundschaftsbegriff folgendermaßen: "Friends
are not the same nor do they seek to remark one another in their own image. Rather,
they acknowledge and appreciate one another's distinctiveness". Und auch: "Our
friends are those who can assess our actions, provide counsel to us, and *increase our
self-understanding* precisely because they are simultaneously bound to us and *other
from us*" (Warnke 2012, 9). Aus dieser Interpretation lässt sich eine Vorstellung
ableiten, dass sich durch das Zusammenleben mit dem anderen sein Selbstverständnis und Verständnis für den anderen gegenseitig erweitern und vertiefen lässt. Ferner

meint die australische Theoretikerin, dass wir von unseren Freunden lernen können, wie sie uns verstehen, und dass wir mit den anderen verbunden sind und "that we are bound to others whose otherness we must grant if we want to discover or to understand ourselves" (ebd., 12). Fehlt aber nicht die Perspektive, dass der andere auch zum Relativieren vonnöten und auszunutzen ist, damit man durch den anderen sich selbst verstehen kann?

Des Weiteren schreibt Warnke: "Gadamer thinks we need consciously to disclose for one another these communities of solidarity to which *we already belong*" (ebd., 12). Diese Solidarität soll jedoch anders als bei Rorty weder unter den *Menschen wie wir* eingeschränkt, noch dadurch erweitert werden, den anderen Gruppen, die davor nicht solidarisch waren, nachträglich die Ähnlichkeiten hinzufügen. So betonen Warnke und Walhof, dass die Solidarität bei Gadamer nicht "created", sondern "discovered" werden soll. Hier möchte ich allerdings folgende Frage aufwerfen: Setzt diese Ansicht nicht voraus, dass ein anderer, mit dem man dadurch Solidarität üben will, die Unterschiede gegenseitig anzuerkennen und zu verständigen, schon "one of us" sein soll, die/der mit uns die Ähnlichkeiten oder Gleichartigkeiten teilt, als sie/er ein anderes Wesen mit Andersheit und Fremdheit ist, wenn auch nicht "one of us" in einem so engen Sinne wie bei Rorty (und: Ist es nicht relevant, wer – entweder bei Rorty oder bei Gadamer – eine beschränktere Vorstellung von "wir" hat)?

Um zu erklären, warum dem Menschen Freundschaft und Solidarität vonnöten sind, zieht Warnke Gadamers Beschreibung aus "Freundschaft und Selbsterkenntnis" heran und stellt die Vollkommenheit Gottes dem Menschen gegenüber:

> Why should we think we need or ought to learn from others? (…) In connection with friendship, Gadamer uses this injunction to contrast a god's self-sufficiency to our own lack of it. Gods need no friends because they already possess full self-knowledge, and they do not need the other or others to save them from illusions. The same does not hold for us. We need friends at least in part because they understand us and help us to understand ourselves in a way we could not accomplish without them. (Warnke 2012, 18; die Kursivierung ist von mir).

Wird es auch im obigen Zitat die Gefahr versehen, dass der Andere zwecks eines Selbstverständnisses zum Relativieren genutzt wird? Dass man zum Selbstverständnis einen anderen braucht, ist das schließlich nicht dasselbe, wie Gadamer in *Wahrheit und Methode* Aufklärung kritisiert und dann später bei der Debatte mit Habermas nochmal betont hat, dass das Selbstverständnis durch die Reflexion am Ende mit eigennütziger Stellungnahme bzw. egoistischem Selbstzweck verbunden sei, dass man selber durch den anderen bzw. die Perspektiven des anderen, also durch die Ausnutzung des anderen mehr Wissen gewinnt?

3.4. Endlichkeit und Tradition

Aus der obigen Analyse wird ersichtlich, dass bei Gadamer sowohl hinter der Freundschaft als auch hinter der Solidarität die Endlichkeit des Menschen steckt. Hierbei ist interessant zu beachten, dass Warnke "Tradition" bei Gadamer als einen *Schlüssel* ansieht, *der uns den Mangel an menschlicher Selbstgenügsamkeit als Endlichkeit aufmerksam bzw. bewusst macht.* Ferner schildert Warnke: "Here the reminder that we are no gods is a reminder that the traditions to which we belong lack self-sufficiency. They need others and need to explore the specific contours of otherness because they are prey to illusions and cannot vet their beliefs and prejudices entirely on their own" (Warnke 2012, 18). Gott hat keinen Freund aber braucht diesen auch nicht. Anderes als Gott ist dem Menschen jedoch weder ein vollständiges Erkennen noch Selbstgenügsamkeit möglich. Wegen dieser Unvollständigkeit und Endlichkeit braucht der Mensch Sprache und Solidarität[8]. Auch wenn Warnke einräumt, dass in der modernen Ethik und politischen Theorie Solidarität im Allgemein höheren Stellenwert als Tradition genießt, misst sie dem Traditionsbegriff bei Gadamer mehr Gewicht bei: "Traditions include the potential for expansion whereas solidarities react to external forces" (ebd., 21). Ihr Argument ist, dass sie die Beziehung zwischen Vergangenheit und Zukunft in Gadamers Traditionsbegriff parallel zur Beziehung unter den Freunden und Menschen in Solidarität begreift. Das liegt daran, dass sie die Tradition bei Gadamer sowohl aus dem Blick der Vergangenheit auf die Gegenwart als auch aus dem Blick der Gegenwart auf die Vergangenheit konstruiert sieht (ebd., 16). Wie sie in ihrem Aufsatz unterstreicht, ist das menschliche Erkennen kein permanentes, sondern es hat Potenzial, sich der Zukunft und neuem Verständnis zu öffnen. Liest man ihrer Beschreibung "traditions are fusions of horizons both vertically, as fusions of past and present, and horizontally, as fusions of distinct traditions" (ebd., 16-17), bedeutet die Tradition, die Warnke heranzieht, auf keinen Fall eine fixierte, unveränderbare. Auch Gadamer schreibt zur Erklärung der Horizontverschmelzung: "Im Walten der Tradition findet ständig solche Verschmelzung statt. Denn dort wächst Altes und Neues immer wieder zu lebendiger Geltung zusammen, ohne daß sich überhaupt das eine oder andere ausdrücklich voneinander abheben" (Gadamer 1990, 311-312). Zumal ist der Begriff des Horizonts in *Wahrheit und Methode* eben eingeführt, um die Endlichkeit des Menschen auszudrücken (ebd., 307ff). Der *Horizont* und *Anrede/Angesprochensein* von der Vergangenheit und dem Text, das sind die Begriffe bei Gadamer, die John

---

[8] Gleichzeitig weist Warnke interessanterweise darauf hin, dass Solidarität auch den Feind hervorbringen kann: "solidarities also create intransigent enemies" (Warnke 2012, 21).

Caputo für sein Konzept "structural friendship" nutzt, das im Folgenden näher in Betracht gezogen wird.

3.5. Gadamer und Derrida überbrücken: *Horizont* und *structural friendship*

In "Good will and the hermeneutics of friendship: Gadamer and Derrida" beabsichtigt Caputo, die Freundschaftsbegriffe bei Gadamer und Derrida zu skizzieren und die Gemeinsamkeiten und Unterschieden beider Philosophen darzustellen.

Zunächst geht Caputo davon aus, dass sowohl Gadamer als auch Derrida den "intersubjektiven Charakter" der Sprache unterstreichen, und dies hält er für eine Gemeinsamkeit, die die beiden von Heidegger trennt. Derrida interessiert sich laut Caputo für Verantwortlichkeit für den anderen und gegenüber dem anderen und legen wie Gadamer auf jeweils verschiedene Art und Weise großen Wert auf die Sprache im Verhältnis zu dem anderen (Caputo 2002, 512-513). Was bei der sprachlichen Auseinander-setzung mit dem anderen nötig ist, ist bei Gadamer z.B. "Horizont" und bei Derrida "Freundschaft(sliebe)". In den beiden Fällen handle es sich um "structural friendship". Was ist unter diesem Konzept zu verstehen?

> In order to understand each other, we must ask each other to listen and we must try to be understood. Let us say that our exchange requires an air, a horizon, a field of amity or friendship, which is not necessarily a matter of personal good feelings, but rather of a *structural* friendship. It is as if every time we hear something said, or pick up a book, or read a sentence, there is an invisible or inaudible prefatory clause attached to what we read or hear, an implicit vocative or in vocation, which takes the form of an apostrophe that says, 'O my friends.' It is as if every sentence comes in the form, 'O my friends, listen to what is said, read, what is written,' as if that is *a structural feature* of every mark or trace. (Ebd., 512-513)

Aus dem Wort "mark" und "trace" lässt sich herauslesen, dass Caputo diese "structural friendship" auf Grundlage von Derrida eingeführt haben will. Anschließend schreibt er selber, "That, I will shortly demonstrate, is exactly the position Derrida takes" (ebd., 512-513). Anzumerken ist, dass das obige Zitat diejenige, die Gadamer lesen, an die folgenden Sätze in *Wahrheit und Methode* erinnert: "Das eigentliche Geschehen ist dadurch aber nur ermöglicht, nämlich daß das Wort, das als Überlieferung auf uns gekommen ist und auf das wir zu hören haben, uns wirklich trifft, als rede es uns an und meine uns selbst" und "Vielmehr liegt darin auch dies, daß, wer angeredet wird, hören muß, ob er will oder nicht" (Gadamer 1990, 465-466).

Zudem gibt es die Stelle, die Caputo als Derridas Ansicht präsentiert, aber den Ausführungen Gadamers, die dieser bereits in *Wahrheit und Methode* oder bei der Auseinandersetzung mit Derrida geäußert hat, sehr ähnlich ist:

> Every sentence comes to us with a friendly supplication, asking us to 'incline our ear', as it is said so beautifully in the Scriptures, to bend down before what we hear or read so as to let it come, let it be heard. Indeed, the language of the Scriptures is very helpful when it comes to understanding this ethics of hearing, this ethics of friendship required for understanding one another. And not only this ethics, but also this politics of friendship, for every polity depends for its very life upon a civility, a civil amity, in order to conduct its business and protect its decision-making process from violence. Every utterance takes the form of a supplication or, one might even say, a *prayer. Every time I open my mouth, I pray you, hear me; every time you open your mouth, you pray me, listen. We pray each other's patience, hospitality, openness, receptiveness.* **I pray you, give me your ear**. (Caputo 2002, 513)

Der letzte Satz erinnert uns an Gadamers Antwort auf Derrida aus dem Jahr 1981: "Wer der Mund auftut, möchte verstanden werden. Anderenfalls würde er weder reden noch schreiben" (Gadamer 1984, 59). Interessant finde ich hierbei, dass Caputo die mehr oder weniger Gadamer'sche Behauptung als Derridas Position vorstellt. Caputo fasst so zusammen, dass bei Derrida "a civility, a civil amity" den Entscheidungsprozess der Bürger vor Gewalt schützt[9]. Diese Stelle erinnert uns wiederum an die Gadamer-Derrida-Auseinandersetzung, und zwar Derridas Kritik an Gadamers gutem Willen, dass guter Wille dabei als "Axiom", "die absolute Verbindlichkeit im Bestreben nach Verständigung" (Derrida 1984, 56) fungiert und dies die Gewalt des Willens sei. Wird diese Vorgeschichte berücksichtigt, ist wohl eine Gegenüberstellung, nämlich guter Wille (ethics) vs. civil friendship (amity) vorstellbar. Dennoch scheint der letzte Satz des obigen Zitats "*I pray you, give me your ear*" in hohen Maßen mit Gadamers Position zu überlappen, wie auch Caputo schreibt: "These biblical requirements of friendship and hearing correspond quite closely, I think, to Gadamer's demand for 'good will' expressed in the Paris exchange" (Caputo 2002, 514). Darüber hinaus lässt sich überzeugen, dass Gadamer am Ende seiner Antwort auf Derrida so gesagt hat, "Ich glaube mich gar nicht so fern von Derrida" (Gadamer 1984, 61), wenn man folgende Beschreibung Derridas liest, die Caputo als Derridas damalige aktuelle Diskussion vorstellt:

---

[9] Allerdings ist auch die Anmerkung zu "Entscheidung" bei Derrida von Dominik Busch nicht zu übersehen. (Busch 2016, 254)

> *You cannot address the other, speak to the Other, without an act of faith, without testimony.* What are you doing when you attest to something? You address the Other and ask, 'believe me.' Even if you are lying, even in a perjury, you are addressing the Other and asking the Other to trust you. This 'trust me, *I am speaking to you' is of the order of faith, a faith that cannot be reduced to a theoretical state-ment, to a determinative judgment; it is the opening of the address to the other. So this faith is not religious, strictly speaking; at least it cannot be totally determined by a given religion.* (Caputo 1997, 22; die Kursivierung ist von mir).

Die kursiven Stellen entsprechen in weiten Teilen Gadamers Ansicht. Zudem über-rascht uns Caputos Anmerkung "Derrida goes so far as to describe the 'O my friends', this apostrophe that implicitly precedes every sentence, as a *prayer*" (Ca-puto 2002, 515-516), wie ähnlich beide Philosophen in dieser Hinsicht sind. So stellt Caputo mit seinem Konzept "structural friendship" eine Brücke zwischen Gadamer und Derrida her, die meist als sehr verschieden angesehen werden.

4.   Solidarität und Zugehörigkeit

Bisher werden Gadamers Freundschafts- und Solidaritätsbegriffe analysiert und deren Probleme aufgezeigt. Oben werden die Ähnlichkeiten zwischen der "structural friendship", die Caputo anhand Derrida behauptet, und Gadamers Ansicht in *Wahr-heit und Methode* herausgearbeitet. Schließlich möchte ich darauf aufmerksam machen, dass bereits in *Wahrheit und Methode* eine prototypische Struktur dessen, was Gadamer später Solidarität nennt, zu finden ist. Meine These lautet, dass die Solidaritäts- und Zugehörigkeitsbegriffen bei Gadamer miteinander verbunden sind und darin das Konzept der Offenheit zu sehen ist. Dabei soll zunächst daran erinnert werden, dass Gadamer in *Wahrheit und Methode* Zugehörigkeit als "das Moment der Tradition" und "die Bedingung des geisteswissenschaftlichen Verstehens" an-sieht und schreibt: "So erfüllt sich der Sinn der Zugehörigkeit, d. h. das Moment der Tradition im historisch-hermeneutischen Verhalten, durch die Gemeinsamkeit grundlegender und tragender Vorurteile. Die Hermeneutik muß davon ausgehen, daß wer verstehen will, mit der Sache, die mit der Überlieferung zur Sprache kommt, verbunden ist und an die Tradition Anschluß hat oder Anschluß gewinnt, aus der die Überlieferung spricht" (Gadamer 1990, 300). Nach Gadamer gehört nicht die Tradi-tion uns zu, sondern wir gehören der Tradition zu. Zur Tradition gehören, bedeutet bei Gadamer die Überlieferung, nämlich Anrede aus der Vergangenheit zuzuhören und das heißt, von der Überlieferung und dem Text *etwas reden zu lassen*. Aber was bedeutet das denn?

Zwar redet ein Text nicht so zu uns wie ein Du. Wir, die Verstehenden, müssen ihn von uns aus erst zum Reden bringen. Aber es hatte sich gezeigt, daß solches verstehendes Zum-Reden-Bringen kein beliebiger Einsatz aus eigenem Ursprung ist, sondern selber wieder als Frage auf die im Text gewärtigte Antwort bezogen ist. Die Gewärtigung einer Antwort setzt selber schon voraus, daß der Fragende von der Überlieferung erreicht und aufgerufen ist. Das ist die Wahrheit des wirkungsgeschichtlichen Bewußtseins. Es ist das geschichtlich erfahrene Bewußtsein, das, indem es dem Phantom einer völligen Aufklärung entsagt, eben damit für die Erfahrung der Geschichte offen ist. Seine Vollzugsweise beschrieben wir als die Verschmelzung der Horizont des Verstehens, die zwischen Text und Interpreten vermittelt. (Ebd., 383)

Text lesen bedeutet für Gadamer, dass der Interpret den Text zum Reden bringt und zuhört. Dies stellt zudem eine dialektische Beziehung dar, in der der Interpret beim Lesen das Angeredetsein aus der Überlieferung fragt und darauf antwortet. Wenn dies berücksichtigt wird, lässt sich nicht sagen, dass die Zusammengehörigkeit von Interpreten und Text im Akt des Lesens, mit anderen Worten, *eine strukturelle Solidarität* – will ich so nennen – bereits in *Wahrheit und Methode* beschrieben wird? Zudem istin dieser strukturellen Solidarität auch die Offenheit am Werk.

Vielmehr, wer sich überhaupt etwas sagen läßt, ist auf eine grundsätzliche Weise offen. Ohne eine solche Offenheit füreinander gibt es keine echt menschliche Bindung. Zueinandergehören heißt immer zugleich Auf-ein-ander-Hören-können. Wenn zwei einander verstehen, so heißt das ja nicht, daß einer den anderen 'versteht', d.h. überschaut. Ebenso heißt 'auf jemanden hören' nicht einfach, daß man blindlings tut, was der andere will. Wer so ist, den nennen wir hörig. Offenheit für den anderen schließt also die Anerkennung ein, daß ich in mir etwas gegen mich gelten lassen muß, auch wenn es keinen anderen gäbe, der es gegen mich geltend machte. Hier liegt die Entsprechung der hermeneutischen Erfahrung. Ich muß die Überlieferung in ihrem Anspruch gelten lassen, nicht im Sinne einer bloßen Anerkennung der Andersheit der Vergangenheit, sondern in der Weise, daß sie mir etwas zu sagen hat. Auch das verlangt eine grundsätzliche Art der Offenheit. (Ebd., 367; die Kursivierung ist von mir).

Der wortspielerische Sinnzusammenhang von Zugehörigkeit, Zueinandergehören, Aufeinanderhören und Zuhören, worauf Gadamer hinweist, funktioniert selbstverständlich nur dank der deutschen Sprache. Ferner gesagt, bringt Gadamer die Solidarität in seinem späteren Werk selbst nicht unbedingt in Verbindung mit seiner Aussage in *Wahrheit und Methode.* Trotzdem, aus der Aussage im obigen Zitat, Warnkes Augenmerk auf Tradition, Caputos "structural friendship", aus diesen Bausteinen möchte ich deduzieren, wenn auch der Ausdruck Solidarität nicht verwendet wird, wird schon in *Wahrheit und Methode* "echt menschliche Bindung" in Form *der strukturellen Solidarität* beschrieben. Allerdings soll die Solidarität hier keine politische oder soziale sein, sondern eine, die eine "hermeneutische Situation" voraussetzt. Hier ist an Gadamers Satz in *Wahrheit und Methode* zu erinnern: "In Wahrheit gehört die Geschichte nicht uns, sondern wir gehören ihr. Lange bevor wir uns in der Rückbesinnung selber verstehen, verstehen wir uns auf selbstverständliche Weise in Familie, Gesellschaft und Staat, in denen wir leben" (Gadamer 1990, 281). Das heißt, was in der "echt menschliche(n) Bindung", als Solidarität gilt, ist Zugehören zur Geschichte, Tradition und Überlieferung und dies bedeutet im konkreten, Geschichte, Tradition und Überlieferung zum Sprechen komme lassen und zuhören. Das ist Zusammen-gehören. Aus dieser Perspektive lässt sich herauslesen, dass auch in Gadamers Solidaritätsbegriff das Konzept der Offenheit, die das Augenmerk der vorliegenden Arbeit darstellt, gefasst ist.

Anschließend möchte ich erneut meine These in diesem Paper zusammenfassen: Erstens setzte sowohl der Freundschafts- als auch der Solidaritätsbegriff Gadamers die Endlichkeit des Menschen (im Vergleich zu Gott) voraus, aber gerade darin findet sich die Offenheit. Zweitens, auch wenn die Diskussion über Solidarität erst in den 70er Jahren in Gadamers Texten vorkommt, lässt sich bereits in *Wahrheit und Methode* ein Prototyp dessen, was Gadamer später Solidarität nennt, finden, was ich strukturelle Solidarität nenne. Dabei handelt es sich um einen wortspielerischen Sinnzusammenhang von Zugehören – Zusammengehören – (Aufeinander-)Hörenkönnen. Außerdem deutet Gadamer diesen Zusammenhang in "Logos und Ergon im platonischen 'Lysis'" selbst an: "Die Frage, was Freundschaft sei, zielt letzten Endes darauf zu begreifen, was rechte Gemeinsamkeit ist" (Gadamer 1985, 176). Auf diese Frage wird weder in Gadamers genannten Text noch in Platons *Lysis* geantwortet. Ich hingegen vertrete die These, dass diese "rechte Gemeinsamkeit" bei Gadamer Sprache ist, in der man mit dem anderen zusammen-(zu)gehört.

Assoc. Prof. Dr. Maya Shiratori,
Tokyo Univeristy of the Arts, maya.shiratori@gmail.com

Literaturangaben

Bernstein, Richard. 1982. "What is the Difference That Makes a Difference? Gadamer, Habermas, and Rorty." In *PSA: Proceedings of the Biennial Meeting of the Philosophy of Science Association,* Vol.2: 331-359.

Bernstein, Richard. 2008. "The Conversation that Never Happened." *The Review of Metaphysics*, Vol. 61, No. 3: 577-693.

Busch, Dominik. 2016. *Begrenzung und Offenheit. Die Seale-Derrida-Debatte*, Wien: Passagen Verlag.

Caputo, John D (ed.). 1997. *Deconstruction in a Nutshell: A Conversation with Jacques Derrida.* New York: Fordham University Press.

Caputo, John. 2002. "Good will and the hermeneutics of friendship: Gadamer and Derrida." *Philosophy & Social Criticism*, vol 28, no 5: 512-522.

Dasenbrock, Reed Way. 1994. "Taking It Personally: Reading Derrida's Responses." *College English*, Vol. 56, No. 3: 261-279.

Derrida, Jacques. 1984. "Guter Wille zur Macht (1)." *Text und Interpretation* herausgegeben von Philippe Forget. München: Wilhelm Fink Verlag: 56-58.

Derrida, Jacques. 1986. *Schibboleth pour Paul Celan.* Paris: Galilée.

Derrida, Jacques. 2002. "Wie recht er hatte! Mein Cicerone Hans-Georg Gadamer." *Frankfurter Allgemeine Zeitung*, 23.03.2002, Nr. 70, 41.

Derrida, Jacques. 2004. "Der ununterbrochene Dialog: zwischen zwei Unendlichkeiten, das Gedicht." *Der ununterbrochene Dialog* herausgegeben von Martin Gessmann. Frankfurt am Main: Suhrkamp: 7-50. (Derrida, Jacques. 2003. *Béliers. Le dialogue ininterrompu : entre deux infinis, le poème*, Paris: Galilée.)

Derrida, Jacques. 2007. *Jedes Mal einzigartig, das Ende der Welt.* Wien: Passagen Verlag.

Di Cesare, Donatella. 2004. "Stars and Constellations: The Difference between Gadamer and Derrida." *Research in Phenomenology*, 34 (1), Brill: 73-102.

Forget, Philippe. 1984. "Leitfäden einer unwahrscheinlichen Debatte." *Text und Interpretation* herausgegeben von Philippe Forget. München: Wilhelm Fink Verlag: 7-23.

Figal, Günter. 2011. *Hans-Georg Gadamer. Wahrheit und Methode.* Berlin: Akademie Verlag.

Gadamer, Hans-Georg. 1982. *Gesprochener Originaltext in Paris 1982, 'Text und Interpretation'.* Deutsches Literaturarchiv Marbach. Mediennummer: HS005316761.

Gadamer, Hans-Georg. 1986. *Wer bin Ich und wer bist Du? – Ein Kommentar zu Celans 'Atemkristall'.* Frankfurt am Main: Suhrkamp.

Gadamer, Hans-Georg. 1990. Wahrheit und Methode [*Gesammelte Werke 1*]. Tübingen: Mohr Siebeck.

Gadamer, Hans-Georg. 1987. "Der Denker Heidegger.", In *Gesammelte Werke3*. Tübingen: Mohr Siebeck: 223-228.

Gadamer, Hans-Georg. 1985. "Logos und Ergon im platonischen 'Lysis'." *Gesammelte Werke 6*. Tübingen: Mohr Siebeck: 171-186.

Gadamer, Hans-Georg. 1993. "Sinn und Sinnverhüllung bei Paul Celan." *Gesammelte Werke 9*. Tübingen: Mohr Siebeck: 452-460.

Gadamer, Hans-Georg. 1976. "Was ist Praxis? Die Bedingungen gesellschaftlicher Vernunft." *Vernunft im Zeitalter der Wissenschaft.* Frankfurt am Main: Suhrkamp Verlag: 54-77.

Gadamer, Hans-Georg. 1983. "Die Erfahrung des Todes." *Gesammelte Werke 4*. Tübingen: Mohr Siebeck: 288-294.

Gadamer, Hans-Georg. 1984. "Text und Interpretation" und "Und dennoch: Macht des Guten Willens". *Text und Interpretation* herausgegeben von Philippe Forget. München: Wilhelm Fink Verlag: 24-55, 59-61.

Gadamer. Hans-Georg. 1991. "Freundschaft und Selbsterkenntnis." *Gesammelte Werke 7*. Tübingen: Mohr Siebeck: 396-406.

Gadamer, Hans-Georg. 2000. "Freundschaft und Solidarität." *Hermeneutische Entwürfe*. Tübingen: Mohr Siebeck: 56-65.

Heidegger, Martin. 1927/1967. *Sein und Zeit*. Tübingen: Max Niemeyer Verlag.

Inazu, Asoka. 2009. "The 'First Friend' and Oikeion Plato's lysis", *Historia philosophiae*, The Society of Philosophy of Tokyo Metropolitan University: 23-45.

Michelfelder, Diane P. and Richard E. Palmer (ed.). 1989. *Dialogue and Deconstruction: The Gadamer-Derrida Encounter*. Albany: State University of New York Press.

Misgeld, Dieter and Graeme Nicholson (ed.). 1992. *Hans-Georg Gadamer on Education, Poetry, and History. Applied Hermeneutics*. State University of New York Press.

Rorty, Richard. 1989. *Contingency, Irony, and Solidarity*. Cambridge: Cambridge University Press.

Walhof, Darren R. 2006. "Friendship, Otherness, and Gadamer's Politics of Solidarity." *Political Theory* (34) No. 5: 569-593.

Warnke, Georgia. 2012. "Solidarity and Tradition in Gadamer's Hermeneutics." *History and Theory* (51) No. 4: 6-22.

VLADIMIR LAZURCA (Vienna)

Modelling Speech and Speakers: Gadamer and Davidson on dialogue, agreement, and intelligible difference

Abstract

This paper examines Gadamer's and Davidson's dialogical models of interpretation. It shows them to be comparable, but importantly dissimilar with respect to the kind of agreement they require for communication to be possible. It is argued that this difference entails different concepts of alterity: they model not only how we talk, but implicitly who we can intelligibly talk to. Another important contribution of this paper is to uncover a distinction in Gadamer between two kinds of agreement missed so far by all commentators. The final section of this paper defends a second thesis, namely that the degree of agreement required by the models is proportional to the conceptual difference it can make intelligible. Hence, the extent of graspable cultural difference is not only an empirical matter, but is entailed by our choice of model.

Keywords: Gadamer, Davidson, dialogue, agreement, alterity, other, intelligibility, cultural difference

No consensus is likely to be reached on the formula for a philosopher's impact factor. The scales for measuring philosophical importance vary so widely with the measurer's interests, affinities and membership in philosophical traditions, that few are likely to strike an agreement. Many might concur, however, that a variable in the equation would be the degree to which a philosopher's views are brought into contact with other philosophers. It may therefore not be too controversial to state that a measure of Gadamer's impact is the frequency and relevance of his comparison with other philosophers, especially from other philosophical traditions and currents. Gadamer's role in Frankfurt school polemics, in endorsements and critiques from poststructuralists and deconstructivists, to name a few, is well-known. Less so, however, is a focus of comparison from the analytical tradition which has been gaining traction in recent decades, namely Donald Davidson's philosophy of interpretation. Indeed,

the Gadamer-Davidson encounter is for some the most promising rapproche-
ment of the two traditions of Western philosophy, the continental and the analytic (see Braver 2011, 149; Føllesdal 2011, xii).

Within the broad orbit of philosophy of language, Hans-Georg Gadamer's
and Donald Davidson's points of intersection are many and not exhaustively
charted. Both develop extensive treatments of the topics of interpretation, understanding and truth, and, despite starting from incommensurable backgrounds,
eventually arrive in the same intellectual neighborhood (see Davidson 1997). My
focus in this paper is Gadamer's and Davidson's respective models of dialogue. I
argue that their dialogical theories of communication impinge not only on what
they are theories of, but determine the picture of our interlocutors: their models of
speech implicitly model other speakers. I structure my paper as follows.

In the first section, I show how both Gadamer and Davidson endorse com-
parably similar dialogical models of communication. In the second section, I argue
that both models share an important condition of possibility: agreement between
the speakers. I claim, however, that the kind of agreement required is radically
different: the Davidsonian model presupposes an agreement *posterior* to linguistic
interaction, whereas the Gadamerian requires one *prior* to it. Finally, I argue for
the first thesis of this paper: the two models entail different pictures of our conver-
sational interlocutor. Davidson models the other as linguistically singular, Gadamer as plural. In the third section, I argue for my second thesis: the degree of
agreement and semantic conformity between speakers postulated by each model is
proportional to that of the conceptual and semantic difference it can make intelligible. In this section, I develop an example showing that Davidson's theory exces-
sively restricts the context of significance making it insufficient to account for the
correct interpretation of the other. I then argue that Gadamer's alternative can
satisfactorily deal with the case and thus allows for more intelligible conceptual
divergence between speakers. I conclude that Gadamer's model is better equipped
for making sense of cultural difference than Davidson's.

1. Dialogue

Dialogue as the paradigm of linguistic understanding and communication
is among the better covered aspects of Gadamer's philosophical hermeneutics.
As is well known, *Dialog* or *Gespräch* designates for him the very "structure of
linguistic understanding" (1972b, 474) and, since for Gadamer understanding is
essentially linguistic, "the basic model of all understanding" (1968, 116). Famously, Gadamer fashions his conception of dialogue after the example of Pla-

tonic dialectic (Gadamer 1985, 368-384)[1]. In fact, Gadamer's entire hermeneutic project is oriented to Socratic dialogue, the *elenchus* (1973, 497), which he considers paradigmatic of every dialogue (Gadamer 1985b, 370). In the following, I will assume the reader knows the Gadamerian conception of dialogue in its broad outline and will confine myself to aspects relevant for my purposes here.

The basic model of the hermeneutical situation, the dialogue, is first of all not conceived as a binary relationship between interlocutors. Its configuration is instead triadic, as it includes the two partners as well as the subject matter of the conversation, its *Sache*. Only this completes the dialogical triad. Understanding is then conceived as an agreement reached between interlocutors concerning the subject matter (Gadamer 1985, 297): its joint possession, its being held in common by the partners, is what secures understanding.

Additionally, the great insight Gadamer discovers in Platonic, and especially Socratic dialogue, is the structure of question and answer, which for him describes the essence of all hermeneutic or interpretive experience (Gadamer 1985, 373, 383). According to him, we can only ever understand an item if we understand it as an answer to a question: "no assertion is possible that cannot be understood as an answer to a question, and assertions can only be understood in this way" (1966b, 226; translation from Gadamer 2007, 84). The hermeneutical priority of the question has important consequences for the concept of meaning. If we only understand an assertion by grasping it as an answer to a question, then its meaning will be relative to the question it answers. Consequently, only by asking the right questions can we truly understand all that the other – our conversation partner, whether person or text – has to say to us. As such, question and answer are thoroughly interconnected: just as an answer is relative to a specific question, so a question can only be understood in relation to what might be an answer to it (1981b, 46). The logic of question and answer is in fact a dialectic of question and answer where they are ultimately "dissolved in the movement of understanding" (ibid., 47).

Furthermore, since an answer's meaning is relative to the question it answers, what one interlocutor means in dialogue depends on the response of the other, and vice versa. As such, what we mean depends on what others can make of what we mean and vice versa.[2] There is no such thing as a meaning-in-itself, an ideal currency exchanged between conversation partners: meaning is always

---

[1] Gadamer 1985 refers to the German edition of *Truth and Method* and Gadamer 1989 to the English translation. When quoting from the latter, I give the page for both the original and the translation.

[2] See Kertscher (2002, 144-146) for a more detailed analysis of this idea in Gadamer.

relative to the interpreter (Gadamer 1985, 477). This explains why, for Gadamer, "words exist at all only in conversation" (Gadamer 1985b, 371) and language "is only fully what it can be when it takes place in dialogue" (Gadamer 1996, 128; see idem 1985, 449; 1972a, 207). The dialectic of question and answer ultimately describes the mechanism by which partners achieve a fusion of their different horizons. Only through this dialectic can we gain a common understanding of the subject matter and achieve that dialogical transformation "in which we do not remain what we were" (Gadamer 1985, 384; idem 1989, 371).

In several later essays, Davidson also elaborates on the connection between Socratic dialogue and his own thinking. He too will see in the *elenchus* a model of the only method available for arriving at an understanding of other creatures, for coming to an agreement with them on the meaning of their concepts and achieving clarity about what we mean ourselves (Davidson 1992a, 250). Elsewhere, he describes it as "a model of every successful attempt at communication" and a "microcosm of the ongoing process of language formation itself" (Davidson 1994b, 254, 248). Davidson echoes Gadamer very closely when stating that dialogue, "particularly in the form of the elenchus, provides the forum in which alone words take on meaning" (ibid., 250). In addition, what the Socratic *elenchus* models so well, for Davidson, in the way in which it leads, seemingly of its own momentum, to lexical clarification and conceptual change: it is "an event in which the meanings of words, the concepts entertained by the speakers, evolve and are clarified" (ibid., 254). New meanings and novel concepts are created through dialogical intersubjective exchanges, through the "interaction of minds in which words can be bent to new uses and ideas progressively shaped" (ibid., 255).

A fortuitous but illuminating coincidence has it that both Davidson and Gadamer use events in the smithy to illustrate the process by which dialogue allows overcoming difference. Like the blacksmith's foundry, dialogue is for Davidson a "crucible in which some of our most important words, and the concepts they express, are tested, melted down, reshaped, and given a new edge" (ibid., 258). In dialogue, speaker and hearer must adapt to each other's idiosyncrasies, they must understand their partner's words as they were intended. And whether they understand them in concert, and hence understand each other, or mean anything intelligible at all, "only the process of question and answer can reveal" (ibid., 255). This closely parallels Gadamer's description of understanding as a 'fusion of horizons' which can only be achieved through the dialogical interplay of question and answer.

Davidson would thus second Gadamer's claim that "dialogue has a transformative force" (Gadamer 1972a, 211). For Davidson, both participants potentially stand to gain greater conceptual clarity through dialogue, thus not remaining as they were (Davidson 1994b, 254). Another core principle of Davidson's view is that meaning as an abstract entity has "no demonstrated use" (Davidson 1967, 21) in the study of language. Davidson is thus in agreement with Gadamer that "people mean what others can take them to mean; to learn what we mean *is* to learn what others we talk with mean" (Davidson 1992a, 250; see idem 1990, 62)[3].

Though Davidson makes these connections later in his career, the dialogical model of communication, in one form or another, has been a constant feature of his thinking at least since the early 70s. Indeed, it is an essential feature of his analysis of radical interpretation, specifically regarding the evidence necessary to support interpretations of a speaker. As is well known, the evidence Davidson requires is the behaviorally manifested attitude of holding a sentence true under specified conditions at certain times. Davidson's chief claim is that this will yield correct (radical) interpretations absent a shared language (see Davidson 1973, 135-137; 1991, 157-159). It is therefore an essential feature of his project that the knowledge required for interpretation is built up exclusively from evidence gathered in the dialogical interactions between speakers and the interpreter.

Later in his career, Davidson will elaborate on the interpersonal exchanges required for radical interpretation. Additionally, with the development of his thinking, the model of the dialogue will grow in significance beyond this initial project. In Davidson's so-called 'triangulation papers', in fact, interpersonal interaction becomes necessary for the very possibility of thought and language. In his paper "Three Varieties of Knowledge" (1991), Davidson offers a more detailed picture of the interlocutors' engagement in radical interpretation. This requires that an interpreter find a regularity in a speaker's behavior which he can correlate with objects or events in their environment. Absent this condition, the interpreter cannot discover any thought or meaning behind the speaker's utterances. Therefore, it provides a determination that the behavior observed is indeed linguistic:

> For until the triangle is completed connecting two creatures, and each creature with common features of the world, there can be no answer to the question whether a creature [...] is discriminating between stimuli at the sensory surfaces or somewhere further out, or further in. Without this sharing of reactions to common stimuli, thought and speech would have no particular content—that is, no content at all. (1991, 159; see 1992b, 263)

---

[3] See Glüer (2018) for more on the interpreter's role in determining meaning in the radical interpretation papers.

Triangulation, then, is the process by which interlocutors locate the common cause of their reactions, which in turn allows each to correlate observed reactions of the other with their own stimuli from the world. Interpersonal engagement with others is alone what gives content to thought and speech: "interaction among similar creatures is a necessary condition for speaking a language" (Davidson 1992b, 264). Although Davidson requires quite a different triadic framework to Gadamer's, they agree on the essential point that unless two interlocutors correctly identify the object talked about as common to both, determining whether they are saying anything at all is impossible.

The most explicitly dialogical conception of communication appears in Davidson's so-called 'anti-conventional papers'. In this series of papers, spanning more than a decade, Davidson motivates his rejection of the idea that communication requires semantic conventions. The general model of communication he provides in his (1986) and (1994a) centers exclusively on the dynamic of *speaker* and *hearer/interpreter* and aims to fully explain linguistic communication in the absence of shared language (see Davidson 1982, 276-267; idem 1986, 96, 103; idem 1994a, 115, 110, 119). We will dwell on this model in greater length in the next section.

For now, I would like to draw the reader's attention to some fundamental points of convergence between Gadamer's and Davidson's dialogical conceptions of understanding. First, the dialogue is not a dyad, but a triad, comprising the two interlocutors and what, very broadly, they speak about. Secondly, the speakers' utterances are interconnected in that their content depends on the interlocutors' responses to them: the meaning of what is said depends on the hearer's interpretation of it. The process of linguistic interpretation, modelled as dialogue, constitutes the content of the *interpretandum*: in other words, there is no meaning outside the dialogue. And so, "a language cannot have a life of its own, a life apart from its users" (Davidson 1994b, 258; see also idem 1993, 170; idem 1994a, 120, 122; Davidson and Glüer 1995, 81).

As mentioned, this is a point of agreement between Davidson and Gadamer. In a paper written for the *Library of Living Philosophers'* volume on Gadamer, Davidson expresses approval for the latter's view that

> Language has its true being only in conversation, in the exercise of understanding between people." This saying of Gadamer's goes far beyond the linguist's insistence on the primacy of spoken over written words, for it implies that only in the context of discussion does language come to have a content, to be language. (1997, 274)

Where he disagrees with Gadamer, however, is on whether conversation requires a shared language. For Gadamer, "every conversation presupposes a common language, or better, creates a common language" (Gadamer 1985, 384; idem 1989, 371). Davidson's position, as mentioned, is that it does not:

> It seems wrong to me to say agreement concerning an object demands that a common language first be worked out. I would say: it is only in the presence of shared objects that understanding can come about. (Davidson 1997, 275)

While scholars agree that Davidson misunderstood Gadamer's position and has thus misplaced the true locus of their disagreement, they have not reached a consensus on where it lies. Certainly, they are right to indicate that Gadamer is not a conventionalist in the sense Davidson seems to assume (Malpas 2011b, 209; Vessey 2012, 35; Lynch 2014, 361). In fact, Gadamer led an attack on a version of conventionalism decades before Davidson did (see Gadamer 1985, 405-410). As he later states, agreeing with recent developments in linguistics and implicitly Davidson himself:

> The term "[linguistic] competence" ... cannot be described simply in terms of the application of rules or merely as the rule-governed manipulation of language. (1985a, 5/6; translation from Gadamer 1997, 42)

Nevertheless, it is true that one affirms what the other rejects. However, their concepts of language differ so substantially that one's requirement of shared language cannot easily be compared with the other's denial. As such, many have argued that the essential divergence is to be found in their accounts of language, and in fact their positions are not in tension with respect to the common language issue (Malpas 2002, 210; idem 2011b, 267; Lynch 2014, 368). Moreover, some have suggested that Gadamer might even subscribe to Davidson's view that communication does not presuppose shared language (Braver 2011, 149; Malpas 2002, 210; Vessey 2012, 37; Lynch 2014, 368; but see Dostal 2011, 181 against this view) and that the true difference lies in their different accounts of conversation (Braver 2011, Vessey 2011, 254; idem 2012, 36, 38; Fultner 2011, 227-228).

In the following, I will reorient this debate and argue that the disagreement is less about whether language must be shared for communication, than the kind of sharing required. Although Davidson and Gadamer concur that some form of agreement is a necessary condition for language and understanding, their conceptions differ radically. The next section will detail these differences and establish their consequences for the concept of the *other*. I argue here that the two models of speech differently model the other speaker, beginning with Davidson's views.

2. Agreement

2.1. Davidson

For Davidson, the exclusive requirement for communication is that speaker and hearer share an understanding of the speaker's words. Agreement on what the speaker's uttered sounds mean is the necessary and sufficient condition for understanding (1994a, 110). For communication to succeed, "speaker and hearer must assign the same meaning to the speaker's words." (Davidson 1982, 277; see idem 1986, 96; 1991, 157)

That communication should require speakers to hold something in common is not only etymologically perspicuous, but an ancient idea[4]. Davidson's famous innovation comes however in detaching communication from the idea of sharing a language, hence not reducing the required agreement to shared semantic conventions. Accordingly, the resulting concept of agreement is one that is not *prior* to the interaction. A core principle of Davidson's philosophy of language in general is that linguistic competence is best modelled as a theory. Put in these terms, the idea is that speaker and hearer need not share a theory for interpreting each other's words before an utterance is made. Instead, their theories must coincide "*after* an utterance has been made, or communication is impaired" (Davidson 1982, 278).

Davidson provides a more detailed account of this process in 'A Nice Derangement of Epitaphs' (1986). Here, he differentiates between 'prior' and 'passing' theories. As they enter a linguistic interaction, speaker and interpreter both possess a 'prior theory' for one another. This corresponds, for the interpreter, to how he is prepared to interpret an utterance by the speaker, while for the speaker, it expresses what she believes the interpreter's prior theory to be. Understanding is then achieved when speaker and hearer both understand the speaker's words in the way she intended them to be understood. And the way a speaker intends to be understood corresponds to the theory she intends her interpreter to apply. This will then be the 'passing' theory, namely, for the interpreter, the theory he uses to interpret the speaker, and, for the speaker, the theory she intends the interpreter to use. Communication succeeds if and only if these coincide.

With each successful interaction between speaker and hearer, their prior theories for one another may adjust, preserving elements of the coinciding passing theories. But they need not. There is no reason, at least not one relevant for communication, why any speaker should persist in speaking the way they have been doing. If communication doesn't require interlocutors to speak the same

---

[4] See Aristotle *De interpretatione* 16a.

language, neither does it require them to remain constant in their idiolect. As such, Davidson's view is more radical: communication doesn't demand that the two participants share a language at all, either ahead of their interaction of after it. Consequently, the theories used by interpreters to understand speakers are "geared to the occasion" and thus remain occasion-dependent (Davidson 1986, 101).

Davidson's illustration of this procedure with the well-known malaprop example does not need to be rehearsed here. What must be retained from these considerations is that for him understanding presupposes an agreement between speaker and hearer on what the speaker's words mean which is both *posterior* and *momentary*: it needn't be in place *before* the interaction nor persist after it. The prior/passing theory mechanism of communication explains it sufficiently without presupposing or enforcing linguistic homogeneity.

But there is an additional type of agreement which Davidson considers necessary for interpretation. In several papers from the 1970's, he develops the position that "understanding can be secured only by interpreting in a way that makes for the right sort of agreement" (1984a, xvii). This sort of agreement is not a shared understanding of what the words used mean, but an agreement *in beliefs*. The main driving force of these arguments is that absent such an agreement, disagreement would be impossible because meaningful content could not be individuated. In other words, no evidence could allow an interpreter to distinguish between unintelligible noise and meaningful utterance. As is well known, these arguments are intimately connected to the Principle of Charity and the methodology of radical interpretation. But in order not to complicate matters I will not bring these issues up, focusing instead exclusively on the notion of agreement at play here.

Now, Davidson is not implying in these papers that agreement is the goal of interpretation. The purpose of communicating is to understand; agreement or disagreement on what is spoken are subsidiary issues. The point in emphasizing agreement is instead that disagreement is only intelligible against a wider, shared, background (Davidson 1974a, 153). What Davidson is after, therefore, is explaining the possibility of meaningful disagreement (Davidson 1974b, 196, 197; idem 1977, 200). If speakers had nothing in common, there could be no telling what they disagree about. And the more things a speaker and an interpreter will agree on, the better they'll understand their points of disagreement (see Davidson 1973, 137 and also 1974b, 184).

Moreover, the beliefs interlocutors must agree on are mostly true: Davidson takes it for granted that "belief is in its nature veridical" (Davidson 1983,146). He argues that what individuates a belief is its location in a doxastic pattern, which determines the belief's content. As such, "there must be endless true beliefs about the subject matter" for anything to become a subject matter at all (Davidson 1975, 168). If this vast agreement generally remains invisible, it is because the "shared truths are too many and too dull to bear mentioning" (Davison 1974a, 153; see idem 1977, 200). The imagery frequently used by Davidson in these arguments is visual. As believers we may of course be wrong. But if we were not generally right in what we believed, we could not tell what, if anything, we were wrong about. In other words, "the more things a believer is right about, the sharper his errors are. Too much mistake simply blurs the focus." (Davidson 1975, 168; see idem 1974b, 197)

Davidson argues that this kind of agreement is necessary for radical interpretation and, since he generalizes this account to all linguistic understanding, for any understanding whatsoever. The question now emerges: is agreement in beliefs equally posterior and momentary? It is immediately obvious that it cannot be momentary. Speakers cannot agree on what they believe for the duration of an interaction and then radically change their views. This would be in tension with their being mostly right. Moreover, to judge that an interlocutor has changed their mind about something, an interpreter must still identify the matter at hand, which requires, as mentioned, a vast background of shared beliefs.

But the other aspect of our question demands further examination: must we *already* be in an intersubjective agreement before a communicative interaction? It would seem so, given Davidson's requirement that people's beliefs be predominantly constant and true for them to be intelligible creatures at all:

> We must find others largely consistent and right in what they believe as a condition of making them intelligible, that is, as having thoughts at all. But since what we find is what is really there, it follows that rational creatures, creatures with thoughts, must be largely consistent and correct in their beliefs. (Davidson 1992a, 245; see also idem 1980, 7)

Elsewhere, Davidson again claims that any language must "depend upon a largely correct, shared, view of how things are" (Davidson 1977, 199) and that successful communication proves that such a view exists. Coupled with the claim that radical interpretation depends on massive overlap in beliefs between interlocutors, we may surmise that all creatures must possess a shared, and mostly true, worldview, which would make communication between them possible. If humans generally have true beliefs and share most of them, they must share them before any new interaction. Not infrequently, in fact, interpreters[5] have read Davidson as claiming that understanding depends on this sort of prior

---

[5] See Malpas 2011b for a brief overview of this interpretation of Davidson.

commonality, embodying something like a common human nature, and that the requisite agreement couldn't be posterior, but would have to be prior, communitarian.

I do not share the view. Summarizing his arguments in "On the Very Idea of a Conceptual Scheme" (1974b), Davidson insists that what he has shown is not that communication is possible in the absence of a prior shared conceptual background or scheme, simply because there is no basis on which to establish their difference. We simply could not discover others had beliefs or concepts radically different from our own. But "if we cannot intelligibly say that schemes are different, neither can we intelligibly say that they are one" (ibid., 198).

This conclusion is strengthened by later developments. The triangulation papers, in fact, as we saw briefly already, provided a picture of the dependence of thought, language, and hence beliefs, on mutual interaction and successful communication between rational creatures. There must be interaction for there to be interpersonal agreement about anything, whether it be the common causes of our perceptions, our beliefs, or the meanings of our words. And so, it is successful triangulation that determines the contents of our thoughts, beliefs and sentences, not vice versa.[6]

Not few commentators emphasize the continuity of Davidson's views on the agreement required for communication and the associated picture of the social. On this view, Davidson presents a diverse but unified body of work on the social nature of language and thought, the central tenet of which is that the kind of agreement necessary for understanding is not prior to the interaction. Davidson's departure from this more common idea involves the claim that social, linguistic, or behavioral regularities in fact develop in the interaction between people instead of enabling it. The view he endorses is well formulated by Malpas: "*understanding*, whether of others or the world, cannot depend on the existence of any form of preexisting, determinate, "internalized" *agreement*" (Malpas 2011b, 260; see Malpas 1999, 139; idem 2010, 270; Brandom 1994, 39, 599, 659n50). The only form of agreement, in beliefs or meanings, that counts for communication and linguistic understanding is therefore *posterior* to the interaction.

2.2. Gadamer

Gadamer shares Davidson's commitment to agreement as a necessary condition for understanding. However, the sort of agreement he requires is diametrically opposed to Davidson's. Contrary to what some interpreters suppose,

---

[6] This is a version of semantic externalism that Verheggen calls interpersonal externalism (see Myers and Verheggen 2016, 65).

Gadamer is committed to a concept of agreement prior to the dialogical interaction.

Before examining Gadamer's views, we must note that behind 'agreement', as found in most translations of Gadamer's texts, lie several German words. Conceptually the most important are *Einverständnis* and *Übereinkunft*, which can be decompounded as 'one understanding' and 'coming over to become one', respectively.[7] In the following, however, I will keep referring to them in the original. My intention is to draw attention to a conceptual distinction missed, to my knowledge, by commentators. In this section, I will examine the kinds of agreement Gadamer considers necessary for communication, starting with *Einverständnis*.

We already noted that Gadamer establishes a tight conceptual link between agreement and understanding. In *Truth and Method*, *Einverständnis* is described as the goal of communication (Gadamer 1985, 297). Interlocutors will understand one another if they reach an agreement, i.e. a shared understanding, or 'one understanding', of the matter at issue. Consequently, for Gadamer, "understanding is, primarily, agreement (*Einverständnis*)" (Gadamer 1985, 183; idem 1989, 180). As such, 'goal' here has the sense of *telos*, rather than 'purpose': *Einverständnis* describes the relation between the conversation partners concerning the subject matter once understanding is achieved. Understanding demands *Einverständnis* since reaching an understanding with a partner is impossible unless the two agree on what is at issue.

This account, however, is not straightforwardly at odds with Davidson's. If understanding demands agreement on the subject matter of the exchange, it is not necessary that it should precede it. In fact, in *Truth and Method*, Gadamer seems sometimes to veer in a direction consistent with Davidson on this matter. And there have been scholars making this argument (Malpas 2011; idem 2002, 210). However, as Gadamer clarifies his views over subsequent decades, the real distance between the two becomes much clearer.

In his later work, most often in explicit opposition to Schleiermacher, Gadamer returns to the notion of *Einverständnis*. Naturally, this paper would not be the place for rehearsing Gadamer's criticism of Schleiermacher, were it not for the fact that it brings out illuminating points of contact between him and Davidson. As is well known, Schleiermacher's hermeneutics depends on the assumption that "misunderstanding results as a matter of course and understanding must be desired and sought at every point" (Schleiermacher 1998, 22). The task he sets a theory of understanding is to explain how a fundamental disunity

---

[7] I borrow these translations from Dostal 2022, 122.

between interpreter and interpreted can be methodically bridged. Consequently, he defines it starting from *misunderstanding*, which makes this concept theoretically and logically fundamental.

Gadamer concedes that Schleiermacher's description is not entirely wrong: surely the strangeness and unfamiliarity of the *interpretandum* can easily lead to misunderstandings (Gadamer 1966b, 222, 223). Indeed, he sees the problem of overcoming alterity as a central motif of any hermeneutics (Gadamer 1976a, 285), as well as "the most difficult of human tasks" (Gadamer 1990, 346). Gadamer claims, however, that the analysis of understanding must be divorced from a picture which prioritizes the disturbances, disruptions, and obstacles: this for him restricts (Gadamer 1966b, 222, 223; 1967, 233) and distorts the hermeneutic phenomenon (Gadamer 1978, 313). What must be recognized, instead, is that prior to any misunderstanding there is *ein tragendes Einverständnis*, a sustaining agreement (Gadamer 1966b, 223; see 1970a, 187-188; 1978, 317).

It is therefore impossible to actively and methodically seek to avoid misunderstanding in advance. Instead, "agreement is presupposed wherever there is a disruption of agreement." (Gadamer 1970a, 186)

The appeal to a Schleiermacherian "targeted search for understanding" is motivated only by the relatively rare obstacles in the pre-existing agreement (ibid.). Even *addressing* another in dialogue, before any understanding occurs, presupposes a deep agreement between interlocutors (Gadamer 1966b, 223). Misunderstanding and otherness are hence not primordial, to be overcome by an interpreter, but it's the other way around: "it is firstly the support of the familiar and agreement that makes the venture into the alien possible" (Gadamer 1966b, 230; translation from Gadamer 2007, 87, slightly modified).

Note the obvious affinity to Davidson's argument. Gadamer anticipates here the Davidsonian claim that disagreement is inconceivable without a shared background in agreement. Misunderstanding and disagreements require that conversation partners agree on an overwhelming number of items for understanding to be possible. The real distance between Gadamer and Davidson however lies in the claim that the agreement reached in interaction, as *telos*, is not sufficient for understanding. Communication, for Gadamer, is grounded in an agreement which is explicitly *prior* to the conversation:

> [E]very effort at grasping meaning [...] must already rest on a general agreement that is binding, if it is to come about that one understands and is understood. (1968, 114-115; translation from Gadamer 2007, 68, modified)

Without a prior *Einverständnis*, in other words, understanding is not possible. Where no agreement unites the two partners, a dialogue cannot be achieved, and hence, to add the superfluous, neither can understanding of any sort: "coming to an understanding can only succeed on the basis of an original agreement" (1972b, 465; idem 1989, 569). In the postscript to the 3rd edition of *Truth and Method*, he articulates what such agreement consists in:

> All coming to understanding in language presupposes agreement not just about the meanings of words and the rules of spoken language; much remains undisputed with regard to the "subject matter" as well—i.e., to everything that can be meaningfully discussed. (ibid.)

We may want to ask, however, in what sense this prior agreement is consistent with Gadamer's account of interpretation and *Gespräch*. We saw that for him dialogue designates an interpretive event which constitutes the meaning of what is interpreted. But if there are no meanings outside of dialogue, then the question whether two people, independently of interpretation, agree on a given item, is left with no determinate answer. Simply because disagreement requires massive agreement, we are not justified in assigning any determinate content to a prior 'sustaining agreement'. There is therefore a tension between the statement that interpretation can never reveal massive disagreement and the inference that hence interlocutors must agree prior to it.

For Gadamer, dialogue has an additional dimension Davidson ignores. Every *Gespräch* is such that it transcends any single interaction: Gadamer speaks of 'the infinite dialogue ... that we are' (Gadamer 1966b, 230; translation from Gadamer 2007, 88). Conversation therefore constitutes not only the meaning of what is said, but the being of the speakers. We are therefore already engaged in conversation before any new interaction, we are, as Gadamer puts it, *mitten im Gespäch* (1992, 408). The inference from the impossibility of massive disagreement to the priority of agreement is hence justified by the speakers' prior participation in the endless conversation that goes on in and through tradition. Gadamer can meaningfully speak of an agreement prior to any new interaction because he conceives of language as a "repository of understandings that have settled into it" and which are shared and passed down through tradition (Sokolowski 1997, 228).

This makes it plain that *Einverständnis* is unfit for explaining all instances of understanding, because it cannot account for interlingual communication. To apply it to cross-linguistic exchanges would miss the point that *Einverständnis* only describes the kind of agreement existing in a particular language and culture and required for linguistic interaction in it. So, acquiring another language cannot presuppose it. It would also be wrong to conclude that cross-linguistic understanding does not depend on any prior agreement. This would obviously conflict with the claim that understanding within a language does. It is in order to preserve the necessary priority of agreement in both cases that safeguarding the Gadamerian distinction between these concepts – which, when discussed at all, are always fused into one (see Di Cesare 2007, 190; idem 2016, 232; Dostal 2022, 122) – is so important. I now turn to the concept of *Übereinkunft*.

Übereinkunft plays in Gadamer's conceptual apparatus a different role compared to *Einverständnis* and it surfaces in a different range of arguments. In *Truth and Method*, this notion first appears as a translation of the Greek *syntheke* in Aristotle's conception of language. Gadamer introduces it when discussing the relation of language to the world. He stresses that Aristotle does not isolate the sphere of linguistic meanings from the world they refer to, expressing agreement with his view that signs are meaningful in virtue of their being *symbola*, which are not natural, but *kata syntheken*, an expression usually rendered as 'by convention'[8] (see Aristotle, *De Interpretatione* 17a). Gadamer however stresses that Aristotle is not describing an instrumental theory of signs:

> Rather, *Übereinkunft*, according to which the sounds of language or the signs of writing mean something, is not an agreement on a means of understanding—that would already presuppose language; it is the agreement on which human community … is founded. (Gadamer 1985, 435; idem 1989, 430, translation modified)

Übereinkunft therefore is a necessary condition for language because it is presupposed by human community. Accordingly, Gadamer continues, the more restricted kind of agreement manifested in the usage of linguistic signs and sounds (what elsewhere he calls *Einverständnis*), is an expression of this more foundational agreement (*Übereinkunft*) on which it depends:

> "*Syntheke*" should express only the basic structure of linguistic understanding and linguistic communication: mutual agreement [*Übereinkommen*]. (1985c, 353; translation from Gadamer 2000a, 12)

Few pages later, shortly before returning to the concept of *Übereinkunft*, Gadamer discusses the intimate connection between social life and language: "All forms of human community are forms of linguistic community" (Gadamer 1985, 450; idem 1989, 443, modified). He brings out this interdependence by considering artificial languages. Such made-up languages, he claims, are never

---

[8] This is also how the English translators construe *Übereinkunft* here, as *convention* (TM 430). For Gadamer's critique of this translation of *syntheke*, see his 1985c, 353.

actual languages, because they necessarily presuppose a community of life, in which there is lived understanding between partners in a living dialogue. Any agreement reached in an artificial language belongs in fact to a natural language. But:

> In a real community of language ... we do not first decide to agree but are always already in agreement [*übereinkommen sind*]. (Gadamer 1985, 450; see 1960, 73-75)

Therefore:

> Without our having always already come to an agreement [*übereingekommen sind*] in this sense, no speech would be possible. ... Language is a communicative event in which human beings have come to an agreement [*übereingekommen sind*]. (1981a, 260)

Gadamer's formulation is very revealing here. That an agreement is 'always already' presupposed indicates that *Übereinkunft* is prior and "there is in it no first beginning" (Gadamer 1985c, 354; see idem 1985, 436). It is not something one picks up, but a commonality on which any learning and socializing depends. The reader will identify here a similarity with Davidson. For him too, the possibility of teaching depends on interaction:

> Interaction ... demands that each individual perceives others as reacting to the shared environment much as he does; only then can teaching take place and appropriate expectations be aroused. (Davidson 1994a, 125)

In fact, however, Gadamer is here in opposition to Davidson. For Gadamer, interaction means engagement in *shared* practices. Gadamer's essay *Zur Phänomenologie von Ritual und Sprache* (1992) is perhaps the clearest working out of the idea that the commonality of language and conversation is grounded in the commonality of ritual, communal practices and common engagement. For reasons of space, this may only be indicated here.

Much remains to unpack regarding this notion and its relationship to *Einverständnis*. However ungratifying in general, the following summary should satisfy the demands of this paper. First, we saw that *Übereinkunft* is presupposed by language and that *Einverständnis*, as an agreement on the uses of words, is a manifestation of it. Moreover, we noted that it characterizes the nature of the sociality that defines language. Additionally, insofar as it is presupposed by communication, *Übereinkunft* is obviously a prior agreement consisting of mutual engagement in shared practices, which always already, logically and chronologically, precedes language.

Summing up, this section detailed the different kinds of agreement pre-supposed by Davidson's and Gadamer's dialogical models of communication. They outlined contrasting accounts of the kind of sociality required for linguistic communication. Both, Gadamer and Davidson, argue that language is essentially social. For Davidson, "interaction among similar creatures is a necessary condition for speaking a language" (1992b, 264). But the required group does not necessarily contain more than two members. In addition, Davidson does not conclude that these demands shared linguistic practices. Instead, the only requirement is that members of the social group are able to interact with one another and understand the linguistic practice followed by the others. This rests on an agreement constructed in the interaction, rather than preceding it. For Gadamer, instead, it is a condition of possessing language that members of social bodies follow shared practices, including linguistic ones. The group, therefore, must be largely homogeneous in their use of language. They must be exactly what Davidson so vehemently denies: "rough linguistic facsimiles of their friends and parents" (Davidson 1982, 278), i.e., share a language.

Davidson and Gadamer therefore endorse two very different pictures of the sociality of language. To employ a terminology proposed by Robert Brandom, who was inspired by Davidson's work, Davidson argues for an *I-thou* picture of sociality, whereas Gadamer upholds an *I-we* account (see Brandom 1994, esp. 598-607)[9]. Consequently, the Davidsonian and Gadamerian dialogical paradigms of interpretation entail different concepts of the *other*. Davidson's account models the interlocutor as linguistically *singular*. There is no reason, Davidson urges, "why speakers who understand each other ever need to speak, or to have spoken, as anyone else speaks, much less as each other speaks" (1994a, 115). For Gadamer, instead, our partner in dialogue is never a mere solitary individual, but plural, conceptually inseparable from a wider linguistic group:

> There is nothing like an I and a thou as isolated, substantial realities. (Gadamer 1966b, 223; translation from Gadamer 2007, 81)

Language, according to Gadamer, belongs "not to the sphere of the I, but to the sphere of the we" (Gadamer 1966a, 151) and it presupposes an agreement which enables it and "constitutes the 'we' that we all are" (Gadamer 1966b, 223; translation from Gadamer 2007, 81). Accordingly, Davidson has an *I-thou* model of alterity, whereas Gadamer advocates for an *I-they* model.

---

[9] See also McDowell (2002) for a defense of the Gadamerian version of the *I-we* picture against some criticisms by Brandom.

In the remainder of this paper, I will argue that this difference bears not only on how these models conceive of dialogue and its interlocutors' relationship to one another and other potential conversation partners, but also that it has important implications for interpretation and interpretability.

3. Understanding the other

Gadamer's hermeneutics has often been criticized that it improperly conceptualizes understanding the *other*. According to many, Gadamer's emphasis on agreement implies that the other is always made to conform to the interpreter's perspective. Understanding thus reduces the other to the self (see Kogge 2001; Kapsch 2007). Gadamer recognizes this as "the weightiest objection" to his philosophy, but nevertheless stands his ground (1972b, 465). In opposition to it, Davidson's *I-thou* model seems superior insofar as it does not presuppose a prior agreement between self and other. My aim in this section is not directly to defend Gadamer against this criticism, though this will be one of its results. Instead, it argues for the unintuitive thesis that the degree of agreement and semantic conformity between speakers postulated by each model of alterity is proportional to that of the conceptual and semantic difference it can make intelligible. The more conformity we presuppose, the more deviation we can detect.

The way towards this conclusion starts in the interpretive situation and the interpreter's point of view. This choice is explained by considerations internal to the models, namely that the bounds of intelligibility are shaped by what an interpreter can understand. A good method for testing these limits is by analyzing cases of interpretive equivocity and the theoretical interpreter's choice between interpretations. Forced to choose, he will have to use everything at his disposal to tell the right interpretation apart from the wrong. Failure to judge correctly is a good test of a model's adequacy, since it entails inability to lead to understanding.

Let's imagine, therefore, a dialogue where an ambiguity arises in the interpretation of a sentence s uttered by the speaker. On one interpretation, call it I_1, the interpreter understands the speaker as uttering s with meaning M_1, whereas on another interpretation I_2, as uttering it with M_2. I_1 and I_2 are mutually exclusive and exhaustive: they are incompatible and the only possible interpretations of s. Furthermore, let M_2 be the intended meaning of the speaker's utterance of s, and hence I_2 its correct interpretation. For ease of distinction between the two situations, let *Donald* play the role of the interpreter in the Davidsonian model, and *Hans* be his Gadamerian counterpart. I begin with the former.

When faced with two possible interpretations of an utterance, Donald may call upon evidence of two kinds for narrowing down its intended meaning. First, he may prompt further utterances from the speaker. He may ask her for instance what she meant on that occasion, or to elaborate on her utterance of *s*, to explain it differently, to employ a synonym, and so on. Assume this fails to resolve the ambiguity. At this point, Donald will have a different sort of evidence at his disposal, namely that of his own beliefs. Before considering this option however, let us analyze the Gadamerian situation.

Now, Hans seems to have access to a further kind of evidence for distinguishing wrong from right interpretations. Given Gadamer's requirement that speakers of a language conform in their use of it, Hans will be able to rely on this conformity in verifying his assumptions. Unable to assign a unique meaning to *s*, Hans can therefore attend to other speakers' utterances of *s*, call upon them to explain its meaning, its use by other speakers, etc. If, in the case of most others, I_2 is the predominantly more likely interpretation of utterances of *s*, or if I_1 is excluded by some other factors, then Hans seemingly has good reason to prefer I_2 as the correct interpretation of the utterance of *s* above. The conformity required by the model, and the exclusivity of I_1 and I_2, dictates that it must be correct.

However, it is clear that the kind of evidence Hans has is essentially negative: useful in discounting faulty comprehension and narrowing down interpretive options, but unfit for picking out the right one. The discovery that speakers radically conflict in their use of words and concepts, under some interpretation, is good indication for Hans that his attribution of meaning is mistaken in at least one case. The requirement of conformity demands that it be revised to account for both. Nevertheless, his evidence will never count *in favor of* some interpretation: no amount of conformity will confirm that one is correct. Even if some interpretation could unambiguously be given to all speakers' utterance of a sentence, it remains in principle open-ended and susceptible to revision.

We may conclude, then, that Hans has a wider evidentiary base than Donald's which, by steering him away from misinterpretations, can make for better results. The more regularity between the members of the relevant community Gadamer presupposes, the more evidence Hans will have at his disposal to sharpen his interpretive capacities. But this is of course not to say that Donald's can only be too dull. While we may suppose that Hans is in a markedly better position, practically speaking, or even that Donald – due to contingent facts about speakers' abilities to explain themselves to an interpreter – will frequently be unable to go very far in his attempts, we have not thus identified a fault with the Davidsonian model.

This is because whatever amount of negative evidence is available to the interpreter simply corresponds to the amount of conformity required by the model. As such, Davidson may in fact grant Hans' abundance of evidence while insisting that it is superfluous. As we saw, for him all that is in principle relevant to interpreting s as uttered by a speaker is internal to the interaction between her and the interpreter. The context of significance is the interaction, which is sufficient for determining the meaning of s. And so, while Hans may rely on several interactions to hone his interpretive skill, the chief claim Davidson makes is that there is no need for many where one was in principle enough. The interpretation of one speaker should not therefore have any bearing on the interpretation of another. Consequently, the challenge Davidson presents us in reply is to show that Donald could not *in principle* get from a single speaker, or communicative interaction, what Hans can get from many.

Let's therefore modify the example to fit the challenge. We may preserve the general outline of the case: the speaker utters s and the interpreters find her utterance consistent with (only) two incompatible interpretations. I_1 wrongly assigns meaning M_1 to s, whereas I_2 correctly assigns it M_2. Moreover, assume that according to I_1 the speaker is understood as saying something truthful and expressing a correct belief, by the interpreter's own lights, whereas I_2 reveals her to be holding a false belief. The perceived relative truth value of s will soon come into play. Furthermore, grant that the evidence Hans has access to, all other utterances of s, remains inconclusive with respect to I_1 or I_2. Hans now runs into the same ambiguity in his interpretation of the many, as Donald faces in the one.

Under this description, all the advantage of the Gadamerian model seems to dissipate. For even though Hans has more evidence at his disposal and a wider background to check his interpretations against, this now makes no difference to his ability to correctly attribute meaning. Hans' evidence, for all its abundance, is evidence merely for the indeterminacy of utterances of s, hence powerless in ascertaining the correctness or otherwise of I_1 or I_2. Therefore, it indeed seems superfluous.

This *prima facie* vindicates Davidson's claim that one interaction provides all the evidence needed for interpretation. Because it appears that both interpreters must appeal to identical resources to decide the case. If further interactions with the speaker (or speakers, for Hans) leads both to the same crossroads, then the only alternative evidence is that of their own beliefs. The truth, what we hold to be right, is then the last arbiter where no further interaction can determine whether our interlocutor is wrong, or we've misinterpreted them. It seems, therefore, that Gadamer's *I-they* picture fares no better than Davidson's more austere *I-thou* model. They are both left, in this case, with a single leg to stand on, the evidence of their own beliefs. And so, both Hans and Donald seem to have good reason for choosing I_1, because it chimes with what they believe to be true. Neither model, therefore, is sufficient to account for understanding here. In the following, I will argue that this is not true for the Gadamerian model.

But first, let us consider the Davidsonian arguments underlying the choice of I_1. As noted, Davidson requires rational creatures to be consistent and mostly right in their beliefs. This justifies the inference from the interpreter's *beliefs* to the speaker's *meanings*: if speakers mostly have, and therefore express, true beliefs, interpretation can assume that beliefs coincide while decoding the idiom expressing them. Accordingly, Davidson states that the task of interpretation is accomplished by "assigning truth conditions to alien sentences that make native speakers right when plausibly possible, according, of course, to our own view of what is right" (Davidson 1973, 137). Certainly, the assigned truth values are not excluded from amendment: as new evidence comes in, interpretations needing revision will receive it. But the basic principle remains that "a good theory of interpretation maximizes agreement" (Davidson 1975, 169; see idem 1974b, 197)[10]. Therefore, Donald is forced into a state of pseudo-agreement, since he does not have sufficient resources to tell an expression of a wrong belief apart from a wrong interpretation. The model thus cannot account for comprehension in this case.

Now, much like Davidson, Gadamer also assumes most of our beliefs must be true. He couches this insight in terms of the positivity and inescapability of prejudice as a condition of all understanding (Gadamer 1985, 270-290). Our insight and comprehension, Gadamer argues, are perpetually guided by the anticipatory structure of our prejudices and fore-understandings. As such, they make up our historical situation and horizon (Gadamer 1985, 281). Prejudices, however, are obviously not always positive and certainly do not always lead to correct understanding. And so, the problem of filtering the true from the false remains: even if most of what we unquestioningly hold to be true is in fact so, there is no telling *which* of our beliefs or prejudices are not.

Gadamer formulates this problem immediately after discussing the fore-structure of understanding and introducing his notion of prejudice:

> [T]he fore-meanings that determine my own understanding can go entire-
> ly unnoticed. If they give rise to misunderstandings, how can our misun-
> derstandings of a text be perceived at all if there is nothing to contradict

---

[10] Davidson's later talk of *optimization* instead of *maximization* has no bearing on Donald's choice here, which remains the same.

them? How can a text be protected against misunderstanding from the start? (Gadamer 1985, 273; idem 1989, 271)

For Gadamer, this problem will later become the fundamental epistemological question of hermeneutics, namely: "What distinguishes legitimate prejudices from the countless others which it is the undeniable task of critical reason to overcome?" (Gadamer 1985, 281; idem 1989, 278). As noted in Gadamer's critique of Schleiermacher, a methodical and pre-emptive foregrounding of the distorting and negative prejudices is impossible, as any recognition of distortion can occur only against a background of taken-for-granted agreement. Thus, Gadamer's reply to his own worry will be negative: a text cannot be protected against misunderstandings from the start. Instead, his solution will involve the notion of temporal distance:

> Often temporal distance can solve the critical question of hermeneutics, namely how to distinguish the *true* prejudices, by which we *understand*, from the *false* ones, by which we *misunderstand*. (Gadamer 1985, 304; idem 1989, 298, modified)

What temporal distance provides here are the requisite prompts which solely make us aware that we have inherited merely one of several possible perspectives on reality. Since, for us to become aware of a prejudice, it must be 'provoked' by the encounter with alterity (Gadamer 1985, 304). As Gadamer later came to realize, however, the required distance needn't be temporal. In his *Attempt at a self-critique* (1985a), objecting to his earlier exclusive focus on historical distance, Gadamer admits that the concept of distance in general would have been better suited for demonstrating the significance of the alterity of the other and the fundamental role of dialogue. He insists therefore that not only *historical* distance, and not even strictly *temporal* distance, but distance *simpliciter* may aid us in overcoming the "false overresonances and distorted applications" of our prejudices (1985a, 9; see the emendation in Gadamer 1985, 304n228).

The necessary distance, therefore, can exist between contemporaries, people searching through dialogue for a common ground, for instance, but most of all in cases of cultural and linguistic difference. The productive significance of temporal distance, therefore, as well as its role in eliminating distorting prejudices, also applies to cultural distance: "it not only lets local and limited prejudices die away, but allows those that bring about genuine understanding to emerge clearly as such" (Gadamer 1985, 304; idem 1989, 298). Gadamer thus writes that:

Every encounter of this kind allows us to become conscious of our own preconceptions in matters which seemed so self-evident to oneself that one could not even notice one's naïve process of assuming that the other person's conception was the same as one's own, which generated misunderstanding. (Gadamer 1985a, 9; translation from Gadamer 1997, 45)

In the remainder of this paper, I readopt the interpreter's perspective and fill in the gaps in Gadamer's description of this filtering process. I argue that the Gadamerian model does not fall into the same traps as the Davidsonian, and can account for correct understanding in the case described.

First, it must be noted that the encounter with cultural distance does not rid Hans of his prejudices:

If a prejudice becomes questionable in view of what another person or a text says to us, this does not mean that it is simply set aside and the text or the other person accepted as valid in its place. (Gadamer 1985, 304, idem 1989, 298)

Instead, Hans' situation can be construed as the hermeneutic experience of the foregrounding of false prejudices.

The encounter with otherness, the experienced tension between I_1 and I_2, provokes Hans' awareness of his preconceptions and of cultural distance. This will consequently lead to the suspension of his prejudices, to their being brought into play, the sole means for Hans to experience the truth of the other's claim (Gadamer 1985, 304). This suspending procedure, in turn, will have for Gadamer the logical structure of the question and thus he perceived ambiguity will represent for Hans the dawning of a question, and of different possibilities of being (see Gadamer 1985, 304). For,

When a question arises, it breaks open the being of the object, as it were. (Gadamer 1985, 368; idem 1989, 356)

In our case, of course, the object whose being breaks open is the *Sache* of *s*, what the sentence was about, and the question addressed to it opens up its different possibilities (see Gadamer 1985, 304). The tension between I_1 and I_2, therefore, confronts Hans with the different possibilities of this object. The awareness of I_1 and I_2 as possible interpretations of *s* represents the awareness of two possible answers to the question addressed to its *Sache*. And this is a clear step towards recognizing I_2 as the correct interpretation of *s*:

Recognizing that an object [*Sache*] is different, and not as we first thought, obviously presupposes the question whether it was this or that. (Gadamer 1985, 368; idem 1989, 356)

As already noted, understanding a question requires that one must ask it oneself (Gadamer 1985, 369). Hence, it implies the explicit anchoring of one's presuppositions which determine how the object being questioned shows itself (*ibid.*). Now, Hans' recognition that the object of *s* was different than what he first thought is due to the fact that asking this question presupposed the suspension of his own beliefs. In other words, it required that Socratic *docta ignorantia* essential to genuine dialogue, the knowledge that one does not know (Gadamer 1985, 368-369).

Consequently, once Hans faced the question, in the form of the interpretive ambiguity, the validity of his own prejudices was already suspended: they had already been foregrounded. And this is exactly the crucial step, the idea that distance provokes an awareness of *negative* prejudices. The contact with otherness has the force of an impact which makes Hans aware of what doesn't fit in with his guiding fore-meanings (Gadamer 1985, 372). Distance carries the realization that he misunderstood and a recognition of what he misunderstood.

In other words, it is sufficient for Hans to encounter the tension between I_1 and I_2 to already recognize the former as wrong. Here we may reserve judgement as to which view was true of the *Sache* of *s*. There is nothing in Gadamer's account to suggest it requires the other to be right and express a true belief about the world. Instead, the point to recognize is that it made conceptual difference intelligible *as difference*. Once a challenge to the interpreter's perspective asserts itself in the way described here, it has already, so to say, overthrown its rival. Hans is therefore not in the position of someone choosing between alternatives with equal subjective probability. The correct choice, in a sense, was already given. Distance granted Hans the ability to tell his true prejudices apart from the false, and thus a way to distinguish between an expression of a wrong belief and a wrong interpretation. This is sufficient to account for correct comprehension.

The *I-they* picture of alterity and the extension of the context of significance to the observed community is crucial to this accomplishment. The fact that, after examination of the linguistic group, I_2 remains a possible interpretation of *s* is indication of communitarian agreement. A single utterance contradicting I_2 would be enough to discount it, but its absence leads to the conclusion that I_2 is potentially true of the object, in other words that the speakers can mean *s* with M_2, and hence have the appropriate belief. The persistence of I_2 at a communitarian level is sufficient for Hans to realize that the possible perspectives on the object do not reduce to his own. On the other hand, the equal possibility of I_1 indicates agreement between the observed community and the interpreter's beliefs. Hans' choice of I_2 is justified by the greater probability that a linguistic group be in agreement with one another than that they be in agreement with one another *and* an external interpreter. This is implicit in the idea of the fusion of horizons:

> the interpreter's own horizon is decisive, yet not as a personal standpoint that he maintains or enforces, but more as an opinion and a possibility that one brings into play and puts at risk [...] I have described this above as a "fusion of horizons." (Gadamer 1985, 392; idem 1989, 390)

To summarize, what was crucial in my description of Hans' choice was the idea that communitarian agreement, which is prior to the interaction, is mor significant than what can be reached in it. And so, in cases of persistent ambiguity, the opposing view, so long as it is supported by communitarian evidence, weighs heavier in the balance. For Gadamer, the interpreter's own horizon remains an opinion and possibility even given the opportunity to maximize agreement. This is an inference which, as well as the evidence grounding it, Davidson's *I-thou* picture of alterity excludes. The model rules it out because the relevant context for interpretation is the interaction. We may speak therefore of an *interpersonal contextualism* in Davidson's case. The inference is well supported, on the other hand, by Gadamer's *I-they* picture of alterity because for him the context in which an utterance is meaningful is communitarian. His is a *communitarian contextualism*.

The analysis of the two models' treatment of ambiguity concludes with the proportionality thesis outlined at the start of this section: the amount of agreement and semantic conformity between speakers required by each model is proportional to that of the conceptual and semantic difference it can make intelligible. And this is in turn proportional to the available evidence. As argued, Gadamer's model, in virtue of its *I-they* picture of alterity, can account for more intelligible difference – grounded in more available evidence – than Davidson's *I-thou* model.

4. Conclusion

In this paper, I have shown how both Gadamer and Davidson build their approaches to language on the foundation of those events in which language and understanding play out between intelligent speakers: conversations. I have argued that both models presuppose some agreement between the speakers as a condition of possibility of the interaction, but that the kinds of agreement presupposed differ substantially. Davidson only demands that an agreement exist at the end of an interaction, whereas Gadamer requires it before as well. The distinction between a prior and posterior agreement is shown to entail significant differences in how the two models conceive of alterity and our encounters with it. Finally, I argued that the Gadamerian *I-they* model can make more conceptual alterity intelligible to the interpreter than Davidson's, which is insufficient to account for understanding in the case developed.

Vladmir Lazurca, M.A., PhD Cand., Dept. of Philosophy,
Central European University, Vienna, Lazurca_Vladimir@phd.ceu.edu

References

Aristoteles. 2014. *De interpretatione* (Peri hermeneias). Edited by Hermann Weidemann. Berlin: De Gruyter.

Ball, Derek, and Brian Rabern, eds. 2018. *The Science of Meaning: Essays on the Metatheory of Natural Language Semantics*. Oxford: Oxford University Press.

Brandom, Robert. 1994. *Making it Explicit. Reasoning, Representing and Discursive Commitment*. Cambridge: Harvard University Press.

Braver, Lee. 2011. "Davidson's Reading of Gadamer: Triangulation, Conversation, and the Analytic-Continental Divide." In Malpas (ed.) 2011a. 149-166.

Davidson Donald. 1989. "James Joyce and Humpty Dumpty." In Davidson 2005. 143-157.

Davidson, Donald, and Kathrin Glüer. 1995. "Relations and Transitions. An Interview with Donald Davidson." *Dialectica* 49 (1): 75-86.

Davidson, Donald. 1967. "Truth and Meaning." In Davidson 1984. 17-36.

Davidson, Donald. 1973. "Radical Interpretation." In Davidson 1984. 125-140.

Davidson, Donald. 1974a. "Belief and the Basis of Meaning." In Davidson 1984. 141-154.

Davidson, Donald. 1974b. "On the Very Idea of a Conceptual Scheme." In Davidson 1984. 183-198.

Davidson, Donald. 1975. "Thought and Talk." In Davidson 1984. 155-170.

Davidson, Donald. 1977. "The Method of Truth in Metaphysics." In Davidson 1984. 199-214.

Davidson, Donald. 1980. "Toward a Unified Theory of Meaning and Action." *Grazer Philosophische Studien* 11 (1): 1-12.

Davidson, Donald. 1982. "Communication and Convention." In Davidson 1984. 265-280.

Davidson, Donald. 1983. "A Coherence Theory of Truth and Knowledge." In Davidson 2001. 137-157.

Davidson, Donald. 1984. *Inquiries into Truth and Interpretation*. Oxford: Clarendon Press.

Davidson, Donald. 1984a. "Introduction." In Davidson 1984. xiii-xx.

Davidson, Donald. 1986. "A Nice Derangement of Epitaphs." In Davidson 2005. 89-107.

Davidson, Donald. 1990. "Meaning, Truth, and Evidence." In Davidson 2005. 47-62.

Davidson, Donald. 1991. "Three Varieties of Knowledge." In A. Phillips Griffiths (ed.). *Royal Institute of Philosophy Supplement* 30: 153-166.

Davidson, Donald. 1992a. "The Socratic Concept of Truth." In Davidson 2005. 241-250.

Davidson, Donald. 1992b. "The Second Person." *Midwest Studies in Philosophy* 17 (1): 255-267.

Davidson, Donald. 1993. "Locating Literary Language." In Davidson 2005. 167-181.

Davidson, Donald. 1994a. "The Social Aspect of Language." In Davidson 2005. 109-125.

Davidson, Donald. 1994b. "Dialectic and Dialogue." In Davidson 2005. 251-259.

Davidson, Donald. 1997. "Gadamer and Plato's *Philebus*." In Davidson 2005. 261-275.

Davidson, Donald. 2001. *Subjective, Intersubjective, Objective*. Oxford: Clarendon Press.

Davidson, Donald. 2005. *Truth, Language, and History*. Oxford: Clarendon Press.

Di Cesare, Donatella. 2007. "Das unendliche Gespräch. Sprache als Medium der hermeneutischen Erfahrung (GW 1, 387-441)." In Figal (ed.) 2007. 177-198.

Di Cesare, Donatella. 2016. "Understanding." In Niall Keane, and Chris Lawn (eds.). The Blackwell Companion to Hermeneutics. Hoboken, NJ: Wiley-Blackwell, 2016. 229-235.

Dostal, Robert J. 2022. *Gadamer's Hermeneutics. Between Phenomenology and Dialectic*. Evanston, IL: Northwestern University Press.

Dostal, Robert. 2011. "In Gadamer's Neighborhood." In Malpas 2011a. 167-190.

Figal, Günter. 2007. *Hans-Georg Gadamer: Wahrheit und Methode*. Klassiker Auslegen. Vol. 30. Berlin: Akademie Verlag.

Føllesdal, Dagfinn. 2011. "Foreword." In Malpas 2011a. ix-xiv.

Fultner, Barbara. 2011. "Incommensurability in Davidson and Gadamer." In Malpas 2011a. 219-240.

Gadamer, Hans-Georg. 1960. "Die Natur der Sache und die Sprache der Dinge." In *Gesammelte Werke*, Vol. 2. 66-76.

Gadamer, Hans-Georg. 1966a. "Mensch und Sprache." In *Gesammelte Werke*, Vol. 2. 146-154.

Gadamer, Hans-Georg. 1966b. "Die Universalität des hermeneutischen Problems." In *Gesammelte Werke*, Vol. 2. 219-231.

Gadamer, Hans-Georg. 1967. "Rhetorik, Hermeneutik und Ideologiekritik. Metakritische Erörterungen zu "Wahrheit und Methode"." In *Gesammelte Werke*, Vol. 2. 232-250.

Gadamer, Hans-Georg. 1968. "Klassische und philosophische Hermeneutik." In *Gesammelte Werke*, Vol. 2. 92-117.

Gadamer, Hans-Georg. 1968. "Klassische und philosophische Hermeneutik." In *Gesammelte Werke*, Vol. 2. 92-117.

Gadamer, Hans-Georg. 1970a. "Sprache und Verstehen." In *Gesammelte Werke*, Vol. 2. 184-198.

Gadamer, Hans-Georg. 1972a. "Die Unfähigkeit zum Gespräch." In *Gesammelte Werke*, Vol. 2. 207-215.

Gadamer, Hans-Georg. 1972b. "Nachwort zur 3. Auflage." In *Gesammelte Werke*, Vol. 2. 449-478.

Gadamer, Hans-Georg. 1973. "Selbstdarstellung Hans-Georg Gadamer." In *Gesammelte Werke*, Vol. 2. 479-508.

Gadamer, Hans-Georg. 1976a. "Rhetorik und Hermeneutik." In *Gesammelte Werke*, Vol. 2. 276-291.

Gadamer, Hans-Georg. 1978. "Hermeneutik als theoretische und praktische Aufgabe." In *Gesammelte Werke*, Vol. 2. 301-319.

Gadamer, Hans-Georg. 1981a. "Stimme und Sprache." In *Gesammelte Werke*, Vol. 8. 258-270.

Gadamer, Hans-Georg. 1981b. *Reason in the Age of Science*. Cambridge: MIT Press.

Gadamer, Hans-Georg. 1985-1995. *Gesammelte Werke*, 10 vols. Tübingen: Mohr-Siebeck.

Gadamer, Hans-Georg. 1985. *Wahrheit und Methode. Grundzüge einer philosophischen Hermeneutik*. In *Gesammelte Werke*, Vol. 1.

Gadamer, Hans-Georg. 1985a. "Zwischen Phänomenologie und Dialektik. Versuch einer Selbstkritik." In *Gesammelte Werke*, Vol. 2. 2-23.

Gadamer, Hans-Georg. 1985b. "Destruktion und Dekonstruktion." In *Gesammelte Werke*, Vol. 2. 361-372.

Gadamer, Hans-Georg. 1985c. "Grenzen der Sprache." In *Gesammelte Werke*, Vol. 8. 350-361.

Gadamer, Hans-Georg. 1989. *Truth and Method*. Translation by Joel Weinsheimer and Donald G. Marshall. New York: Continuum.

Gadamer, Hans-Georg. 1990. "Die Vielfalt der Sprachen und das Verstehen der Welt." In *Gesammelte Werke*, Vol. 8. 339-349.

Gadamer, Hans-Georg. 1992. "Zur Phänomenologie von Ritual und Sprache." In *Gesammelte Werke*, Vol. 8. 400-440.

Gadamer, Hans-Georg. 1996. *The Enigma of Health*. Stanford: Stanford University Press.

Gadamer, Hans-Georg. 2000a. "Boundaries of Language (1985)." Translation of Gadamer 1985c by Lawrence K. Schmidt. In Schmidt 2000. 9-18.

Gadamer, Hans-Georg. 2007. *The Gadamer Reader: A Bouquet of the Later Writings*. Edited and translated by Richard Palmer. Evanston, IL: Northwestern University Press.

Gadamer, Hans-George. 1997. "Reflections on my Philosophical Journey." In Hahn (ed.) 1997. 3-63.

Glüer, Kathrin. 2013. "Convention and Meaning." In Lepore and Ludwig (eds.) 2013. 339-360.

Glüer, Kathrin. 2018. "Interpretation and the Interpreter: On the Role of the Interpreter in Davidsonian Foundational Semantics." In Ball and Rabern (eds.) 2018. 226-252.

Griffiths, Phillips A. 1992. *A. J. Ayer: Memorial Essays*. Cambridge: Cambridge University Press.

Hahn, Lewis Edwin, ed. 1997. *The Philosophy of Hans-Georg Gadamer*. The Library of Living Philosophers. Vol. 24. Chicago: Open Court.

Kapsch, Edda. 2007. *Verstehen des Anderen. Fremdverstehen im Anschluss an Husserl, Gadamer und Derrida*. Berlin: Parodos.

Kertscher, Jens. 2002. "'We Understand Differently, If We Understand at All": Gadamer's Ontology of Language Reconsidered." In Malpas, Arnswald, and Kertsch'r (eds.) 2002. 135-156.

Kogge, Werner. 2001. *Verstehen und Fremdheit in der philosophischen Hermeneutik. Heidegger und Gadamer*. Zürich: Hildesheim.

Lepore, Ernest, and Kirk Ludwig, eds. 2013. *A companion to Donald Davidson*. Hoboken, NJ: Wiley-Blackwell.

Lynch, Greg. 2014. "Does Conversation Need Shared Language? Davidson and Gadamer on Communicative Understanding." *The Southern Journal of Philosophy* 52 (3): 359-381.

Malpas, Jeff, and Santiago Zabala, eds. 2010. *Consequences of Hermeneutics: Fifty Years After Gadamer's Truth and Method*. Evanston, IL: Northwestern University Press.

Malpas, Jeff, ed. 2011a. *Dialogues with Davidson. Acting, Interpreting, Understanding*. Cambridge, MA: MIT Press.

Malpas, Jeff, Ulrich Arnswald, and Jens Kertscher, eds. 2002. *Gadamer's Century. Essays in Honor of Hans-Georg Gadamer*. Cambridge, MA: MIT Press.

Malpas, Jeff. 1990. "Locating Interpretation: The Topography of Understanding in Heidegger and Davidson." *Philosophical Topics*: 27 (2): 129-148.

Malpas, Jeff. 2002. "Gadamer, Davidson, and the Ground of Understanding." In Malpas, Arnswald, and Kertscher (eds.) 2002. 195-215.

Malpas, Jeff. 2010. "The Origin of Understanding: Event, Place, Truth." In Malpas and Zabala 2010. 261-280.

Malpas, Jeff. 2011b. "What Is Common to All: Davidson on Agreement and Understanding." In Malpas 2011a. 259-280.

McDowell, John. 2002. "Gadamer and Davidson on Understanding and Relativism." In Malpas, Arnswald, and Kertscher (eds.) 2002. 173-194.

Myers, Robert H., and Claudine Verheggen. 2016. *Donald Davidson's Triangulation Argument: A Philosophical Inquiry*. New York and London: Routledge.

Schleiermacher, Friedrich. 1998. *Hermeneutics and Criticism. And Other Writings*. Cambridge: Cambridge University Press.

Schmidt, Lawrence K. 2000. *Language and Linguisticality in Gadamer's Hermeneutics*. Lanham, Boulder, New York, Oxford: Lexington Books.

Sokolowski, Robert. 1997. "Gadamer's Theory of Hermeneutics." In Hahn (ed.) 1997. 223-235.

Vessey, David. 2011. "Davidson, Gadamer, Incommensurability, and the Third Dogma of Empiricism." In Malpas 2011a. 241-258.

Vessey, David. 2012. "Gadamer and Davidson on Language and Thought." *Philosophy Compass* 7 (1): 33-42.

LABYRINTH Vol. 24, No. 1, Summer 2022

JOSEP MARIA BECH (Barcelona)

On Gadamer's Heteronomy Argument:
The "Irruption" of Reality vs. its "Strategic Excision"

Abstract

The aim of this paper is to find out whether Gadamer is entitled to hold together his finitist commitment to the heteronomy of art and thought, and his advocacy of an "endless conversation with itself" of humankind. We focus on three texts: Gadamer's dismissal of Carl Schmitt's outside-in account of the heteronomy implied by the "irruption of reality" in the play Hamlet and, as Archimedean point, Shakespeare's "excision of reality" according to Stephen Greenblatt, and its inside-out heteronomic consequences. The results: Schmitt's approach restricts Gadamer's argument on the "endless dialogue", Gadamer's rejoinder aggravates his own argumentative fragility, and Greenblatt's perspectivation discloses a non-sequitur. The inspection of these texts attests that heteronomy per se does not entail any openness to "creative" interpretations, that a universalized logos endiéthetos *is a chimera, and that there cannot be any "infinite conversation" which would sustain the Gadamerian interplay of question and answer.*

Keywords: Hans-Georg Gadamer, Carl Schmitt, Stephen Greenblatt, Hamlet, heteronomy, aesthetic consciousness, endless dialogue, finitism

Current philological approaches recognize the heterogeneous, disconnected structure of Gadamer's *Truth and Method*.[1] As a result, the interrelatedness of its central theses, previously taken for granted, have begun to appear problematic. To the unprepared reader, in particular, Gadamer may appear eager to maintain a sober, finitist commitment to the heteronomy of art and thought compatible with the ostensibly nostalgic, neo-Romantic attachment to an idealized "infinite conversation which we ourselves are" (Gadamer 2004, 360 and 1975, 381). Needless to say, this problematic striving coexists with a set of innovative advocacies, such as the "effective" history, the fusion of horizons, the rehabilitation of prejudice, authority, and tradition, or the "application" as chief hermeneutic tool.

---

[1] Prominent in the philological concern with Gadamer's oeuvre is the work of Jean Grondin (see Grondin 1990).

It remains a riddle, though, how Gadamer's opposition to autonomous aesthetics and his account of tradition as an endless but continually productive "dialogue" of humankind with itself could be kept interdependent. The indisputable starting point for overcoming this difficulty is the core position of the aesthetic concern in Gadamer's thought. He opposes tying the experience of art to the framework he calls "aesthetic consciousness", a mindset which peaks in the attribution to aesthetic perception of an immediate, congenial and subjective character (the instant grasping of *Erlebnisse*) of blatantly Romantic origin (Gadamer 2004, 66 and 1975, 61). In Gadamer's view, by insisting on the autonomy of the aesthetic attitude in contrast to other modes of experience, the "aesthetic consciousness" dissociates art and the aesthetic from everyday life.

Gadamer's critique of the abstraction inherent to this attitude lies at the very heart of his thought. He aims at replacing it by a hermeneutic approach to the experience of art which, far from being an isolated part of his doctrine, works in many ways as its chief foundation. It starts by highlighting the extra-aesthetic or un-functionalized aspects of artworks and the practices surrounding their production: games, plays, feasts, rituals, symbolic uses, cultish and religious purposes, everyday roles, life-worldly tasks. According to Gadamer, in short, religious, ritualistic and life-worldly contexts held sway upon the isolating consideration of artworks, which are seen as a compendium of mundane bondages. His main aim, therefore, is to re-functionalize artworks by tying them back to the lived world. It must be kept in mind, however, that Gadamer's rejection of the "aesthetic consciousness" is not confined to the autonomy of artworks because his conception of "understanding" embraces both art and life.

In summary, therefore, Gadamer rejects the "aesthetic consciousness", by which he means aesthetic autonomy and un-functionalized art and sees the subjectivation of aesthetics as its conceptual opposite (Gadamer 2004, 65 and 1975, 60). (He admits, though, that along history art has striven to become autonomous from both reality and convention, as shown by prevailing notions like "sureness of taste" (Gadamer 2004, 33 and 1975, 34). Conversely, Gadamer defends artistic heteronomy and alongside it the primacy of an externalist approach, driven by the idea that "aesthetic truth" (the truth-content of art, as we will see, not merely the truth about art) is to be found in not-aesthetic practices.

II

Gadamer sets "aesthetic in-difference" against artistic autonomy, and this grounding move deserves some scrutiny. By stressing historicity, externalism, facticity, and dependence from the lifeworld, Gadamer signals to the defenders of the aesthetic consciousness that the artworks are not a universe added to the universe, with laws, materials and developments of their own. Conversely, artistic constructions must be traced back to their less abstract, more life-worldly context, for the artwork's way of being consists in practices that originally are not aesthetic (Gadamer 2004, 81 and 1975, 75). Artistic experience is not necessarily the experience of artworks. Experience (*Erfahrung*) is not research (*Erforschung*) fed by methodical-objectivizing procedures. According to Gadamer, nevertheless, truth exists also (or better, in the best Heideggerian descent: above all) outside the sciences originated by these "procedures".[2] In his view, scientism and the idolization of method must give way to an anti-methodical attitude towards artistic traditions that can be un-problematically transferred to the tradition of ideas.

The outstanding consequence of Gadamer's anti-methodologism is that any tradition amounts to the seamless creative supplementation of what are already consolidated artistic or philosophical works, enriched by the subsequent history of their interpretations. Gadamer's idealist tenet of the constitutive uncloseness or *Unabgeschlossenheit* of cultural entities supports this view, reminiscent of the expansive Preromantic views on criticism. A notorious statement of Gadamer clarifies this issue:

> Understanding is not, in fact, understanding better (*kein Besserverstehen*), either in the sense of superior knowledge of the subject because of clearer ideas (*sachlichen Besserwissens durch deutlichere Begriffe*) or in the sense of fundamental superiority (*Überlegenheit*) of conscious over unconscious production. It is enough to say that we understand in a different way, if we understand at all. (Gadamer 2004, 296 and 1975, 280)

Any encounter with an artwork or a text, therefore, "is an encounter with an unfinished event [properly 'with an un-self-contained coming-into-being (*unabgeschlossen Geschehen*)'] and is itself part of this event" [properly 'belongs as well to this coming-into-being (*ist ein Teil dieses Geschehen*)']. (Gadamer 2004, 85 and 1975, 94) The resonance of these Gadamerian views has been massive. For instance, the suggestion that any event is actually present only if interpreted has been neatly expressed by K. P. Liessmann: each artwork or text "in its being also includes the ways of its reception (*in seinem Sein schließt auch die Weisen seiner Rezeption ein*)" (Liessmann 2003, 225). Such glosses underscore the

---

[2] Yet Gadamer believes, on the other hand, that the "autonomous" artworks are surreptitiously congruent with a methodology-bound, objectivizing approach. (Gadamer 2004, XXIX and 1975, XXII).

essential productivity (not the mere reproductivity, as presumed notoriously by Friedrich Schleiermacher) assigned to the interpreter:

> The real meaning of a text, as it speaks to the interpreter, does not depend on the contingencies (*hängt eben nicht von dem Okkasionellen ab*) of the author and his original audience. It certainly is not identical with them (*er geht zum mindesten nicht darin auf*), for it is always co-determined also by the historical situation of the interpreter and hence by the totality of the objective course of history. (Gadamer 2004, 296 and 1975, 280)

This tenet is so crucial in Gadamer's thought that its effects reverberate throughout Truth and Method:

> There is no possible consciousness, however infinite, in which any traditionary 'subject matter' would appear in the light of eternity. Every appropriation of tradition is historically different (*ist eine geschichtlich andere*): which does not mean that each one represents only an imperfect understanding (*getrübte Erfassung*) of it. Rather, each is the experience of an 'aspect' (*einer 'Ansicht'*) of the thing itself. (Gadamer 2004, 468 and 1975, 448)

III

The outstanding role assigned by Gadamer to the productivity of the interpreter supports the hermeneutic understanding of thought. Yet it depends on a motivating background which is also the fine-grained basis of Gadamer's conception of heteronomy and hence deserves close attention. Already the classical vocabulary called "internal logos" the *verbum interius* (Philo of Alexandria's logos endiathétos), i.e., that which wants to be said and, therefore, corresponds to Gadamer's belief that any expression rests on unstated presuppositions (Gadamer 2004, 434 and 1975, 455). Conversely, the *actus exercitus* (*logos prophorikos*) designated what the discourse actually means for both speakers and hearers, that is, the "uttered logos", what in a statement can be logically apprehended. This polarity was originally conceived by Augustine of Hippo (Augustine 2015, 239 and 280) to distinguish the stoic principle of the logos from the outwardness of repetitive commentary.

Yet an unavoidable question comes to mind. Is there really a *logos endiathétos* to which the *logos prophorikos* only imperfectly corresponds, so that an always renewed effort at matching both must be attempted? After all, the *verbum interius* (*logos endiathétos*), summoned by Gadamer as supporting the hermeneutic consciousness, may have the same "occasional" (and hence "accidental") character that Gadamer assigns to the notion of the "original reader", as far as it is prone to be "determined by the course of events (*sich von Gele-genheit zu Gelegenheit ausgefüllt*)". It is exposed, therefore, to the Gadamerian charge of "unsuspected idealization" (*undurchschaute Idealisierung*). (Gadamer 2004, 397 and 1975, 373)

According to Gadamer, in short, the "interior word" is irreducible to stated discourse. A sort of "essential deficit" always occurs. We cannot accomplish in uttered language (the *logos prophórikos*) the full expression (the *logos endi-athétos*) of what we would have to assert in order to be effectively understood. Gadamer summarized this viewpoint in a conversation with Jean Grondin:

> One cannot express everything that one has in mind, the *logos endiathe-tos*. That is something I learned from Augustine's *De Trinitate*. This experience is universal: the *actus signatus* is never fully covered by the *actus exercitus*. (Grondin 1994, xiv)

Yet, the problem posed by a universalized logos endiathétos had already been detected by Leo Strauss shortly after the publication of *Truth and Method*:

> The hermeneutic experience I possess makes me doubtful whether a universal hermeneutic theory which is more than 'formal' or external is possible. I believe that the doubt arises from the feeling of the irretrievably 'occasional' character of every worthwhile interpretation. (Strauss and Gadamer 1978, 5-6)[3]

This perplexity closes our foray into the operative ground of Gadamer's hermeneutic consciousness. The question of whether Gadamerian heteronomy and his endorsement of an "endless dialogue" of humankind can be kept together boils down to ascertaining whether it does make sense to hold on to the *logos propho-rikos*. Does Gadamer's advocation of the *verbum interius* shed light on the process of reflection and correction triggered by the unfolding of tradition? It must be admitted that tradition, understood as a succession of hermeneutic encounters, evinces a healthy fertility, and a continually productive evolution of historical meanings cannot be doubted. Some aspects of this growing process shall become hegemonic, yet other elements will have baffling consequences. They will come up as obstacles preventing our full self-understanding, but paradoxically they can in some way turn us back to ourselves. The Gadamerian dialogism of question and answer, precisely, is a step further in this direction:

---

[3] Letter (in English) of 26th February 1961 sent by Leo Strauss to Gadamer, who blandly replied (in German) that Strauss' dismissal "is no reproach against [my] theory [...], rather an anticipation of this theory itself." (Strauss and Gadamer 1978, 9. Translated by G.E. Tucker).

The apparently thetic beginning of interpretation is, in fact, a response; and the sense of an interpretation (der Sinn einer Auslegung) is determined, like every response (wie jede Antwort), by the question asked. Thus, the dialectic of question and answer always precedes the dialectic of interpretation. It is what determines understanding as an event (das Verstehen als ein Geschehen). (Gadamer 2004, 467 and 1975, 447)

Summing up, Gadamer convincingly rejects the "aesthetic consciousness" (i.e., the de-functionalized view of artworks that undergirds every claim of artistic autonomy) but gives the impression of doing it for the wrong reasons. In his view, declaring artworks autonomous amounts to saying that they are closed or *abgeschlossen*, which prevents any "creative" interpretation (Gadamerian hermeneutics' chief tenet) and merely allows "reproductive" approaches. Pace Gadamer, however, heteronomy per se does not entail any openness or *Unabgeschlossenheit* that would allow "productive" interventions. No "endless dialogue" occurs that could sustain the interplay of question and answer whose outcome would be a ceaseless build-up of commentary. (Against Gadamer's support of an "endless dialogue" of humankind can also be objected that it assumes a prior agreement about the subject matter of such "dialogue" or, in other words, its chief presupposition is sharing a common meaning. This assumption, however, jeopardizes the acknowledgement of differences which often are hard to overcome. Gadamer's "fusion of horizons", in particular, blurs the heterogeneity of traditions and hence conceals their likely conflict. As a result, the Gadamerian "dialogue" appears at bottom coercive and totalitarian. It tends to overshadow differences by producing what outwardly looks like an agreement but is actually a sort of resultant in a parallelogram of forces.)

In conclusion, the current philological reception of Gadamer's work is marked by a disagreement about what aspects of understanding ought to prevail: either its ontological and existential traits, or the problems posed by its validity (Gadamer 1976, 74). Hermeneutics as a philosophical doctrine about the linguistic and historical constitution of our being-in-the-world, or as the procedural confrontation with the difficulties of understanding the texts of the past. We are convinced, however, that the emerging conflicts must be addressed by the attentive reading of specific texts. One of the few concrete expositions of Gadamer's standpoint on heteronomy is his twofold (in the main text of *Truth and* Method and in an *Annex* to the same work) diatribe against Carl Schmitt's approach to Shakespeare's Hamlet. This Gadamerian precedent has led us to focussing our discussion on three main texts: Gadamer's negative reaction to Carl Schmitt's theses about the irruption of reality in the play Hamlet and, as the necessary Archimedean point that allows to mediate between these opposite views, Stephen Greenblatt's revocation of these antecedent positions, to the benefit of innovative insights into Shakespeare's masterpiece. These concrete theses, both related to Hamlet, ground two alternative conceptions of heteronomy, opposed to each other and both incompatible with Gadamer's.

IV

In his book *Hamlet or Hecuba: The Irruption of Time into the Play*, Carl Schmitt advocates a viewpoint that was vehemently disqualified by Gadamer, and which in essence argues that in Shakespeare's Hamlet takes place an "irruption of historical reality" (Schmitt 2006 and 2017). This "breaking-in" consists in "historical facts" embracing the circumstances of King James' access to the throne of England and thus suggesting a similarity between the Stuart family and that of the Hamlets. Both James I's and Hamlet's father were slain, and their mother wed the respective murderer. In a few words, James I's personal history (enmeshed in the historical post-Reformation conflict between Catholics and Protestants) intrudes upon the formal universe of play in Hamlet, altering it in a way that was obvious for the original audience, but which is bound to remain undetected by the modern viewer.

Schmitt perceives the historical reality "breaking into" the drama Hamlet in a twofold way: 1) Queen Gertrude's (Hamlet's mother) unclear guilt or innocence may point out to the likely involvement of James's mother, Mary Queen of Scots, in the killing of her spouse. The Protestant aversion to Catholic Mary is congruent with the guilty role Shakespeare ambiguously assigns to her, but at the same time he implicitly supports James's bid for the throne by hinting at her potential innocence. In fact, both James I and Mary Stuart "are there without being there". 2) The "Hamletization" of the revenge hero (i.e., the transformation of the hero with a mission of vengeance into a dithering, action-shunning melancholicer) is the alternate way in which reality breaks out into the play. Shakespeare gestures toward the broader religious struggles of the Reformation by highlighting Hamlet's indecision, which represents the plight of James, caught between Catholics and Protestants.

Schmitt's argument sheds light on the fragility of Gadamer's tenet about the constitutive un-closeness or *Unabgeschlossenheit* of cultural entities. The outside-in, positive sort of heteronomy advocated by Schmitt poses a crucial dilemma. Does the play Hamlet remain closed (which means that it cannot be "interpreted" any longer) even if the surrounding world irrupts upon it, for this is Schmitt's claim? Or, as Gadamer contends, it is the intrusion of the play into the reality of its own time what becomes represented before us? Evidently, Schmitt's position is incompatible with Gadamer's defence of the heteronomous artwork, destined to be supplemented and "present only in interpretation". Yet Schmitt's move involves a separation of aesthetics and politics, which would seem a regress to the illusion of autonomy were it not for the table-turning irruption of reality that he detects in Hamlet.

Schmitt's stance, therefore, is fiercely anti-hermeneutic: historical facts are immune to interpretation, the reader must stifle his or her decoding impulses, commentary is impossible. In his view, interpretations are intrinsically weak because they never trigger real changes in the interpretandum, a shortcoming that is especially manifest in Hamlet's case. There, the "irrupting exteriority" does not need to be interpreted because it consists in the same historical-epochal event in which both author and public are involved. It makes any hermeneutic request redundant, which dispels the Romantic lure of an "infinite conversation":

> A terrifying historical reality (*eine furchtbare geschichtliche Wirklich-keit*) shed a faint light through the masks and costumes of a theatre play. No interpretation (*Deutung*), whether philological, philosophical, or aesthetic, however subtle (*scharfsinnige*), can change that. (Schmitt 2006, 18 and 2017, 21)

This anti-hermeneuticist mindset suggests that Schmitt's mistrust of an "endless conversation" arose from the link he established between the concept of "dialogue" (*Gespräch*) and the Romantic eagerness for an infinite "productivity" bent to building sociable wordplays upon arbitrary objects.

These issues evoke Schmitt's notorious discussion of the decisionist[4] intervention of the sovereign into political affairs, for the alleged "irruption of reality" amounts in fact to a decision that outwardly seems to make interpretation redundant. Yet Schmitt concedes that "historical objectivation could not put an end to the series of new interpretations of Hamlet [*den immer wieder neuen Hamlet-Deutungen*]" (Schmitt 2006, 9 and 2017, 10). The invocation of a clear-cut historical context does not really exclude innovative interpretations. On this topic, an insight of Andreas Höfele (2016) should be mentioned. In Schmitt's view, Hamlet was the emblem of both the post-war reality and Schmitt's own maverick position in its midst. Through the portrayal of James I, Schmitt's back-broken Hamlet, according to Höfele, stands as well for the schism which, arising from the upheaval of 1848 and continuing to the German defeat of 1918, has steered the European destiny. Hamlet, therefore, aids to understand both Schmitt's general vision of history and his role as thinker of the torn German past.)

---

[4] On the wayward thesis that a hermeneutical spirit permeates Schmitt's decisionism (see Marder 2010, 309).

V

From a wider perspective it can be concluded that when Schmitt opposes the autonomy of art (he underscores "the limits [*Grenze*] constraining the free invention of the author" [Schmitt 2006, 34 and 2017, 37]) he is defending a sort of ideal-typical, externalist approach. The resistance of the aesthetic realm to conceptual formulation is viewed by Schmitt as one of the two aspects of modern experience, the other being abstract quantification. He concedes that the aestheticist approach, claiming the autonomy of the artwork, may be congruent to the creative freedom ascribed to the lyrical poet. (This admission, however, is blurred when he blames the "aesthetic ideology" for depoliticizing all intellectual endeavours, in line with his understanding of politics as existential confrontation.) But he points out that the dramatist's imagination, unlike the poet's case, is constrained by the historical circumstances, the immediate perception of the audience, and the collective consensus spanning author, actors and public. In short, it is grounded upon a shared historical reality and indifferent to the rules and the language of the play.

Yet, how are we to conceive the "time" that, according to Schmitt, breaks-in or intrudes into the play? In his view it cannot be understood in chronological or empirical terms (the public events surrounding the play or, more specifically, the empirical existence and political ascendancy of both James I and Mary Stuart, who after all "are there without being there"), because it consists in an epochal reality that manifests itself precisely through these terms. Alternatively, the "irruption" or "intrusion" that occurs in the play, as Carlo Galli has strongly stated, is "of an immediacy which renders mediation at once real and impossible" (we must keep in mind Schmitt's relentless anti-hermeneuticism) and which he frames as the relation between the concrete political event and the universality of dramatic representation:

> For Schmitt, the immediacy and uniqueness of historical events, the objectivity of the problems to be analysed, place before us, from the very beginning, the theme of Shakespeare's work. [...] By putting aside the interpretive and explanatory accretions that, like a gigantic crust, suffocate the Shakespearian masterpiece, Schmitt faces Hamlet frontally in order to study its 'history'. (Galli 2012, 61 and 64)

Schmitt is careful to avoid misunderstandings on this issue. In his view, what distinguishes tragedy from other forms of drama is a kind of "surplus value" which resides in the objective existence of the tragic action. No human mind has conceived this externally imposed, unavoidable and unalterable reality. The explicit summoning of "real" historical facts limits the writer's imagination and in so doing raises drama to tragedy. Shakespeare's tragedies (in that respect opposite, for instance, to Friedrich Schiller's historical dramas) represent a historical state of emergency that demands a decision. While the play Hamlet decides nothing, it makes indecision intensely real to the audience. It can even be said that Shakespeare, not Hamlet, appears decisive when he displays the state of emergency embodied by 17th century England.

In Schmitt's perception, Hamlet is a tragic figure that represents the historic failure of the Stuarts as reigning dynasty. He embodies the situation of an English prince before the historical emergence of a concrete conception of the political in authors like Thomas Hobbes. And Schmitt also believes that, in Shakespeare's eyes, Hamlet is a figure of barbarism (Schmitt 2006, 54) because his shortcomings as a melancholic and indecisive prince are ancillary to the insular English condition of late 16th century and display the Stuarts' inability to leave the "barbaric" Middle Age behind and take instead the path of Modernity.

Finally, it may be worthwhile to point out that the occasionalist procedure endorsed by Gadamer in his commentary of Schmitt's Hamletian text (a practice both attacked and mutely adopted by Schmitt) has also oriented our approach in the present paper. Convinced that tiny phenomena may throw light on big problems, Gadamer defends the tendency to perceive particular issues as "occasions" leading to far-reaching conclusions:

> Occasionality must appear as a meaningful element within a work's total claim to meaning (*als ein Sinnmoment im Sinnanspruch eines Werkes*) and not as the trace of the particular circumstances (*die Spur des Gelegenheitlichen*) that are, as it were, hidden behind the work and are to be revealed by interpretation. (Gadamer 2004, 498 and 1975, 469)

This same "occasionalism", precisely, has encouraged us to focus the discussion of the present topics on distinctly circumscribed texts. Schmitt's contribution understands Hamlet out of his "concrete situation" (Schmitt 2006, 55), which constitutes the source of "the tragic" deemed as the ultimate "historical reality" and defined as the "intrusion" (*Einbruch*) of historical time into the play. What in Schmitt's view is actually tragic, therefore, is this tangible "breaking in" effected by historical time. It converts the "trespassed" play into a myth (it mythologizes the historical event represented in the play) and so perpetuates transhistorically the very idea of tragedy.

VI

Gadamer addresses Schmitt's standpoint in the section *The Ontology of the Artwork* (p. 141 of *Truth and Method*), and more explicitly in the *Appendix II* of the same book (pp. 498-500). He begins his criticism of Schmitt's theses by denouncing their alleged link to the "aesthetic subjectivity". He energetically reinstates, against Schmitt, the premises of his own heteronomic conception of artworks:

> A work of art belongs so closely to what it is related to (*worauf es Bezug hat*) that it enriches the being of that as if through a new event of being (*dass es dessen Sein wie durch einen neuen Seinsvorgang bereichert*). To be fixed in a picture, addressed in a poem, to be the object of an allusion from the stage, are not incidental and remote from what the thing essentially is (*sind nicht Beiläufigkeiten, die dem Wesen fernbleiben*); they are presentations of the essence itself. (Gadamer 2004, 141 and 1975, 140)

In the *Appendix II* of *Truth and Method* the stakes appear even sharper drawn. The dilemma boils down to whether there is an intrusion of political reality into the play Hamlet, as Schmitt contends, or conversely, as Gadamer states, "what we are really seeing here is the irruption of the play into time (*es ist in Wahrheit der Einbruch des Spiels in die Zeit, der sich hier vor uns* darstellt)". (Gadamer 2004, 499 and 1975, 470)

When Gadamer turns Schmitt's contention around and defends the idea of "the irruption of the play into time", he is merely alluding to Shakespeare's authorial intervention in the political reality of his time. Faithful to his heteronomic standpoint, he cannot see any disparity between the play and the concrete historical events surrounding it. Needless to say, his hermeneutical stance clashes with Schmitt's genealogical bent. In Gadamer's view, Schmitt misses the dramatic concreteness of the play when he converts it into a sort of roman à clef.

Paradoxically, Gadamer's criticism sheds light on the difficulties of viewing tradition as an "endless dialogue". His argument, indeed, backfires: 1) it shows how the alleged un-closeness or *Unabgeschlossenheit* of texts and artworks can be bypassed; 2) it points out the ways of counteracting the Romantic regress to an infinite conversation. While Gadamer asserts that the irruption of political reality into Hamlet suppresses the possibility for this play to ever become a "new" event, in fact this overdetermination closes off the play to our (for we are its virtual present-day audience) lived involvement with it.

Setting Schmitt's views against Gadamer's[5] has resulted in a duck/rabbit perplexity about what is internal to the dramatic representation and what is external to it. We obviously need a contrasting view which, acting as an Archime-

---

[5] In fact, the positions of both Gadamer and Schmitt are ancillary to the Romantic *topos* of the essential "incompleteness" of everything, which entails the necessity of "creatively completing" what we want to experience.

dean point, will contribute to overcoming this quandary. If the outside-in account has proved unconvincing, the search for a tie-breaking tool directs us to
the tradition that arose in Germany with Johann Gottfried Herder and the *Sturm
und Drang* and which perceived in Shakespeare's works (and chiefly in Hamlet)
an invitation to breaking with the theatrical conventions for the benefit of the
authorial self-determination that German aesthetics was bound to adopt. A crucial trait of this tradition has been revived in unexpected ways, as we will see in
the next section, by the inside-out approach to Hamlet (and to Shakespeare's
works in general) authored by Stephen Greenblatt.

VII

In his book *Will of the World: How Shakespeare became Shakespeare*, Stephen
Greenblatt (2004) defends an inside-out, negative form of heteronomy. In his
view, Shakespeare devised in Hamlet a "new technique of radical excision" that,
by taking out a key explanatory element, accomplished an "expulsion of reality
from the play". These insights, arisen from a detailed foray in the Shakespearian
context, upturn our subject matter. Assigning to Hamlet a justified prominence
among the Shakespearian plays, Greenblatt enters the controversy with an array
of startling statements:

> The crucial breakthrough in Hamlet [...] had to do with an intense repre-
> sentation of inwardness called forth by a new technique of radical exci-
> sion. Shakespeare found that he could immeasurably deepen the effect of
> his plays [...] if he took out a key explanatory element, thereby occluding
> the rationale, motivation, or ethical principle that accounted for the action
> that was to unfold. The principle was [...] the creation of a strategic
> opacity. This opacity, Shakespeare found, released an enormous energy
> that had been at least partially blocked or contained by familiar, reassur-
> ing explanations. [Refusing] to provide himself or his audience with a
> familiar, comfortable rationale that seemed to make it all make sense, he
> could get to something immeasurably deeper. The excision of motive [...]
> expressed Shakespeare's preference for things untidy, damaged, and un-
> resolved [...]. (Greenblatt 2004, 324-325)[6]

---

[6] Greenblatt expands these views to the whole Shakespearian oeuvre: "In the years after
Hamlet, Shakespeare wrote a succession of astonishing tragedies that drew upon this
discovery. Repeatedly, he deftly sliced away what would seem indispensable to a coherent, well-made play". This and the following references to Greenblatt's texts belong to
pp. 323-325 of Greenblatt 2004.

Greenblatt supports a non-sequitur view which is worthwhile to explore. His stance can be judged both anti-Gadamerian, as far as it excludes any possibility of "endless dialogue", and pro-Gadamerian as well because it involves an heteronomic approach to art and thought. Let's inspect in some detail this Janus-faced attitude. On the one hand, Greenblatt endorses Gadamer. Already in an earlier work, *Renaissance Self-Fashioning* (Greenblatt 1980), he insisted on preserving "a sense of the larger networks of meaning in which both the author and his works participate", thus the opposite to viewing artworks "exclusively as the expression of social rules and instructions" (Greenblatt 1980, 4 and 6). This approach assigns artworks a fundamentally active role. They mirror the extant cultural formations, but above all they also reflect on them and even contribute to their emergence. This blueprint for historical interpretation undergirds Greenblatt's latter approach to Hamlet. From such viewpoint, his tenet about the "strategic excision" accomplished by Shakespeare makes flawless sense.

On the other hand, in Greenblatt's view the "endless dialogue" endorsed by Gadamer cannot take place (which agrees with the conclusions we attained in Schmitt's case). Greenblatt conceives every historical epoch as a sort of battlefield in which several discourses oppose one another. Some of them either prevail over former opponents or combine with them, while others became sidelined or altogether silenced. As Mark Robson points out, Greenblatt "sees culture as dynamic, contested and conflictual" and poses the anti-Gadamerian question of "how individuals come to terms with, and negotiate between, the competing ideas and possibilities within their culture" (Robson 2008, 54). Any artwork, literary text, or cultural practice, in short, according to Greenblatt emerges at the interface of divergent or even mutually destroying impulses.

Let's focus now on Greenblatt's heteronomic thesis. One of its chief entailments is the view that "Shakespeare wrecked the plot provided by the sources" (Greenblatt 2004, 305). This paradoxical gesture has been eloquently explicated by James Wood:

> Why does Lear test his daughters' love? Why can't Hamlet effectively avenge the death of his father? Why does Iago ruin Othello's life? The source texts that Shakespeare read all provided transparent answers (Iago was in love with Desdemona, Hamlet should kill Claudius, Lear was unhappy with Cordelia's impending marriage). But Shakespeare was not interested in such transparency. (Wood 2009, 10)

Up to this point, the debate around Hamlet amounts to deciding on the following dilemma. Does the play remain closed (which means that it cannot be "interpreted" any longer) even if (or precisely because) "the reality" of its time intrudes upon it? Or, as Gadamer contends, is it precisely the play itself what encroaches on the reality of its own time? Greenblatt's Archimedean position helps to overcome this perplexity. It allows seeing Hamlet as "a highly political play about betrayal and assassination". As a matter of fact, it includes scenes that could "excite a London audience shaken by the events of 1601 [the insurrection that led to the execution of the Earl of Essex]", but which "do not actually constitute a direct reference to them, and that could be easily explained away". (Greenblatt 2004, 310)

However, producing "a highly political play" without "a direct reference to political events" requires a dire recasting in the dramatist's craft. According to Greenblatt, already "by the turn of the century Shakespeare had perfected the means to represent inwardness" (Greenblatt 2004, 299). This upheaval consisted in taking out major clarifying items and thus creating a sort of productive vagueness. He favoured an "inner structure" that replaced the "structure of superficial meanings". As a result, his "brilliant practice of strategic opacity" became a primary "aesthetic resource". It happened, in sum, that "an opacity shaped by Shakespeare's experience of the world and of his own inner life" inspired his withdrawal of a recognisable justification. This restraint gave sense to the whole play without diminishing its "inward logic and poetic coherence" (Greenblatt 2004, 377).

Greenblatt is particularly convincing when he points out that Shakespeare's ground-breaking practice of removal (the controlled exclusion of reality in the play) led him to rethink "the amount of explicit psychologic rationale a character needed to be compelling". This recasting culminated in Hamlet, where a "daring transformation of Shakespeare's whole way of writing" brought about a momentous "break in his career" (Greenblatt 2004, 307).

It is worth mentioning that Greenblatt's concern with the dramatic power of ambiguity has long been active. Already in his book *Hamlet in Purgatory* (2001), Greenblatt declared his desire to "bear witness to the intensity of Hamlet", a feature he ascribed to Shakespeare's decision to deliberately leaving the status of the Ghost of King Hamlet open to interpretation (Greenblatt 2001, 4). The reason of this ambivalence is that it cannot be decided whether the Ghost is "a spirit of health or goblin damned", or otherwise put, whether it proffers a call to revenge or to remembrance (Greenblatt 2001, 239-40). In so doing, Greenblatt concludes, Shakespeare mobilizes the controversy about Ghosts that pervaded the Elizabethan society. The very undecidability that surrounds the Ghost, in consequence, furnishes the key to the play's dramatic thrust.

In general terms, Greenblatt agrees with Schmitt: a determining lack does inhabit the play Hamlet. But they are at odds over the reasons for this absence: contemporary events in Schmitt's case, Shakespeare's expressive strategy in

Greenblatt's. In Carlo Galli's words, Schmitt sees in Hamlet "a shadow or lacuna that cannot be explained from inside the text, but only in reference to a core of contemporary historical events" (Galli 2012, 65). We may well imagine that this is the contention that Schmitt, if anachronistically confronted with Greenblatt, would oppose to the belief in a Shakespearean scrapping of motive.

Applying Greenblatt's insights to the problem we have been addressing, we conclude that the "productive ambiguity (*produktive Vieldeutigkeit*)" highlighted[7] by Gadamer is in no way "productive". That Hamlet amounts to "a courtyard of the indeterminate (*ein Hof des Unbestimmten*)", does not attest its "essential capacity to become an event again (*neu zum Ereignis zu werden*)". Just the contrary is what happens. If the *Unbestimmheit* makes up the aesthetic value of the play, in fact closes it to new, "productive" interpretations while outwardly demanding updated commentaries.

VIII

Schmitt's account not only disables Gadamer's argument on the issue of the endless conversation but emerges as its very opposite. And Gadamer's rejoinder, as we have seen, merely aggravates the fragility of his own position. Finally, Greenblatt puts their antagonism in perspective. Both Schmitt's and Greenblatt's conceptions of heteronomy, though opposite to each other, attest Gadamer's inconsequence when he holds together the endlessly productive drive of human-kind's "dialogue" and a finitist persuasion[8] of Heideggerian descent:

> In fact, our fundamental experience of beings subject to time (*als zeit-liche Wesen*) is that all things escape us, that all the events of our lives fade more and more (*dass alle Inhalte unseres Lebens uns mehr und mehr verblassen*), so that at best (*aus fernster Erinnerung*) they glow with an almost unreal shimmer in the most distant recollection. (Gadamer 1986, 114 and 1997, 78)

This finitist credo conceals a blessing in disguise because, according to Gadamer, precisely the inconclusiveness of our experience generates endless innovative understandings.

---

[7] The references to Gadamer's text in this paragraph belong to Gadamer 2004, 499 and Gadamer 1975, 471.

[8] We can only disagree with this attempt at conciliation: "Dialogue or conversation is the form of recovery, not from the one sidedness of dialectical thinking, but in Socratic fashion, from the soul fallen into the finitude of bodily existence." (Risser 2002, 91).

In our experience we bring nothing to a close [...] and the special significance of the human disciplines ensues from this inconclusiveness (*Unab-
schliessbarkeit*) of all experience. [Accordingly,] we come upon [re-
newed] insights. That means that we return from the blindnesses
(*Verblendungen*) that held us captive. (Gadamer 1993, 32)

Both the anti-hermeneutic renown of Schmitt's views, alongside Gadamer's
negative reaction to them, and Greenblatt's insight on the "excision of reality"
achieved by Shakespeare in his plays, reflect the contemporary sway of
Gadamer's thought. His finitist alchemy, however, cannot curtail the evidence
that heteronomy per se does not entail any openness to "creative" interpretations. A universalized *logos endiathétos* is a chimera, and there cannot be any
"endless conversation" that would sustain the Gadamerian interplay of question
and answer and so give raise to unlimited accumulations of commentary.

Prof. Dr. Josep Maria Bech,
University of Barcelona, jmbech@ub.edu

References

Augustine of Hippo. 2015. *The Trinity (De trinitate)*. Translated by Edmund Hill, 2nd
ed. New York: New City Press.

Gadamer, Hans-Georg. 1976. "Zur Problematik des Selbstverständnisses". In *Kleine
Schriften I. Philosophie. Hermeneutik*. 2nd ed. Tübingen: Mohr/Siebeck.

Gadamer, Hans-Georg. 1986. "On the Contribution of Poetry to the Search for
Truth". In *The Relevance of the Beautiful and Other Essays*, ed. by R. Bernasconi. New
York: Cambridge U.P. Original edition: Gadamer, Hans-Georg. 1997. "Über den Beitrag
der Dichtkunst bei der Suche nach Wahrheit." In *Gesammelte Werke*, vol. 8. Tübingen:
Mohr/Siebeck.

Gadamer, Hans-Georg. 1993. *Gadamer im Gespräch*, edited by Carsten Dutt. Heidelberg: Carl Winter.

Gadamer, Hans-Georg. *Truth and Method*. 2004. Translated by Joel Weinsheimer
and Donald Marshall, 2nd revised ed. New York: Crossroads Publishing. Original edition: Gadamer, Hans-Georg. 1975. *Wahrheit und Methode*. 4th ed. Tübingen:
Mohr/Siebeck.

Galli, Carlo. 2012. "Hamlet: Representation and the Concrete." In *Political Theology and Early Modernity*, edited by G. Hammill and J. R. Lupton. Chicago: Univ. of Chicago Press: 60-83.

Greenblatt, Stephen. 1980. *Renaissance Self-Fashioning*. Chicago: Univ. of Chicago Press.

Greenblatt, Stephen. 2001. *Hamlet in Purgatory*. Princeton: Princeton U.P.

Greenblatt, Stephen. 2004. *Will of the World: How Shakespeare became Shakespeare*. New York: Norton.

Grondin, Jean. 1990. "Sulla composizione di 'Verità e metodo'." *Rivista di Estetica* (39): 3-21.

Grondin, Jean. 1994. *Introduction to Philosophical Hermeneutics*. Translated by J. Weinsheimer. New Haven: Yale U. P.

Höfele, Andreas. 2016. *No Hamlets: German Shakespeare from Nietzsche to Carl Schmitt*. Oxford: Oxford U.P.

Liessmann, Konrad Paul. 2003. "Die Sollbruchstelle". In *Gadamer Verstehen / Understanding Gadamer*, edited by M. Wischke and M. Hofer. 211-231. Darmstadt: Wissenschaftliche Buchgesellschaft.

Marder, Michael. 2010. "Political Hermeneutics, or Why Schmitt Is Not the Enemy of Gadamer." In *Consequences of Hermeneutics. Fifty Years After Gadamer's Truth and Method*, edited by J. Malpas and S. Zabala. 306-323. Evanston: Northwestern University Press.

Risser, James. 2002. "In the Shadow of Hegel: Infinite Dialogue in Gadamer's Hermeneutics." *Research in Phenomenology* (32): 86-102.

Robson, Mark. 2008. *Stephen Greenblatt*. Abingdon: Routledge.

Schmitt, Carl. 2006. *Hamlet or Hecuba: The Irruption of Time into the Play*. Translated by Simona Draghici. Corvallis: Plutarch Press. Original edition: Schmitt, Carl. 2017. *Hamlet oder Hekuba. Der Einbruch der Zeit in das Spiel*. 6th ed. Stuttgart: Klett-Cotta.

Strauss, Leo and Gadamer, Hans-Georg. 1978. "Correspondence Concerning Wahrheit und Methode." *The Independent Journal of Philosophy* (2): 5-12.

Wood, James. 2009. *How Fiction Works*. London: Macmillan.

KARL LANDSTRÖM (Coventry)
On hermeneutical openness and wilful hermeneutical ignorance

Abstract

In this paper I argue for the relevance of the philosophy of Hans-Georg Gadamer for contemporary feminist scholarship on epistemic injustice and oppression. Specifically, I set out to argue for the Gadamerian notion of hermeneutical openness *as an important hermeneutic virtue, and a potential remedy for existing epistemic injustices. In doing so I follow feminist philosophers such as Linda Martín Alcoff and Georgia Warnke that have adopted the insights of Gadamer for the purpose of social and feminist philosophy. Further, this paper is positioned in relation to a recent book chapter by Cynthia Nielsen and David Utsler in which they argue for the complementarity, and intersecting themes and concerns of Gadamer's hermeneutics and Miranda Fricker's work on epistemic injustice. However, Nielsen and Utsler solely focus on Fricker's conception of epistemic injustice and the two forms of epistemic injustice, testimonial injustice and hermeneutical injustice, that she identifies. In this paper I expand their analysis by considering other forms of epistemic injustice such as wilful hermeneutical ignorance and contributory injustice. Thus, this paper contributes to the budding literature on the relevance of Gadamer's work for the debates pertaining to epistemic injustice and oppression by expanding such analysis to other forms of epistemic injustice, and by further arguing for the strength of Gadamer's work in terms of offering relevant insights for the reduction and remedy of existing epistemic injustices.*

Keywords: Gadamer, hermeneutics, epistemic injustice, wilful ignorance, hermeneutical openness

1. Introduction

This article is primarily an argument for the relevance of Hans-Georg Gadamer's (2004, 1976) hermeneutics for contemporary scholarship on epistemic injustice and oppression. Specifically, I argue for the Gadamerian notion of *hermeneutical openness* as a hermeneutic virtue, and a potential remedy for existing epistemic injustice and oppression. In doing so I follow feminist philosophers such as Linda Martín Alcoff (2005), Georgia Warnke (2015) and Lauren Swayne Barthold (2016) who draw upon the insights of Gadamer in their social and feminist philosophy. This article is positioned in direct relation to a recent book chapter by Cynthia Nielsen and David Utsler (2022), in which they argue for the complementarity and intersecting themes of Gadamer's hermeneutics and Miranda Fricker's (2007) work on epistemic injustice. I expand Nielsen & Utsler's (2022) analysis beyond the initial Frickerian conception of epistemic injustice and consider further forms of epistemic injustice. The forms of epistemic injustice that are the main focus of this article are wilful hermeneutical ignorance as identified by Gaile Pohlhaus (2012), and contributory injustice as defined by Kristie Dotson (2012). I argue that we can understand cases of wilful hermeneutical ignorance as cases where the hearer fails to exercise appropriate hermeneutical openness, which in turn also situates such a failure as a partial cause of contributory injustice. Thus, this article contributes to the nascent literature on the relevance of Gadamer's work for the debates pertaining to epistemic injustice and oppression by considering other forms of epistemic injustice, and by further arguing for the strength of Gadamer's work in terms of offering relevant insights for both identifying the wrongs in cases of epistemic injustice, but also for offering pathways towards the reduction and remedy of existing epistemic injustices.

This article proceeds in the following manner. The second section consists of a brief overview of feminist engagements with Gadamerian hermeneutics before turning to the recent scholarship that combines the insights of Gadamer with feminist theories of epistemic injustice and oppression that has inspired this article. Section 3 is dedicated to outlining hermeneutical openness as a hermeneutical virtue of both epistemic and ethical significance. In section 4 the two forms of epistemic injustice that are the focus of this article, wilful hermeneutical ignorance and contributory injustice, are introduced. In the penultimate section, section 5, I argue that hermeneutical openness can serve as a counterfactual that makes it possible to pin down the epistemic, and ethical failure of the wilfully ignorant and that the virtue of hermeneutical ignorance would serve well as a corrective to the agential dimension of cases of wilful hermeneutical ignorance and contributory injustice. Thus, the virtue of hermeneutical openness has a role to play in the alleviation of such epistemic injustices. The article then concludes in section 6, where I summarize the arguments made, and their contribution to the existing scholarship on the intersection of Gadamer's hermeneutics and epistemic injustice.

2. Gadamerian hermeneutics, feminist philosophy and epistemic injustice

Feminist philosophers have had an ambivalent relationship to the philosophy of Hans-George Gadamer. Gadamer has been criticized by feminists for his failure to address issues of power and privilege, the inaudibility of marginal voices in his work, the lack of attention paid to embodiment, his attempt to rehabilitate prejudice and tradition, as well as for his view that philosophy is politically incompetent (Code 2003; Warnke 2015). Lorraine Code (2003) has argued that for feminists who are aware of the social and political exclusion and oppression of women throughout history it is hard work to find a social-political ally, or even a silent friend of feminist projects in Gadamer. This leads Code (2003) to suggest feminist readers of Gadamer often read him "against the grain". That is, they read Gadamer beyond the omission of women and the marginalised Other in order to unearth valuable insight and tools from the Gadamerian approach to language, history, knowledge and the arts. Similarly, Veronica Vasterling (2003) has argued that while there is much for feminisms to resist in the thought of Gadamer, there is also much to gain from reading him. The Gadamerian project shares many themes and presuppositions with feminist thinking, which makes it less surprising that at least some feminist philosophers have turned to Gadamer rather than discounting him as a source of insight. Lorraine Code (2003) argued already in 2003 that that turning to Gadamerian hermeneutics, if critically enacted, opens the possibility of developing a responsible, situated knowing.

Gadamer (2004) illustrates in *Truth and Method* that hermeneutic understanding is complex and multifaceted, both historically conscious and conscious of its own historicity. Lorraine Code (2003) argues that Gadamerian hermeneutics, in which knowing is thought of as engaged, situated, dialogic and sensitive to history offers important tools and insights for feminist theorists of subjectivity, agency, history, and knowledge. However, while the scholarship on epistemic injustice is explicitly situated at the intersection of epistemology and ethics, it is important to note that Gadamer himself, at least in his early work, did not conceive of his hermeneutics as an epistemology (Code 2003). However, considering how central notions such as understanding and interpretation are for Gadamer, it is no surprise that feminists interested in epistemology have found value in his hermeneutics. One prominent feminist philosopher who have drawn upon Gadamer's hermeneutics for the purposes of feminist epistemology is Linda Martín Alcoff (1996; 2003; 2005). Alcoff (2003) argues that there is plenty of value in Gadamer's hermeneutics and highlight, among other things, his openness to alterity and the move from knowledge to understanding as of particular interest for feminists. Likewise, Susan-Judith Hoffman (2003) argues that many of Gadamer's ideas are in solidarity with feminist theorizing. Hoffman (2003) similarly to Alcoff (2003) highlights how Gadamer's emphasises the importance of difference, but also his notion of understanding as an inclusive dialogue, his account of prejudices as positive conditions of an understanding that must always remain provisional, and his account of language as on-going, developing project.

The literature on the intersection of Gadamerian hermeneutics and epistemic injustice is relatively small, albeit growing. The existing engagements with the philosophy of Gadamer in relation to questions of epistemic injustice has so far has primarily been concerned with the two types of epistemic injustice identified by Fricker in her seminal book from 2007, testimonial injustice and hermeneutical injustice. Cynthia Nielsen & David Utsler's (2022) account is the primary focus in this paper, and they are mainly concerned with testimonial injustice. Georgia Warnke's (2015) analysis is primarily focused on hermeneutical injustice, and Burke (2022) engages with both testimonial injustice and hermeneutical injustice. However, scholars of epistemic injustice have identified a range of different types of epistemic injustice beyond the initial two forms identified by Fricker (2007). In the last few sections of this paper, I expand the analysis offered in the existing literature on Gadamer and epistemic injustice by considering two further forms of epistemic injustice: Wilful Hermeneutical Ignorance as theorised by Gaile Pohlhaus (2012), and contributory injustice as theorised by Kristie Dotson (2012). In doing so, I aspire to not only expand the scope of the literature, but also to illustrate the relevance, and strength of Gadamer's thought as both a diagnostic tool for identifying the wrong in epistemic injustices, but also for offering action-guiding proposal towards possible remedies to existing epistemic injustices.

Nielsen & Utsler (2022) argue that while the work of Gadamer, Fricker and Axel Honneth (1995) constitute important contributions to the theorisation of mutual recognition on their own, the three accounts also complement each other. For the purposes of this article, I will focus on their account of the complementarity between Gadamer's hermeneutics and Fricker's theorisation of epistemic injustice in order to identify and spell out the virtue of hermeneutical openness. Nielsen & Utsler (2022) highlight several intersecting themes and concerns between the Gadamerian, and the Frickerian projects. One such intersecting theme is the role of prejudice in our epistemic lives.

For Gadamer (2004) prejudice is both inescapable and can have positive value. Prejudice orients hermeneutical engagements, functions as a condition for understanding and can serve a corrective role for understandings once they become exposed in interactions with others. James Risser (1997:68) has described Gadamer's view on prejudice as one in which "prejudice need not be taken in its pejorative sense as one-sided distortion of the truth, but is simply that condition in which we at first experience something". For Gadamer (2004, 1976), the role of prejudice in hermeneutical engagements intersects with his emphasis on how historical situatedness, language, tradition, and community shapes one's understanding of oneself and the world. Nielsen & Utsler (2022) emphasises that for Gadamer human beings are historically and socially shaped beings who inherit various prejudices, customs and practices, which in turn can be revised and changed through our interactions with others. However, one alone does not control the various ways which in which one's understanding is culturally, historically and communally shaped (Nielsen & Utsler 2022).

Warnke (2015) argues that Gadamer's rehabilitation of prejudice and tradition is more benign than what the somewhat provocative terminology might suggest. Warnke (2015) posits that for Gadamer 'tradition' signals shared understandings that history pass onto us, and prejudices reflect the pre-orientations, or pre-judgements that it offers us. Warnke (2015) elaborates the Gadamerian view starting from the recognition that one cannot escape or deny participating in history. Rather, one comes to one's projects in media res, that is within a world that one did not create, and that has already formed interpretations of its possibilities and limitations. It is possible to intervene in this world, and to rethink and change these interpretations but one cannot begin anew. Thus, we are inescapably prejudiced, in the sense that prejudice means historically situated and always direct towards that which we are trying to understand. However, our historical traditions are themselves clearly not benign (Warnke 2015). While Gadamer (2004) is primarily concerned with the richness of what history brings, such as ideals to aspire to and values and norms worth preserving. Historical traditions also undoubtedly include problematic aspects such as racism, sexism, homophobia among many other troubling dimensions (Warnke 2015). It is this, the more problematic aspects of shared understanding that Fricker (2007) targets with her conception of hermeneutical injustice. She targets lacunae in the collective hermeneutical resource available to individuals and groups to articulate their experiences.

Gadamer (2004) offers an account of prejudice that highlights the function of prejudice as a condition for understanding, and for correcting misunderstanding. Nielsen and Utsler (2022) describes this corrective dimension as one that takes place when our prejudices are revealed to be flawed or problematic when exposed to the claims of the others, and thus in need of revision. That way prejudice can facilitate opportunities for greater understanding, as they make possible further understanding. This stands in contrast to Miranda Fricker's focus on the role of prejudice in instances of epistemic injustice. In her seminal book *Epistemic Injustice: Power and the Ethics of Knowing* (2007), Miranda Fricker shines a light on ethical aspects of two basic epistemic practices: conveying knowledge to others through telling them and making sense of our own social experiences. Fricker's (2007) aim is to develop an account of a type of injustice that is distinctively epistemic. An injustice that consists fundamentally of a wrong done to someone in their capacity as a knower, such as being mistreated, dismissed or put at an unfair disadvantage as a knower. Fricker (2007) identifies two forms of distinctively epistemic injustice, testimonial injustice and hermeneutical injustice. Testimonial injustice occurs when a hearer gives less credibility to a speaker's word than they ought to due to an identity prejudice. Hermeneutical injustice occurs at a prior stage to testimonial injustice, it occurs when a gap in collective hermeneutical resources puts someone at an unfair disadvantage when it comes to making sense of, or expressing their social experience. Fricker's conception of epistemic injustice posits that they are both epistemic, and ethical wrongs. With her conception of hermeneutical injustice, Fricker's analysis goes beyond just considering the ways tradition shape collective understanding, to instead consider the conditions of how those understandings were generated. Thus Fricker illuminates how shared hermeneutical resources can be skewed to the advantage of some, and to the disadvantage of others. Following Fricker one might want to fault Gadamer's attempt to rehabilitate prejudice and tradition for ignoring damaging prejudices that marginalize certain groups and preventing them from contributing to tradition and its projections of meaning. In this sense, traditions are not only sets of collective hermeneutic resources, but also products of power, exclusion and misrepresentations (Warnke 2015). However, as Warnke argues, it is not clear that Gadamer was as indifferent to these issues as one might think as a great of deal his work is concern with the possibility of going beyond one's hermeneutic limits and assumptions. A key to doing so for Gadamer is rejecting the kind of epistemic relations of power that Fricker is concerned with (Warnke 2015).

At the heart of Fricker's paradigmatic cases of testimonial injustice lies what she calls negative identity prejudices. That is prejudices with a negative valence held against some people qua their social type. These prejudices distort the hearer's perception of speakers from that social type, and thus their credibility judgement of the testimony of those speakers (Fricker 2007, 35-36). Nielsen & Utsler (2022) similarly describe this type of prejudice, as a type of prejudice that decide in advance what specific groups of people are, and what they are capable of as knowers. They argue that these identity prejudices function as distorting lenses that impede genuine exchanges between speaker and hearer. That is, the distorting lens shapes the hearer's perception such that the claim of the other is forced to conform to the hearer's perception of, and prejudice towards, the Other. Thus, testimonial injustice forecloses the possibility for dialogue in which the hearer can learn and be challenged by the testimony of the speaker as the speaker is assigned less credibility than they are due, and thus effectively silenced.

While Fricker herself doesn't cite Gadamer, she is aware of the role that prejudice plays in our everyday epistemic lives. She is aware of the ubiquity of prejudice and argues that without prejudgments and heuristics it would not be possible to achieve the spontaneity of everyday testimonial exchanges (Fricker 2007, 32). Further, she suggests that much of everyday testimony requires the hearer to put speakers into social categories, and that prejudice and stereotypes 'grease the wheels' in testimonial exchanges (Fricker 2007, 32). However, with questions of how individuals and groups can be wronged being the main occu-pation of Fricker's (2007) project, it is unsurprising that her focus his primarily on negative social stereotypes and how they affect our epistemic lives. Nielsen & Utsler (2022) highlight an important difference between Fricker's work and that of Gadamer. Fricker's analysis sheds light on identity prejudices that are direct towards a person qua their belonging to a particular social group. In cases of the testimonial injustice, the unfair credibility deficit is imposed upon the person's testimony because the belong to a particular social group. In contrast, in his discussions of genuine dialogical engagements Gadamer (2004) is primarily focused on the subject at hand, rather than on prejudgements about the episte-mic, and moral status of the speaker.

However, as Nielsen & Utsler (2022) point out, this does not necessarily mean that Fricker's and Gadamer's accounts of prejudice are fundamentally at odds or incompatible. They instead argue that we ought to keep in mind the different aims of the two projects. Fricker's is primarily interested in cases whe-re dialogues break down and fails, while Gadamer primarily is focused on what counts as genuine dialogue. Thus, Nielsen & Utsler (2022) suggest that we can think of Fricker and Gadamer's engagements with prejudice as not in contention, but rather as complementary and mutually strengthening. Fricker's analysis of the detrimental epistemic, and ethical consequences of identity-prejudicial cre-dibility deficits that go beyond Gadamer's focus on the role of prejudice in genu-ine dialogues, is on Nielsen & Utslers (2022) view a complement, and a welco-me addition to Gadamerian hermeneutics, as it offers a substantial analysis of engagements in which the voice of the Other is silenced. Nielsen & Utsler (2022) astutely points out that while Gadamer's project in *Truth and Method* did not focus on negative stereotypes, or identity prejudice in the Frickerian sense, he was not unaware of harmful unequal relations of power, manipulative dis-courses, and exploitation that harm both humans (Nielsen & Utsler 2022). Rather, Nielsen & Utsler find in Gadamer an emphasis on openness, and antici-patory listening that is directed towards a different way of being in the world. A being in which others are not seen as mere resources or means, but rather as irreplaceable others from whom one can learn.

3. Hermeneutical Openness as a hermeneutical virtue

By bringing together Gadamer and Fricker, Nielsen & Utsler (2022) develops an answer to critiques levied against Fricker's project by scholars such as Linda Martín Alcoff (2010) and the aforementioned Warnke (2015). Both Alcoff (2010), and Warnke (2015) are troubled by Fricker's move to put neutrality at the centre of her considerations pertaining to identity, justice, and virtue. A neutrality, or absence of prejudice, that Gadamer would reject the possibility of. This neutrality according to Fricker (2007) is one where one is able to correctly, and fairly assess the credibility of the speaker, and when doing so one is able to discern cases in which identity, and identity prejudice, is at play and when they are not. Both Alcoff (2010) and Warnke (2015) has criticized these appeals to neutrality, and Fricker's claim that it is possible to discern the appropriate amount of credibility that would have been given were it not for identity prejudice. Warnke (2015) emphasises that for Gadamer, rather than neutralizing or rising above one's prejudices, one ought to suppose the truth of what one reads, or what the Other says in order to find out what one's prejudices are. One's prejudices become apparent when challenged, and by supposing the truth of what one reads or hears, one put one's prejudices up for being challenged. Further, doing so also constitutes a concession that one's prejudices may be inadequate and in need of revision. It is in acknowledging one's ignorance and limitations that one puts one's prejudices up for challenge, and allows them to be confirmed, rejected or shown to be in need of revision (Warnke 2015).

To respond to these critiques Nielsen & Utsler (2022) suggest to read Fricker's (2007) appeals to 'neutralise' as counteracting the effects of negative prejudicial judgements, rather than as appeals to true neutrality. Such a reading brings the call for 'neutrality' away from the notion of credibility judgements completely free from prejudice, which Gadamer undoubtedly would reject, to a call for neutralising the influence of identity prejudices on credibility judgements. Doing so would bring Fricker's account much closer to Gadamer's (2004) emphasis on assuming that the other has something meaningful to say, and thus might challenge the hearer's prejudices. Such a reading allows Nielsen & Utsler (2022) to conclude that despite Fricker's emphasis on neutrality, one can foreground other aspects of her account to alleviate some of the tension between her and Gadamer's (2004) accounts.

Nielsen & Utsler (2022) find further support for their reading of Fricker (2007) in Fricker's account of the virtue of testimonial justice. In setting out the virtue of testimonial justice, Fricker (2007, 92) argues that the virtuous hearer is one that neutralises the impact of prejudice in their credibility judgements. In line with their alternate reading of Fricker's call to neutralise, they suggest to read the virtue of testimonial justice, as one that when developed and practiced makes the hearer increasingly aware of how identity prejudices operate in dialogical exchanges, and one that calls of intentional habituation towards adopting positive prejudices towards the speaker, and their credibility (Nielsen & Utlser 2022:20). This brings their reading of Fricker very close Gadamer's call to assume that the speaker has something meaningful and truthful to say, and that hearer might be wrong, and thus might need to revise their prejudgements. As Warnke (2015) has argued, both Gadamer (2004) and Fricker (2007) conceive of listening to the Other as both a virtue, and an epistemic demand (Warnke 2015). Likewise, Alcoff (2003) argues that Gadamer's philosophy widens the debates pertaining to what virtues are the most valuable for achieving reliable knowledge. One of the core arguments of Fricker's (2007) book is that cases of epistemic injustice are both ethical and epistemic wrongs. This intersection of ethics and epistemology is also not unknown to Gadamer who conceives of openness to the Other as not only an epistemic good that provides the hearer with a corrective to their own prejudices, but also as of ethical significance. Gadamer (2004) argues that hearers can fail to treat speakers ethically in two distinct manners. They can objectify them by explaining their claims as symptoms of some underlying cause or issue. Further, hearers can patronize speakers and claim that they know what the speaker is trying to convey better than the speaker themselves. By objectifying the other, Gadamer argues that one treats the Other as a means, and in patronizing the other one robs the Other's claim of its legitimacy. Warnke (2015) argues that each of these two wrongs reflect perpetuations of relationships of power, and in each of them the hearer fails to display the appropriate openness, and thus for Gadamer (2004) there is no 'genuine bond' between speaker and hearer.

Bringing together Fricker and Gadamer in this manner leads Nielsen & Utsler (2022) to argue that deeper understanding, and acknowledgment of prejudgments will lead to the openness, and anticipatory listening emphasised in Gadamer's project. Simultaneously, if one understands the reality of prejudgements, one is in a better position to hear the voice of the other and conceiving of the other as someone who has something meaningful, and truthful to say. Hermeneutical openness and anticipatory listening, they argue is the basis for Fricker's virtue of testimonial justice. They argue that it is possible to conceive of cases of testimonial injustice as cases in which prejudgements work in a negative manner resulting in a lack of openness to the other as a genuine, and meaningful interlocutor (Nielsen & Utsler 2022).

Nielsen & Utsler (2022) conceive of hermeneutical openness as a hermeneutical virtue, and one that is of relevant for issues of epistemic injustice and oppression. They argue that the hermeneutical openness they find in Gadamer's work functions as a hermeneutical virtue, paralleling Fricker's (2007) turn to virtue epistemology (Nielsen & Utlser 2022). Hermeneutical openness and anticipatory listening are excellences or virtues for hermeneutical practice that constitute an orientation toward the other that makes possible for one's prejudices to be challenged so that they might be corrected and thus improve one's understanding. Further, hermeneutical openness constitutes an orientation towards the other that respects their alterity and their status as an interlocutor with something important and meaningful to say. Nielsen & Utsler (2022) bring this intersection of the philosophies of Gadamer and Fricker into conversation with that of Axel Honneth (1995) to argue that a combination of the three would serve well in the development of a theory of recognition. While that is seemingly a promising project, I will not follow them in that regard. Rather, for the rest of this paper focus will remain on the Gadamerian virtue of hermeneutical openness, and I will argue for its relevance both in the identification of epistemic injustices, but also for its potential contribution to their remedy. Starting from Nielsen & Utsler's (2022) account, I will expand their analysis by considering other forms of epistemic injustice, thus further illustrating the relevance of Gadamer's philosophy for the debates pertaining to epistemic injustice, and epistemic oppression.

Nielsen & Utsler (2022) turn to Gadamer's later works further demonstrates that his emphasis on openness is sensitive to relations of power in its respect for alterity. Gadamer (1992) explicitly calls for respect for the other, and non-exploitative relationships between humans, and between humans and nature in his 1992 essay *The Diversity of Europe: Inheritance and Future*. Illustrating that Gadamer himself was not ignorant of exploitation, abuses of power and manipulation, even if that was not his core concern in *Truth and Method*. Nielsen & Utsler (2022) argues that Gadamer's emphasis on openness is in contrast with treating others as mere means to an end, or silencing them as one has decided ahead of time that one knows better. Rather, Gadamer sets out a pathway to a co-existence with others in which they are seen as irreplaceable Others from whom one can learn, rather than an Other of one's own making.

Hermeneutical openness is based upon one's respect for the alterity of the other and hermeneutical openness is demonstrated in one's willingness to take seriously what the Other has to say, and to regard their claims as potential correctives to one's own prejudice and present understanding (Nielsen & Utsler 2022). That being said, hermeneutical openness does not imply that one must agree with the Other. Rather, through the interaction with the Other, one might or might not come to agree with them. Hermeneutical openness does not entail giving up one's own views or barring one from defending them. Rather, it does entail remaining open to the possibility that one is wrong, and that one's present understanding can be improved by learning from the other. Hermeneutical openness is to situate oneself, and one's own understanding, in relation to the meaning of the other. In doing so one puts one's own prejudice to the test in relation to the claims of the Other. Nielsen & Utsler (2022) points out that doing so necessitates the exercise of a different hermeneutical virtue, namely that of hermeneutical humility. Further, as Nicholas Davey (2006) has argued, hermeneutical practice is not easy. Genuine hermeneutical engagement demands openness to taking part in hard and at times uncomfortable conversations, to self-discipline and to engagement. Of similar importance is that, as Nielsen & Utsler (2022) notes, both Gadamer (1992) and Fricker (2013) recognize that genuine transformation requires not only the exercise of virtues and change in one's individual practices and ways of seeing the Other, but also requires structural changes in practice and policy.

There is a wider, growing interest in Gadamerian virtues, and their relevance for issues of epistemic injustice. Beyond Nielsen & Utsler's (2022) recent work, Haley Irene Burke (2022) has argued in a recent paper that reading Gadamer & Fricker together elucidates the possibly for ethical development through the cultivation of virtues that promotes understanding. Burke (2022) argues that the cultivation of such virtues can counteract injustices wherein recognition of, or the articulation of reality is at stake. While Burke herself never discusses hermeneutical openness as conceived of here, I hope to show in this article that hermeneutical openness would be one such virtue that would both promote understanding and play a role in counteracting injustice. Similarly, we find explicit references to the notion of hermeneutical openness in José Medina's excellent book *The Epistemology of Resistance* (2013). Medina himself never discusses or cites Gadamer directly, but like Nielsen & Utsler (2022) he finds in Fricker (2007) an account of hermeneutical virtue that includes the obligation to confront one's interpretative limitations and vulnerability in order to cultivate hermeneutical openness, echoing the Gadamerian emphasis on openness and challenging one's prejudices. Likewise, it would be a mistake to not mention the existing literature on the relationship between virtue and vice epistemology and issues of epistemic injustice and epistemic oppression. Beyond

Fricker's engagement with virtue epistemology, authors such as José Medina (2013) and Heather Battaly (2017) among others have in great detail described the relationship between epistemic virtues and vices, and epistemic injustice. The virtue of hermeneutical openness that is the focus of this paper, while distinct, undoubtedly shares some qualities with the epistemic virtue open-mindedness which has received extensive attention in the subfield of virtue epistemology.

4. Wilful Hermeneutical Ignorance & Contributory Injustice

In the years since Fricker's (2007) ground-breaking book was published plenty of philosophers have dedicated their time to questions of epistemic injustice and oppression. Some have set out to identify epistemically unjust practices and structures in different areas of the social world (See for example: Carel & Kidd 2014; Kidd & Carel 2017; Landström 2021). Other philosophers have criticized the narrowness of Fricker's (2007) account and set out to identify further forms of epistemic injustice. Two such examples are Gaile Pohlhaus' (2012) work on wilful hermeneutical ignorance, and Kristie Dotson's (2012) work on contributory injustice.

Pohlhaus (2012) argues that there are two senses in which the sociality of knowers is epistemically significant: their situatedness and their interdependence. The social situatedness of the knower is epistemically significant as it draws their attention to particular aspects of the world. For Pohlhaus (2012) situatedness is fundamentally about how relations to others positions the knower in relation to the world. Likewise, the interdependence of knowers is epistemically relevant as the epistemic resources needed to make sense of the world are collective. Epistemic resources such as language, concepts and criteria for evaluation on lie beyond any one individual. Of particular importance for Pohlhaus is that these resources are not equally equipped for making sense of all experience. For example, in socially unequal and stratified societies some individuals are situated in positions that allow their experiences to play a larger role in the development and circulation of epistemic resources. This, Pohlhaus argues, illustrates the significance of the relationship between the situatedness of the knower, and their interdependence as the standards for knowing the world well is determined by what is salient in the experienced world itself, and one's experience of the world will depend on one's situatedness. For Pohlhaus, the relationship between the knower's situatedness and their interdependence is dialectical and can produce tensions. When these tensions are resolved, they can lead to an expansion of both shared, and possible knowledge. However, the dialectical relationship between the knower's situatedness and interdependence can also lead to a distinct form of epistemic injustice, particularly in socially unequal and stratified societies. Pohlhaus calls this form of epistemic injustice wilful hermeneutical ignorance.

Pohlhaus argues that because of the dialectical relationship between situatedness and interdependence, marginally situated knowers are more likely to find gaps in predominant sets of epistemic resources for making sense of their experience based in their marginalised situatedness. She gives two arguments for this. First, due to their marginalisation, the marginalised knower must be aware of the concerns of those dominantly situated, while those dominantly situated need not to know about the concerns of the marginalised. This has the consequence that it behoves the marginalised to acquire and draw upon the epistemic resources that follow from being dominantly situated, while the epistemic resources of the marginalised is not immediately of use for those dominantly situated. Pohlhaus second argument is that social situatedness allows some to develop and disseminate epistemic resources more easily than others. In such cases, the interdependence between knowers is asymmetrical due to the relations of power between dominantly situated and marginally situated knowers. From this starting point Pohlhaus argues that those epistemic resources that become predominantly recognized are those which originate from the experienced world of dominantly situated knowers. This does not mean that those who are marginally situated are epistemically disadvantaged. Rather, Pohlhaus argues that those marginally situated are often well situated to know that there are whole parts of the world for which dominantly held epistemic resources are not well suited.

The problem that Pohlhaus identifies, and targets in her discussion of wilful hermeneutical ignorance is that while marginalised knowers are well situated to develop epistemic resources adequate for making sense of more parts of the experienced world, they often face problems when trying to convince those dominantly situated of the usefulness and importance of those epistemic resources. Pohlhaus provides two reasons as to why this is the case. The first is that dominantly situated knowers are not required by their situatedness to learn to navigate and investigate parts of the world based on the concerns of others. Further, it is not in the interest of the dominantly situated to acquire and maintain epistemic resources calibrated by those marginally situated since doing so would move epistemic power away from the dominantly situated.

Distinguishing situatedness and interdependence in this manner allows Pohlhaus to develop a picture in which she maintains that being marginally situated can be epistemically advantageous, while also holding those dominantly situated responsible for their ignorance of the experienced world of the marginally situated. The dominantly situated can not step outside their situatedness, however they can learn to draw upon and use epistemic resources developed from the experiences of marginalized knowers (Pohlhaus 2012). According to Pohlhaus, learning when and how to use the epistemic resources of the marginalised requires engagement with those who are skilled in their use, and to place oneself in encounters where it makes sense to draw upon them, making mistakes and being corrected. Here there are parallels between Pohlhaus (2012) account and Gadamer's (2004) emphasis on encounters with alterity, dialogue and learning from the other. However, as Davey (2006) said of genuine hermeneutical practice, learning to draw upon the epistemic resources of the marginalised is a difficult endeavour for dominantly situated knower. Pohlhaus mentions a few reasons as to why this is, including that it is disorienting, it opens one's eyes to aspects of one's situatedness that are hard to stomach such as unearned privilege, and marginalised knowers might not welcome the dominantly situated to the use of the epistemic resources that they have worked hard to develop.

Pohlhaus argues that even when it is seemingly the case that the dominantly situated knower appears to be open to the claims of those in marginalized positions, they can pre-emptively dismiss the epistemic resources necessary to make sense of those claims due to the dialectical relationship between interdependence and situatedness. Good epistemic resources make sense of the experienced world, and if one's situatedness does not make salient those aspects of the world for which those epistemic resources are useful, the dominantly situated knower can employ that fact in order to dismiss those resources before learning to use them. Pohlhaus (2012, 722) suggests that this sort of pre-emptive dismissal can be seen in the dismissal of concepts such as 'date rape', 'heteronormativity' and 'white privilege' by dominantly situated knowers. It is this kind of dismissal, and the dominantly situated knower's refusal to learn to use the epistemic resources developed from marginalised situatedness that Pohlhaus calls wilful hermeneutical ignorance. Pohlhaus suggests that wilful hermeneutical ignorance both falls under what the late Charles Mills (1997) has called 'epistemology of ignorance' and is a type of epistemic injustice. However, as Fricker (2007) in her original account does not consider different epistemic relations working in conjunction, the type of epistemic injustice that Pohlhaus (2012) identifies exposes a lacuna in the Frickerian account of epistemic injustice.

Wilful hermeneutical ignorance picks out instances in which dominantly situated knowers dismiss the possibility that there is something new to know about a particular aspect of the world and any epistemic resources to do so, despite marginally situated knowers holding, or developing, epistemic resources for knowing that particular aspect of the world based on their experience (Pohlhaus 2012). Thus, wilful hermeneutical ignorance picks out cases in which marginally situated people cannot demonstrate to dominantly situated people that there is a part of the world that their epistemic resources are inadequate to know, and in which the marginally situated cannot call the attention of dominantly situated knowers to those parts of the experienced world because the epistemic resources necessary to do so are pre-emptively dismissed. That way, dominant groups with a vested interest in ignoring certain parts of the world can maintain their ignorance by simply refusing to recognize, and actively undermine newly developed epistemic resources that attend to aspects of the world that they are vested in ignoring. Further, it is important to note that these instances are not based in some sort of inherent inability on the part of the dominantly situated, but rather is a wilful act. It is an exercise of power in the relationships of interdependence to undermine, or to refuse to acknowledge the epistemic resources developed by those marginally situated in order to remain ignorant. Wilful hermeneutical ignorance is a wilful refusal to acknowledge, and to acquire the necessary tools for knowing and understanding parts of the world (Pohlhaus 2012, 729).

Pohlhaus (2012) draws on Sandra Harding's (1991) work to argue that one is not doomed to ignorance because of one's social position. Rather ignorance is something that one chooses to maintain. If those dominantly situated take active interest in how the world is experienced and understood from those marginally situated, they can participate in what Harding calls a critical standpoint. That is, a position in which there is a tension between the epistemic resources one draws upon and one's experienced world that signals a need to change the epistemic resources one draws upon, or create new epistemic resources for knowing the world more adequately. Both wilful ignorance and critical standpoints stem from the interest, or disinterest, one takes in the Other and their experiences, not from one's social position, to determine what one can know (Pohlhaus 2012). Pohlhaus argues that it is by considering the relationship between situatedness and interdependence that one can show that this is possible. If one genuinely aspires to know something about the world as experienced from those situated differently than oneself, one must draw upon the epistemic resources suited to, and developed from those differently situated. Doing so requires both allowing these resources to be developed well by those situated to do so, but also, to trust them to have done so well and to take an interest in learning from them how to utilize those epistemic resources. Thus, on Pohlhaus picture, even though one cannot leave one's social position, one can acquire the epistemic resources that show that which is not obvious from where one is situated. Refusing to allow the development, or refusing to acknowledge epistemic resources for knowing the world from different situations from one's own, contribute both to maintaining one's own ignorance but also to epistemic injustice.

Kristie Dotson (2012) has identified a separate type of epistemic injustice that arise out of wilful hermeneutical ignorance. She calls this type of epistemic injustice contributory injustice. Contributory injustice is caused by an epistemic agent's wilful hermeneutical ignorance, both in maintaining structurally prejudice hermeneutical resources and in utilizing them, resulting in epistemic harm to the epistemic agency of particular knowers. Contributory injustice is both structural and agential as both the structurally prejudiced hermeneutical resources of the dominantly situated, and the agents own situated and wilful ignorance function as catalysts for the epistemic harm. Contributory injustice occurs because there are different hermeneutical resources that a hearer could utilize beyond the structurally prejudiced hermeneutical resources of the dominantly situated, and the hearer wilfully refuses to acknowledge or acquire the necessary tools for knowing the world that the speaker utilizes, thus effectively silencing them as their testimony does not get the appropriate uptake. The hearer in cases of contributory injustice wilfully refuses to recognize or acquire the requisite alternative hermeneutical resources to understand and give appropriate uptake to the testimony of the speaker. This refusal is what Pohlhaus (2012) has called wilful hermeneutical ignorance. Wilful hermeneutical ignorance produces contributory injustice when the epistemic agent's wilful hermeneutical ignorance maintains and utilizes structurally prejudiced resources thwarts a knower's ability to contribute to the shared epistemic resources within a particular epistemic community. Thus, compromising their epistemic agency. Contrary to hermeneutical injustice, contributory injustice does not render certain experiences equally unintelligible. Rather, the victims of contributory injustice are able to articulate their experiences, but those articulations fail to gain appropriate uptake due to the wilful ignorance of the hearer. Thus, thwarting the epistemic agency of the speaker.

5. Hermeneutical openness and wilful hermeneutical ignorance

So how is the virtue of hermeneutical openness relevant for thinking about wilful hermeneutical ignorance, and in extension contributory injustice? In this section I will outline two suggestions for such relevancy. The first being that hermeneutical openness can serve as a counterfactual that makes it possible to pin down the epistemic, and ethical failure of the wilfully ignorant. The second suggestion is that the virtue of hermeneutical ignorance would serve well as a corrective to the agential dimension of cases of wilful hermeneutical ignorance and contributory injustice, and thus has a role to play in the alleviation of such epistemic injustices.

Cases of wilful hermeneutical ignorance occur because a hearer actively chooses to ignore some sets of hermeneutical resources and instead chooses to solely relies on structurally prejudices sets of hermeneutical resources, thus refusing to acquire the necessary tools for knowing parts of the world. The follow-on injustice of contributory injustice occurs when a hearer's wilful hermeneutical ignorance thwarts other knower's ability to contribute to the shared hermeneutical resources within a particular epistemic community, thus compromising their epistemic agency. The speaker's epistemic agency is thwarted as even though they are able to articulate their experience, those articulations fail to gain appropriate uptake as the ignorant hearer chooses to ignore the hermeneutical resources that the speaker draw upon to remain ignorant about a part of the experienced world of the Other. As Alcoff (2003) points out, for Gadamer coming to an understanding with another person is to engage in a dialogue in which each interlocutor has agency. An attitude of genuine epistemic openness is central to such a dialogue, and for expanding one's horizons of understanding. Alcoff argues that Gadamer better captures the actual process of knowing than traditional analytic epistemology, as Gadamer (2004) centres the complex process of interpretation. What is at stake in cases of epistemic injustice is the agency of the interlocutor, and as argued in the previous section wilful hermeneutical ignorance and contributory injustice are each forms of epistemic injustice in which the epistemic agency of the speaker is thwarted by the wilful ignorance of the hearer.

In a counter-factual case to that of wilful hermeneutical ignorance, where the hearer displays the appropriate openness towards Other rather than being wilfully ignorant, the wilful hermeneutical ignorance and the follow-on injustice of contributory injustice no longer takes place. Exercising appropriate hermeneutical openness towards the speaker would at its very least involve not choosing to remain actively ignorant of the testimony of the Other, and the hermeneutical resources they employ. By exercising the appropriate hermeneutical openness, one makes it possible for one's prejudices to be challenged so that they might be corrected and thus improve one's understanding. Further, hermeneutical openness constitutes an orientation towards the other that respects their alterity and their status as an interlocutor with something important and meaningful to say. By taking the speaker seriously as someone with something relevant and truthful to say, respecting their alterity and acknowledging the hermeneutical resources that they draw upon, both the epistemic and the ethical wrongs are avoided as the hearer opens up the possibility for genuine dialogue, for prejudices to be challenged and for learning from the Other rather than choosing to ignore the speaker and the hermeneutical resources they draw upon. Thus, making possible the expansion of understanding, and for the revision of prejudices. Rather than thwarting the epistemic agency of the Other, a virtuous hearer would support the epistemic agency of the Other by making it possible to share their experiences and understanding without being effectively silenced, thus contributing to their ability to contribute to the shared hermeneutical resources. The counter-factual case, as well as cases of wilful hermeneutical ignorance, illustrates Pohlhaus' (2012) point that both wilful ignorance and critical understanding stem from the interest, or the disinterest, one takes in the experiences of the Other. The hermeneutically open hearer takes an interest in the Other as someone who has something both important, and truthful to say and thus can develop a critical understanding based in the Other's experience of the world. The wilfully ignorant dismisses the Other as a knower, and thus both morally wrongs them, and causes epistemic harm to both themselves and the Other.

I propose conceiving of the hearer in cases of wilful hermeneutical and contributory injustice, as failing to exercise the appropriate hermeneutical openness. That is, the hearer has failed to demonstrate their willingness to take seriously what the Other has to say, and to regard their claims as potential correctives to one's own prejudices and understanding. As the hearer does not exercise the appropriate openness towards the speaker, and the hermeneutical resources they draw upon the hearer perpetuates both epistemic harm, an ethical wrongs. Similar to Nielsen & Utsler (2022) analysis that the epistemic injustice of testimonial injustice forecloses the possibility for genuine dialogue, so does wilful hermeneutical ignorance. As Pohlhaus (2012) has argued, refusing to acknowledge epistemic resources for knowing the world from different situations from one's own, contribute both to maintaining one's ignorance, but also to the perpetuation of epistemic injustice. The epistemic harm consists of the hearer losing out on understanding about certain parts of the world around them as they refuse to listen and learn from the Other. The ethical wrong consists of the hearer wronging the speaker by effectively silencing them, and preventing them from contributing to collective understanding, thus unfairly thwarting their epistemic agency due to their refusal to acknowledge other hermeneutical resources that the structurally prejudiced one they draw upon. As Pohlhaus suggests, by identifying the epistemic and ethical failing of the hearer they can be held responsible for their ignorance. By positing that the hearer in cases of wilful hermeneutical ignorance and contributory injustice acts in a hermeneutically vicious manner, contrary to meeting the Other with appropriate hermeneutical openness, their epistemic and ethical failings become clear.

There are grounds for thinking that the virtue of hermeneutical openness could serve well as a corrective to wilful hermeneutical ignorance and the follow-on injustice of contributory injustice. As suggested earlier, by taking the speaker seriously as someone with something relevant and truthful to say, respecting their alterity and the hermeneutical resources that they draw upon, both the epistemic and the ethical wrongs are avoided as the hermeneutically open hearer makes possible genuine dialogue, for prejudices to be challenged and for learning from the Other. In contrast to the wilfully ignorant hearer who forecloses the possibility for genuine dialogue and learning from the Other. However, remember that both Pohlhaus (2012), and Dotson (2012) stressed that wilful hermeneutical ignorance and contributory injustice each includes both an agential dimension and a structural dimension. The individual virtue of herme-neutical openness would do little to address epistemic inequalities and injustice at a structural level. As discussed earlier in this paper, Nielsen & Utsler (2022) notes that both Fricker and Gadamer while focusing on the virtues of individual hearers, recognize that changing the structural dimensions of epistemic injustice would require more radical structural changes. Following this insight, I put forth hermeneutical openness as a virtue that can function as a corrective to the agential dimension of wilful hermeneutical ignorance and contributory injustice. To tackle both dimensions of wilful hermeneutical ignorance and contributory injustice, individual virtues would have to be combined with more radical structural change.

6. Conclusion

Scholarship at the intersection of Gadamer's hermeneutics and epistemic injus-tice and epistemic oppression is limited, and there is plenty left to explore. In some ways, Gadamer's thought goes beyond the existing scholarship on episte-mic injustice in interesting ways that deserve to be further explored. Warnke (2015) has already argued that Gadamer goes beyond Fricker's work both ethi-cally and epistemically, and one could likewise argue that Gadamer's (2004) emphasis on historical situatedness adds another relevant dimension to the pro-jects of feminist such as Fricker (2007), Pohlhaus (2012) and Dotson (2012) who are primarily concerned with social situatedness and its relation to the ethics of knowing. In this article I contribute to this nascent project by arguing that Hans-Georg Gadamer's (2004, 1976) hermeneutics offers relevant insights for contemporary scholarship on epistemic injustice and oppression. Specifically, I have argued for the Gadamerian notion of *hermeneutical openness* as a hermeneutical virtue that can play a role in remedying the agential wrongs in epistemic injustices such as testimonial injustice, wilful hermeneutical ignorance and contributory injustice. In doing so, I expand Nielsen & Utsler's (2022) analysis of testimonial injustice by considering further forms of epistemic injustice. I argue that we can understand cases of wilful hermeneutical ignorance and contributory injustice as cases where the hearer fails to exercise appropriate hermeneutical openness, and in doing so does something epistemically and ethically wrong. Further, I have argued for hermeneutical openness as a hermeneutical virtue that can function as a corrective to the agential dimension of wilful hermeneutical ignorance and contributory injustice. However, tackling both the agential and the structural dimensions of wilful hermeneutical ignorance and contributory injustice would require individual virtues such as hermeneutical openness to be combined with more radical structural change. In doing so I aspire to have illustrated not only the relevance of Gadamer's philosophy for scholars of epistemic injustice, but also its potency in both offering diagnostic tools for identifying the wrongs in specific forms of epistemic injustice and offering potential remedies to existing epistemic injustices.

Karl Landström, MA, Phd. Cand., Centre for Trust,
Peace and Social Relations, Coventry University,
Landstrk@coventry.ac.uk

References

Alcoff, Linda Martín. 1996. *Real Knowing: New Versions of the Coherence Theory.* Ithaca: Cornell University Press.

Alcoff, Linda Martín. 2003. "Gadamer's Feminist Epistemology". In Code, Lorraine (Ed.) *Feminist Interpretations of Hans-George Gadamer*. University Park, Pennsylvania: The Pennsylvania State University Press. 231-258.

Alcoff, Linda Martín. 2005. *Visible Identities: Race, Gender, and the Self.* New York: Oxford University Press.

Alcoff, Linda Martín. 2010. Epistemic Identities. *Episteme*. Volume 7, Issue 2. 128-137.

Barthold, Lauren Swayne. 2016. *A Hermeneutical Approach to Gender and Other Social Identities*. New York: Palgrave MacMillan.

Battaly, Heather. 2017. "Testimonial Injustice, Epistemic Vice, and Vice Epistemology," in Kidd, Ian James, Polhaus, Gaile and Medina, José (eds.) *The Routledge Handbook of Epistemic Injustice*. New York: Routledge. 223–231.

Burke, Haley Irene. 2022. Developing Gadamerian Virtues Against Epistemic Injustice: The Epistemic and Hermeneutic Dimensions of Ethics. *Journal of Applied Hermeneutics*.

Carel, Havi & Kidd, Ian James. 2014. Epistemic injustice in healthcare: a philosophi-
al analysis. *Medicine, Health Care and Philosophy*. 17(4), 529-540.

Code, Lorraine. 2003. "Introduction: Why Feminists Do Not Read Gadamer". In
Code, Lorraine (Ed.) *Feminist Interpretations of Hans-Georg Gadamer*. University Park,
Pennsylvania: The Pennsylvania State University Press. 1-36.

Davey, Nicholas. 2006. *Unquiet Understanding. Gadamer's Philosophical Hermeneutics*. Albany: SUNY Press.

Dotson, Kristie. 2012. "A cautionary tale: On limiting epistemic oppression". *Fron-
tiers: A Journal of Women Studies*. 33: 24–47.

Fricker, Miranda. 2007. *Epistemic Injustice: Power and the Ethics of Knowing*.
Oxford: Oxford University Press.

Fricker, Miranda. 2013. Epistemic Justice as a Condition of Political Freedom? *Synthese*. Vol. 190, Issue 7. 1317-1332

Gadamer, Hans-Georg. 1976. *Philosophical Hermeneutics*. Translated by D. E. Linge
(ed.). Berkeley: University of California Press.

Gadamer, Hans-Georg. 1992. 'The Diversity of Europe: Inheritance and Future', in
Misgeld, Dieter & Nicholson, Graeme (Eds.), and Schmidt, Lawrence & Reuss, Monica
(trans.) *Hans-Georg Gadamer On Education, Poetry, and History: Applied Hermeneutics*. Albany: SUNY Press.

Gadamer, Hans-Georg. 2004. *Truth and Method*. 2nd Edition. Translated by J.
Weinsheimer and D. G. Marshall. New York: Continuum.

Harding, Sandra. 1991. *Whose science? Whose knowledge? : thinking from women's
lives*. Ithaca, N.Y.: Cornell University Press.

Hoffman, Susan-Judith. 2003 "Gadamer's Philosophical Hermeneutics and Feminist
Projects". In Code, Lorraine (Ed.) *Feminist Interpretations of Hans-George Gadamer*.
University Park, Pennsylvania: The Pennsylvania State University Press. 81-108.

Honneth, Axel. 1995. *The Struggle for Recognition: The Moral Grammar of Social
Conflicts*. Translated by J. Anderson. Cambridge: Polity.

Kidd, Ian James & Carel, Havi. 2017. Epistemic injustice and illness. *Journal of applied philosophy*. 34(2), 172-190.

Landström, Karl. 2021. Archives, Epistemic Injustice and Knowing the Past. *Ethics
and Social Welfare*, 15(4), 379-394.

Medina, José. 2013. *The Epistemology of Resistance*. New York: Oxford University
Press

Mills, Charles. 1997. *The racial contract*. Ithaca, N.Y.: Cornell University Press.

Nielsen, Cynthia R., and Utsler, David. 2022. 'Gadamer, Fricker, and Honneth: Testimonial Injustice, Prejudice, and Social Esteem', in Giladi, Paul and McMillan, Nicola.
(eds.) *Epistemic Injustice and the Philosophy of Recognition*. London: Routledge.

Pohlhaus Jr., Gaile. 2012. "Relational Knowing and Epistemic Injustice: Toward a Theory of '*Willful Hermeneutical Ignorance*'". *Hypatia* 27 (4): 715–35.

Risser, James. 1997. *Hermeneutics and the Voice of the Other: Re-reading Gadamer's Philosophical Hermeneutics*. Albany: SUNY Press.

Vasterling, Veronica. 2003. "Postmodern Hermeneutics? Toward a Critical Hermeneutics". In Code, Lorraine (Ed.) *Feminist Interpretations of Hans-George Gadamer*. University Park, Pennsylvania: The Pennsylvania State University Press. 159-180.

Warnke, Georgia. 2015. 'Hermeneutics and Feminism', in J. Malpas and H-H. Gander (eds.) *The Routledge Companion to Hermeneutics*. London: Routledge.

COLINE SÉNAC (Montréal)[1]

L'injustice épistémique : questions de vérité et méthode

Epistemic injustice: questions of truth and method

Abstract

This article proposes the comparison of two methods of analysis, semiotics, and herme-neutics, to address contemporary issues in ethical and political philosophy, through the study of the phenomenon of epistemic injustice. Conceptualized by Fricker (2007), epis-temic injustice is synonymous with the denial of the value of knowledge that an individual possesses because of prejudices about the social group to which he or she belongs or is affiliated. When epistemic injustice is studied in the empirical world, it poses some cru-cial issues in terms of interpreting the meaning that the individual gives to the experience of injustice that he or she experiences.

Although the interpretation of injustice is central to the understanding of the phenome-non itself, little research in ethical and political philosophy addresses these aspects, because of the failure to sufficiently mobilize analytical methods such as semiotics and hermeneutics. However, these two methods, usually used in other fields to deal with these aspects, allow us to question the treatment and the interpretative scope of the epistemic injustice by the different interlocutors involved in the interaction in which it is recon-ducted.

The comparison of these two methods in the analysis of epistemic injustice finally allows us to argue in favor of the hermeneutic method, as defined by Gadamer and rethought by Code (2003), to enhance Gadamer's legacy through the analysis of ethical and political issues in human sciences research.

Keywords: Hans-Georg Gadamer, Lorraine Code, epistemic injustice, semiotics, herme-neutics,

Introduction

Les turbulences sociales des dernières années ont révélé que, malgré les progrès de ces dernières décennies, de profondes injustices persistaient. Des mouve-ments sociaux, comme *#MeToo* ou *Black lives matter*, se sont alors formés pour

[1] Ce projet a bénéficié du soutien financier du Fonds de recherche du Québec en Société et Culture (Bourse de recherche doctorale 2020-B2Z-275831).

rendre compte des nombreuses situations d'iniquité sociale vécues par des individus affiliés à des communautés marginalisées.

Notre recherche traite des injustices dans les interactions sociales, parmi les tissus de communication où les relations se nouent (van Dijk 1997), et au travers desquels des préjudices sont portés sur des individus. Notre intérêt se dirige vers une forme subtile d'injustice, qui demeure pourtant très présente dans nos interactions quotidiennes : l'injustice épistémique, celle relative à l'exclusion de la participation de certains groupes sociaux sur la base de préjugés quant aux connaissances que possèdent les individus qui y sont directement associés (Fricker 2007). Il s'agit par exemple de ne pas prendre d'emblée au sérieux les témoignages de victimes d'agressions sexuelles, de demeurer silencieux face aux propos cohérents émis par un individu qu'on présume atteint d'un trouble de santé mentale, ou de n'accorder aucune crédibilité à de multiples demandes d'assistance de la part d'un individu qui est, à en juger seulement par son apparence, en situation d'itinérance.

Ces injustices ont généralement pour effet de questionner ou d'invalider la capacité des locuteur.rice.s à produire ou à transmettre des connaissances dans une interaction (Kidd et al., 2017), à cause principalement de leurs appartenances ou assignations en tant que membres d'un groupe minoritaire (Lépinard et Mazouz 2020). L'étude de ces situations d'injustice est donc cruciale, notamment pour les organisations et les communautés en quête d'une certaine équité épistémique et sociale, car elles témoignent de la reconduction des relations de pouvoir dans les interactions sociales (Bencherki *et al.* 2019).

L'étude des injustices épistémiques, ayant donné lieu à tout un champ d'études en philosophie politique et sociale grâce notamment aux travaux préliminaires de Fricker (2007), conduit bien souvent les philosophes à déterminer le caractère préjudiciable de l'injustice épistémique. Mais, un constat demeure : les limites épistémologiques et éthiques évoquées en conclusion d'articles se rapportent bien souvent à la question de l'interprétation du préjudice ressenti par les victimes de ces injustices. Pour contrer cet appel à la subjectivité des individus, certains philosophes défendent une conception objective de l'injustice épistémique, ou tentent, tant bien que mal, de déterminer ses conditions générales (Byskov 2021), tandis que d'autres le considèrent comme un facteur uniquement contextuel, relevant des aspects contingents du phénomène social (Beeby 2011).

Malgré la difficulté de saisir le sens que l'injustice épistémique invoque et les effets qu'elle produit, nous admettons que ce phénomène — à cause de son caractère purement social — doit être prioritairement analysé en fonction de la compréhension qui en est produite par les individus. Car une même question ne cesse de revenir, dès lors qu'on étudie les contextes au sein desquels une injustice épistémique s'opère : dans quelle mesure pouvons-nous réellement savoir comment l'injustice épistémique advient dans les interactions sociales, si nous ne questionnons pas, de prime abord, ceux et celles qui le vivent ? Pour rendre compte de ce dont l'injustice épistémique relève, il est donc nécessaire de mobiliser des démarches différentes de celles habituellement élaborées en philosophie sociale et politique, car ces dernières demeurent inopérantes pour étudier la signification et l'expérience vécue par les individus (Renault 2004). Nous devons alors choisir d'autres méthodes, plus portées sur l'interprétation de phénomènes situés au croisement de plusieurs disciplines en sciences humaines, comme la sémiotique ou encore l'herméneutique.

Par la comparaison de la sémiotique et de l'herméneutique au regard de notre sujet de recherche, notre objectif est de tracer les contours d'un cadre théorique qui nous permettrait de bien comprendre l'ampleur et les limites du sens associé à une situation d'injustice épistémique, afin de mieux identifier et saisir ses principales modalités interprétatives. Ce cadrage doit nous amener à porter une attention plus accrue sur la signification et l'interprétation de l'injustice épistémique, de manière à pouvoir mieux saisir les implications sociales et éthiques de l'injustice épistémique par rapport au dialogue qui s'instaure entre les diverses communautés sociales. Mais, comment cadrer l'injustice épistémique de manière à pleinement comprendre ce qu'elle implique au niveau du sens qu'elle évoque, des actions qu'elle provoque, et du dialogue qu'elle initie entre les communautés sociales ?

Ce regard croisé sur des méthodes élaborées en sémiotique et en herméneutique nous permettrait d'identifier laquelle des deux s'avère être la plus pertinente pour rendre compte des enjeux épistémologiques et praxéologiques derrière le phénomène social qu'on étudie, et dont nous cernons l'importance, par sa finalité théorique et pratique, d'en révéler pleinement la compréhension qu'en font les individus. Les approches étudiées ont été sélectionnées sur le principe qu'elles permettent d'analyser de manière approfondie les interactions sociales ; c'est pourquoi elles se situent au croisement de la communication pour la sémiotique (Boutaud 2005), et de la sociologie critique pour l'herméneutique (Code, 2003).

Pour la sémiotique, nous allons principalement nous référer aux travaux précurseurs de Peirce (1978), qui demeure la principale influence des théories sémiotiques élaborées jusqu'à présent. Et, même si nous allons survoler par la suite les différentes théories, et notamment celles aux confluences de la communication, nous allons toutefois centrer notre analyse sur un ouvrage d'Umberto Eco (1992), parce qu'il nous permet de cerner avec acuité les avantages et les inconvénients de la sémiotique, au regard de l'injustice épistémique. Cela nous permettra de mieux comprendre pourquoi la sémiotique, et surtout celle employée en communication, permet de cadrer l'injustice épistémique comme une réinterprétation infinie et une possibilité discursive.

En ce qui concerne l'herméneutique, même si nous allons puiser nos arguments dans les principaux ouvrages de Gadamer (1996a et 1996b), nous articulerons nos propos sur un ouvrage témoignant de l'application féministe possible d'une telle philosophie gadamérienne, dans le but de montrer les enjeux et les limites d'une perspective herméneutique dans l'étude de phénomènes sociaux à partir d'une approche critique, comme celle adoptée par Lorraine Code (2003). De cette manière, nous pourrons mieux saisir en quoi la philosophie herméneutique de Gadamer permet de cadrer l'injustice épistémique comme une réhabilitation des préjugés et une critique sociale.

L'analyse de ces deux démarches nous aidera à penser un cadre idéal pour cerner un phénomène social, l'injustice épistémique, que nous parvenons difficilement à saisir pleinement, même dans ses manifestations les plus visibles, du fait de dépendre principalement de l'expérience de ceux et celles qui le vivent.

L'injustice épistémique : présentation d'un concept

L'injustice épistémique incarne un phénomène social actuellement peu abordé dans le monde académique, alors qu'il se présente pourtant fréquemment dans nos interactions quotidiennes, sitôt que la conversation témoigne d'une situation problématique au niveau de l'accès, de la production et de la transmission de connaissance entre des interlocuteur.rice.s dans une même interaction sociale. Mais, qu'est-ce qu'une injustice épistémique ? C'est par nature un acte de langage (Austin, 1962) ayant comme fonction d'invalider, ou de douter du statut épistémique d'un individu, en jugeant de manière arbitraire, et donc souvent de façon injuste, sa capacité à pleinement saisir et connaitre le monde qui l'entoure. Ainsi, même si ces injustices sont, d'abord et avant tout, à caractère épistémique, et donc principalement lié au domaine du langage, elles ont pourtant des implications réelles sur la constitution et la représentation de certaines communautés sociales, et peuvent engendrer des violences sur les individus les plus touchés par les injustices épistémiques.

La pionnière de ce champ de recherche, Miranda Fricker (2007), établit qu'une injustice épistémique correspond par définition au fait de discréditer les propos d'un individu sur la base de préjugés portés à son égard. Cette définition, quoique abstraite, lui permet alors d'en distinguer deux types : l'injustice testimoniale, qui est le fait de ne pas accorder de crédibilité au témoignage ou à l'expérience de ces individus ; et l'injustice herméneutique — laquelle survient à force de subir à répétition des injustices testimoniales — qui correspond à l'incapacité, notamment pour les victimes, d'accéder aux ressources herméneutiques leur permettant de faire sens avec la réalité qu'ils ou elles vivent. Pour l'expliciter, Fricker (2007, 150-151) prend le cas du harcèlement sexuel : la constante remise en question du témoignage de victimes de harcèlement (i.e. injustice testimoniale) fait en sorte qu'elles finissent même par se demander si ce qu'elles ont vécu est véritablement du harcèlement (i.e. injustice herméneutique).

Grâce à l'ampleur des recherches dans ce champ d'études, d'autres injustices épistémiques ont été conceptualisées depuis, et s'inscrivent dans la continuité des injustices au départ élaborées par Fricker (2007). Des philosophes ont développé des concepts plus orientés sur la mise en doute des connaissances, comme la silenciation épistémique (Dotson 2011), à savoir la réduction au silence d'une personne — par indifférence ou par étouffement — du fait de douter de sa capacité à produire ou à transmettre des connaissances ; ou encore, l'ignorance épistémique (Mills, 2007), soit la résistance cognitive d'un individu à recevoir et accepter la connaissance pourtant indéniable étant transmise par autrui, à cause des préjugés qu'il porte à son égard. D'autres philosophes ont également développé des concepts étant, eux, centrés sur les rapports de pouvoir impliqués dans la reconduction des injustices épistémiques, comme celui de l'oppression épistémique (Dotson 2018), qui est l'exclusion épistémique persistante d'un individu à la transmission et à la production des savoirs ; et celui de l'exploitation épistémique (Berenstain 2016) qui est la contrainte exercée sur les personnes marginalisées d'éduquer les individus privilégié.e.s sur la nature même de l'oppression provoquée par ces dernier.e.s. De plus, certains chercheurs ont mobilisé des concepts issus d'autres domaines, pour enrichir le champ d'études des injustices épistémiques. C'est le cas pour le concept de *gaslighting* (Pohlhaus 2020), mobilisé au départ dans les milieux féministes, et ayant été retravaillé pour montrer qu'il consiste plus précisément à tenir un discours qui reporte la faute ou la culpabilité, non pas sur le coupable, mais sur la victime, à cause de préjugés étant généralement associés à cette dernière, comme le fait qu'elle soit faible, folle, vulnérable, etc. ; ou le concept de résistance en sociologie, précisé alors comme étant « épistémique » (Medina, 2013), puisqu'il consiste à réhabiliter les mentalités et les imaginaires, afin d'éviter la reconduction d'injustice sur la prémisse qu'il existe des préjugés à l'égard de certaines communautés sociales.

Grâce à ces nouvelles recherches dans ce domaine, nous constatons que l'injustice épistémique répond généralement d'une répartition inégalitaire des pouvoirs épistémiques étant distribués entre les interlocuteur.rice.s d'une même interaction sociale, sur la base de préjugés liés généralement à leurs assignations ou à leurs revendications identitaires ; ce qui repose, en somme, sur le fait d'être reconnu comme étant légitime ou non de transmettre, de produire et d'accéder à une compréhension adéquate de la réalité sociale. À cause de ce principe de légitimité, les injustices épistémiques instaurent, par conséquent, des rapports d'iniquité contribuant à la reproduction de problèmes systémiques, comme le racisme, le sexisme ou la discrimination, et qui concernent, malgré ce qu'on peut *a priori* penser, l'ensemble des individus.

Pourtant, le terme d'injustice est initialement employé dans un cadre juridique, pour juger — jusqu'à un certain degré — de l'irrespect d'une loi, après l'exécution d'un ou de plusieurs actes allant à l'encontre en principe de la jurisprudence en vigueur. Mais le système juridique comporte toutefois certaines limites évidentes : les injustices nécessitent d'être reconnues comme telles par les instances juridiques, alors que certaines reposent sur des preuves qui ne sont pas estimées suffisamment recevables ou légitimes, tandis que d'autres dépassent le simple domaine du droit, en étant plus largement associées à un reniement ou à un bafouement des conditions collectives dans lesquelles vivent certaines communautés sociales. Les mouvements sociaux comme *Metoo* ou *Black lives matter,* qui dénoncent respectivement le sexisme et le racisme dont sont victimes des individus issus de communautés bien souvent marginalisées, démontre, en fait, de l'existence d'injustices plus larges, faisant alors état de l'existence de rapports d'iniquités parmi les individus, sur le plan économique, social ou politique. Par la dénonciation de ces situations d'injustices, ces mouvements sociaux servent finalement à attester du tort ou du blâme porté sur des individus liés à certaines communautés sociales, sans qu'une reconnaissance formelle soit émise de la part des instances juridiques, à cause de leur incapacité à traiter d'injustices rendant compte des conditions de vie dont souffrent ces individus.

Donc, contrairement à ce qu'affirme Laura Beeby (2011), comme quoi le préjudice ne dépend pas des conditions dans lesquelles vivent les individus, mais uniquement du contexte relatif à une situation d'injustice, nous croyons davantage que ces injustices résultent d'expériences individuelles (Renault, 2004), saisies et interprétées par un ou plusieurs interlocuteur.rice.s dans un contexte interactionnel spécifique, mais que le préjudice qu'ils et elles subissent, dépend plus largement des conditions économiques, sociales et politiques dans lesquelles ils et elles vivent. Certes, ces individus sont directement confronté.e.s à des situations particulières de disqualification de leurs témoignages, de dénigrement de leurs réalités sociales ou même d'exclusion de leurs participations au processus de décision (Byskov, 2021), mais les effets de ces injustices épistémiques dépassent à proprement dit le simple contexte de l'interaction, en reconduisant respectivement des mécanismes de dévalorisation, d'ostracisation et d'exclusion opérant une violence épistémique souvent légitimée, à une plus grande échelle, par les instances du système au pouvoir, comme en témoignent les travaux de Spivak (1988) sur le colonialisme, de Pateman (1988) sur le sexisme, ou de Mills (1997) sur le racisme. Et, parfois dans l'ignorance des interlocuteur.rice.s eux-mêmes (Proctor & Schiebinger 2008), ces mécanismes sociaux garantissent, à une échelle individuelle, le maintien des positions de pouvoir d'un individu sur un autre, et, à une plus grande échelle, des rapports de domination d'un groupe sur un autre. Ainsi, même si ces mécanismes sociaux se manifestent par des gestes et des discours posés à l'encontre d'interlocuteur.rice.s dans un certain contexte interactionnel, il se trouve que la violence subie, ainsi que la souffrance ou le profond sentiment d'injustice qu'ils et elles peuvent ressentir, incarne le poids d'un préjudice qui dépasse en soi leur propre individualité, en pouvant être rapporté à toute une communauté sociale.

Mais, même si ces expressions de signes particuliers proviennent d'un certain contexte interactionnel, qui dépend plus largement de conditions économiques, politiques ou sociales dans lequel les interlocuteur.rice.s vivent, elles prennent tout leur sens, si et seulement s'ils et elles établissent que la situation relève effectivement d'une injustice épistémique. Si l'on s'appuie sur l'exemple de Françoise Vergès dans *Un féminisme décolonial* (2019), l'invisibilisation de la présence des femmes de ménage causée par l'absence d'interaction avec les employé.e.s des entreprises pour lesquelles elles travaillent, pourrait être considéré comme étant de la silenciation épistémique (Dotson 2011), uniquement si ces premières affirment le vivre et l'interpréter ainsi. Donc, par cet exemple, nous réalisons à quel point la présence d'une injustice dépend, de prime abord, de l'expérience de sens et d'affect vécue par les interlocuteur.rice.s concern.é.e.s.

Cela dit, la saisie et de l'interprétation d'une injustice épistémique impliquent également que les individus réagissent différemment face à ce genre de situations. Bien que leurs réactions puissent être diverses et variées, il n'en demeure pas moins qu'elles sont toutes significatives, et se traduisent souvent par un changement perceptible au niveau de leurs comportements, leurs attitudes, leurs expressions (Hepburn 2004; Ruusuvuori 2007), leurs gestes (Ekman 1993), ou leurs discours. Ces changements, causés au départ par le simple fait d'être affecté.e par une situation différente de celles vécues habituellement, peut être interprétée par la suite, en sachant qu'il s'agit effectivement d'une injustice épistémique, comme étant plus difficile ou éprouvante à vivre, ce qui peut alors altérer, de manière plus ou moins visible, la production du sens et la construction de la relation s'établissant entre les différent.e.s interlocuteur.rice.s. Donc, si l'on pense l'injustice épistémique par le biais de l'interprétation qui en est faite, ainsi que des réactions qu'elle suscite, il est alors nécessaire de se demander, au préalable, comment nous pouvons établir que les changements provoqués sont spécifiquement liés à la compréhension même d'une situation d'injustice, et non pas à d'autres facteurs psychologiques ou linguistiques, pouvant dépendre de l'état psychologique des interlocuteur.rice.s, ou de leurs états et capacités cognitives à pleinement saisir les énoncés transmis dans l'interaction sociale. Ainsi, une étude interprétative de l'injustice épistémique nous confronte à certaines limites du concept lui-même, notamment concernant le fait de pouvoir cerner, parmi les altérations qui se produisent, lesquelles résultent spécifiquement de la saisie et de l'interprétation d'une forme d'injustice épistémique.

D'autant plus que l'injustice épistémique recèle un profond paradoxe quand elle est pensée à partir d'un angle interprétatif, car elle implique, par définition, la remise en question de l'interprétation que donne un individu sur sa propre expérience ou connaissance du monde, alors qu'il doit démontrer, pour réagir à cette injustice, qu'il possède une connaissance adéquate du monde — notamment à celui qui a reconduit l'injustice et porté un préjugé sur lui — pour faire valoir le fait qu'il a subi une forme d'injustice épistémique. Ce genre de situation est récurrent, et pose problème, car : comment faire reconnaitre à autrui que nous ayons vécu une injustice épistémique quand, au départ, il remet en question notre propre capacité à bien saisir et interpréter le monde qui nous entoure ? Cette question, de prime abord insoluble, nous invite à étudier l'injustice épistémique à partir de méthodes axées sur la signification et l'interprétation étant prêtées à des expressions de signes, comme le font la sémiotique et l'herméneutique, et qui ont, selon nous, une vocation opérationnelle concrète pour repenser les problèmes interprétatifs susmentionnés. C'est pourquoi nous allons maintenant comparer les démarches de la sémiotique et de l'herméneutique, pour établir lesquelles sont les plus pertinentes pour cadrer l'injustice épistémique, et saisir, en particulier, les altérations qui s'opèrent dans la production de sens et la relation entretenue dans une interaction sociale.

Sémiotique et herméneutique à l'épreuve de l'injustice épistémique

Partant du constat que les démarches sémiotiques et herméneutiques demeurent vraisemblablement plus adaptées que ceux élaborés en philosophie pour repenser spécifiquement la saisie et de l'interprétation de formes typiques de l'injustice épistémique, nous allons dorénavant tester leurs applications concrètes au regard de l'injustice épistémique, dont la particularité est de dépendre de la compréhension des interlocuteur.rice.s pour bien la saisir et l'identifier, et de susciter une variété de significations et d'affects selon l'expérience particulière que les individus vivent, au moment de l'interaction sociale.

Les démarches sémiotiques et herméneutiques relèvent toutes les deux de traditions philosophiques, élaborées, aux alentours du XIXe siècle, aux intersections de la pragmatique, du langage, de l'esthétique et de la phénoménologie, pour étudier des enjeux ayant trait à la signification et à l'interprétation. En dépit de leurs apparentes similitudes, elles se distinguent en ceci que la sémiotique questionne le processus de constitution d'un système de signe et de la signification dont elle relève, alors que l'herméneutique s'interroge en particulier sur le phénomène de l'interprétation et de la compréhension, afin de mieux saisir la manière dont les individus font sens avec leurs expériences.

Les théories sémiotiques, par leur filiation historique à la pragmatique ainsi qu'à la philosophie du langage, accordent une importance cruciale à la logique formelle des énoncés linguistiques, et se focalisent sur la saisie et la production du sens s'opérant au sein d'un système particulier de signes. Les premiers travaux sémiotiques traitant des interactions sociales se centrent sur l'émission et la transmission d'un ensemble de messages et de codes entre un émetteur et un destinataire ; au risque, selon Jakobson (1967 [1963], 94—95 et notes de bas de page), de réduire la fonction du langage à un modèle linguistique n'étant aucunement en relation avec la communication se produisant réellement entre un émetteur et un destinataire. C'est que la transmission implique une certaine réception, qui a été définie au départ comme un simple travail d'encodage et de décodage d'un message (Hall 1994), mais qui a été reconnue par la suite, à mesure que les théories de la réception se sont développées, comme un véritable travail d'interprétation de la part de l'ensemble des locuteur.rice.s (Jauss 1988, voir herméneutique).

Cependant, ces théories de la réception ont tendance à négliger les situations au travers desquelles ces interactions se produisent, alors qu'elles sont pourtant nécessaires pour que les individus parviennent à faire sens avec le monde social qui les entoure (Quéré 1999). Pour y remédier, des chercheurs ont élaboré des théories, situées aux confluences de la sémiotique et de la communication, pour penser alors l'interaction sociale, moins en termes de codes, de messages et de réception, qu'en termes de processus de communication, et de situations d'énonciation (Boutaud 2005 ; Boutaud et Veron 2007 ; Landowski 1997), de manière à pleinement saisir le caractère processuel de l'échange dynamique qui se produit entre des interlocuteur.rice.s, et de la relation sociale qui y est alors entretenue. Parmi elles, des théories nommées « sémiopragmatiques » (Bourrel et Engberink 2018 ; Meunier et Peraya 2010 ; Odin 2000) étudient plus précisément le rapport médiatique qu'entretiennent les spectateur.rice.s, selon leurs connaissances et leurs expériences antérieures, comme celles étant liées au cinéma, en l'occurrence pour Odin (2000).

Ces récentes théories sémiotiques se réclament majoritairement de la pragmatique de Charles S. Peirce (1978 [1931-1935]), ou ce qu'il désigne par « pragmaticisme », lequel développe une logique formelle pour penser le processus sémiotique d'un système de signe qui dépendrait alors des contextes d'énonciation. Malgré son potentiel avorté à incarner une philosophie de la communication, le pragmatisme peircien propose quand même une méthode très efficace pour étudier des phénomènes dynamiques de la signification, ayant été par la suite clarifiés par notamment les travaux d'Umberto Eco (1992, 238), soit : la sémiotique (Peirce, 1978 [1931-1935], 5.488) — l'ensemble des discours théoriques sur les phénomènes sémiosiques ; et la sémiose ou *semiosis* (Peirce 1978 [1931-1935], 5.484)— l'activité au travers de laquelle la signification se produit par la coopération de trois sujets, à savoir un objet, un représentanem et un interprétant. Le processus de la sémiose s'illustre bien par l'exemple de la rose, tel que donné par Eco (1992, 239), du fait que la rose incarne un objet dynamique fréquemment représenté par le terme rose (i.e représentanem) qui, lui-même, peut être interprété par l'énoncé « fleur rouge », par l'image d'une rose, ou bien par une histoire entière qui raconte comment on cultive les roses (i.e interprétant). L'activité sémiosique se produisant alors par la relation entre cet objet, ce représentanem et ces interprétants, comme celle illustrée par la rose, crée un enchainement d'interprétants, ouvrant la signification à un monde infini de possibles interprétations. Car, la rose peut être aussi une couleur, une odeur, une symbolique, etc., et même complètement autre chose.

Quant aux théories herméneutiques, elles reposent bien souvent sur les travaux du pionnier de ce courant, Hans-Georg Gadamer (1996a), qui a tenté, à la suite des travaux de Wilhelm Dilthey (1942), de redonner une importance à l'interprétation dans les sciences humaines, alors qu'elles voulaient, à l'époque, rivaliser avec les sciences naturelles, lesquelles, en se dotant d'une méthode scientifique, prétendaient détenir une vérité objective sur les phénomènes. Le problème toutefois, pour Gadamer, est que cet idéal d'objectivité promu par la méthode scientifique des sciences naturelles a tendance à réduire la vérité à son plus futile dessein, alors que cette dernière incarne, pour Gadamer, le fondement ontologique de toute connaissance, de tout savoir énoncé par les humain.e.s. En fait, dans son ouvrage *Vérité et méthode* (1996a), Gadamer soutient que la méthode scientifique ne doit aucunement primer sur les savoirs humains, et plus largement sur la vérité ontologique des choses, car la connaissance s'acquiert de prime abord par la compréhension que fait l'interprète des phénomènes qu'il ou elle observe. Il précise, par la suite, que seule la méthode de l'esthétique peut libérer les savoirs humains du joug de cette science instrumentale, en ceci qu'elle permettrait aux chercheurs de réaliser que les connaissances ne se forment qu'au travers de l'expérience vécue, par les individus, des objets et des phénomènes qui les entourent, de manière similaire à celle qu'ils et elles vivent au moment de contempler une œuvre d'art.

Quand nous contemplons une œuvre d'art, nous expérimentons en fait ce qui manifestement « ressort » comme une vérité ontologique, car elle suscite un « dévoilement » des choses — au sens heideggérien du terme — du simple fait de remarquer la présence de l'œuvre en cet « ici et maintenant » que nous pouvons parfois ressentir au moment de l'appréhender et de la saisir. L'œuvre d'art nous offre alors une expérience esthétique nous faisant prendre connaissance, le temps d'un bref instant, d'une vérité dépassant même parfois notre entendement. Donc, à l'inverse de ce que revendique la méthode scientifique, comprendre les choses ne s'apparente pas au fait d'accéder entièrement à la vérité, ni même de saisir comment elle s'opère, ni de comprendre d'où elle vient, mais plutôt au fait de savoir qu'elle existe quand elle se présente réellement sous nos yeux.

Ce qui se produit au cours de notre expérience dépasse, en ce sens, notre simple subjectivité : cette dernière se laisse emporter par l'attestation même de cette vérité à l'issue de laquelle il en découle une véritable connaissance sur le monde. Il faut ici élargir le sens généralement attribué à la connaissance, qui correspond pour Gadamer à une reconnaissance, au sens où elle nous ouvre les yeux sur ce qui est vraiment là, avec une justesse, tout d'un coup évidente, du monde, tel qu'il se présente réellement à nous. C'est pourquoi l'expérience demeure un élément fondamental dans toute quête d'une connaissance ou d'un savoir : elle contribue à la redécouverte de notre monde comme il est réellement, comme si c'était la première fois que nous le voyons aussi clairement.

Entrer en discussion avec Gadamer exige au préalable de bien comprendre que l'expérience relève au départ, pour les individus empreint.e.s d'une culture et de connaissances sur leur monde, d'une tradition historique de référence — au sens de *Vorurteile* en allemand. La tradition historique se comprend, pour Gadamer, comme l'héritage de savoirs se formant, au travers des siècles, à mesure que les peuples développent leurs cultures et connaissances sur le monde. En même temps, ces connaissances nous forment en tant qu'êtres, autant sur un plan individuel que collectif : elles nous marquent, nous constituent et nous transforment, par-delà même nos existences. Mais, contrairement à l'ambiguïté qu'elle peut suggérer, cette conception n'implique absolument pas la défense d'un traditionalisme (Fleming 2003, 109-133) ou d'un conservatisme (Ipperciel 2004) cherchant à défendre alors les acquis d'un certain héritage culturel et historique ; elle peut aussi susciter une volonté, au contraire, de remettre en question ce qui est considéré comme étant acquis. D'après l'ouvrage de Lorraine Code (2003), la tradition historique permet aussi de contrer l'assimilation constante de la différence, sans qu'il soit fait, au préalable, un véritable travail de reconnaissance, ou une prise de distance nécessaire et suffisante offrant la possibilité d'assurer la prise en compte de tout ce qui serait étrange, différent ou nouveau (Code 2003, 11).

D'un point de vue épistémologique, la considération de la tradition — ainsi que de l'ensemble des déterminations sociohistoriques sous-jacentes — rend visible le fait indéniable, rendu pourtant tacite par cette objectivité à laquelle prétend la science instrumentale, que le savoir est sans cesse en construction. De cette manière, nous gardons toujours à l'esprit qu'il persiste une part de doute dans la connaissance, qui est alors nécessaire à ce que nous puissions sans cesse regarder le monde à partir d'une certaine distance, pour continuer d'y porter attention et de chercher humblement à le connaitre. Cette posture d'humilité est alors synonyme de sagesse, entendue au sens socratique du terme, car il faut d'abord et avant tout reconnaitre son ignorance pour parvenir à s'approcher de cette vérité, de prime d'abord insaisissable, et qui se manifeste finalement à qui sait la voir. À partir de ce principe, Gadamer estime alors que l'interprétation dépend à la fois de l'accès à cette vérité fondamentale, qui est appréhendée, selon l'expérience qui y est vécue, à la lumière de la tradition historique à laquelle les individus appartiennent. Les théories herméneutiques s'appuyant sur les travaux de Gadamer (1996a), et plus récemment sur ceux de Paul Ricoeur (1969) ou de Robert Jauss (1988), proposent donc de concevoir les expériences de vérité des individus, de manière à la fois singulière et universelle, en tenant compte des contextes sociohistoriques qui les sous-tendent.

Ces deux démarches, respectivement sémiotiques et herméneutiques, permettent de réfléchir sur des enjeux portant sur la signification et l'interprétation, et offrent des finalités pratiques similaires, au sens où elles permettent toutes les deux de saisir les modalités de saisie, d'interprétation et d'expression étant mobilisées au sein des interactions sociales. Mais, après un examen minutieux, nous constatons qu'elles marquent certaines oppositions formelles en ce qui a trait au processus derrière la circulation, la saisie et la compréhension du sens véhiculé dans une interaction, et plus précisément à l'activité même de la sémiose. Un débat, étayé par Eco lui-même (1992, 368), sans toutefois le spécifier à la sémiotique et à l'herméneutique, distingue deux conceptions en opposition formelle : celle, hermétique, qui considère que la sémiose dérive d'un interprète particulier — étant souvent le créateur par exemple d'un texte ou d'une œuvre — auquel nous devons nous fier lorsque nous tentons d'en comprendre le sens, et celle, illimitée, qui admet qu'on puisse prêter plusieurs interprétations à des signes, sans nécessairement rester fidèle à l'intention prêtée par le créateur.rice. Donc, on assume finalement du côté des hermétiques, et en l'occurrence ici des herméneutes, qu'interpréter une œuvre, par exemple littéraire ou artistique, signifie mettre en lumière l'interprétation voulue par l'auteur pour reconnaitre ce qui serait l'essence même d'un texte ou d'une œuvre ; tandis que d'un autre côté, pour les sémioticiens, les textes ou les œuvres peuvent être de nouveau interprétés à la lumière de nouvelles saisies du sens émises par différents interprétants. La présentation de ce débat nous invite à nous questionner sur la véritable nature de la sémiose, et à nous demander si elle doit être pensée comme étant univoque ou plurivoque.

Pour l'herméneutique, l'interprétation est tributaire du bagage culturel et historique de l'interprète — soit la tradition à laquelle il appartient — et de son expérience de l'événement vécu, ce qui limite alors le renvoi à de multiples interprétations, car elles se limitent strictement au contexte sociohistorique vécu auquel elles se réfèrent. En particulier, Gadamer exprime, par son idée de vérité, la croyance en la présence d'un signifié transcendantal, qui peut être évoqué au travers, par exemple, des mots et des images, ce qui met, encore une fois, rapidement fin au renvoi infini de signe à signe, car ces dernières ont une vérité profonde qui paraît indéniable, et dans un sens, absolu, pour ceux et celles qui les contemplent.

Pour la sémiotique, la signification dépend de trois sujets, soit le signe, son objet et ses interprétants, et implique une variation illimitée d'interprétations possibles pouvant être hiérarchisées ou limitées uniquement si les individus d'une même communauté parviennent à un accord provisoire les déclarant comme étant temporairement vraies. Mais, l'association spontanée de nouveaux enchainements d'interprétants, et donc, éventuellement, la production de nouvelles interprétations peut rompre cet accord, et amener les individus à questionner ou à remettre en question les interprétations évoquées. Mais, c'est qu'au départ, les sémioticiens ne reconnaissent pas du tout la présence d'un signifié transcendantal : le langage est pris dans un jeu de signifiants multiples ne présentant aucunement de signifiés pouvant être considérés comme étant univoques et absolus. Et même, pour tout peircien.ne qui se respecte, l'indétermination du signifié est ce qui permet d'attester du fait que tout ne demeure qu'une affaire de signes. Car, ce qui entame le mouvement de la signification, c'est ce qui rend impossible son interruption, au sens où un signe ne demeure qu'un signe, et que rien n'existe en dehors de la chaine signifiante qui opère une régression à l'infini (Peirce 1978 [1931-1935], 1.339). Certains sémioticiens — et en l'occurrence ici Boutaud (2005, 38) — considèrent même que le mouvement de la sémiose infinie offre une réflexion philosophique sur la pensée humaine, laquelle est sans cesse entreprise et toujours inachevée, à force de glisser de signe en signe, et de produire une chaine signifiante qui ne reste jamais figée.

Maintenant que nous avons analysé les principes et les particularités de ces deux démarches de recherche, comment doit-on les mettre à l'épreuve et les cadrer au regard de l'injustice épistémique ? Quels sont leurs avantages et leurs inconvénients au regard de notre enquête ?

Les théories sémiotiques offrent un cadre propice à la réinterprétation infinie et à la possibilité discursive, ce qui serait favorable à l'acceptation de la diversité et de la différence, et à l'amélioration du dialogue parmi les diverses communautés sociales. À première vue, nous constatons que la sémiotique offre une conception dynamique des processus de signification, ayant l'avantage de prendre en compte de modalités sémiosiques complexes et variables, tels que le ton, les gestes, les mots, les sons, etc., et qui changent incontestablement selon les contextes interactionnels, notamment quand des injustices épistémiques y sont reconduites. Et, bien que la sémiotique puisse paraître limitée à cause de son attachement, toujours présent, à la linguistique, elle permet néanmoins de s'attarder à tout ce qui se rattache à la signification, ce qui nous permet d'enrichir notre propre compréhension de la pensée humaine, et de ce que les individus éprouvent sur le plan cognitif et affectif, au moment où ils et elles vivent par exemple une situation d'injustice épistémique. Cependant, la position — un peu radicale, telle que précédemment introduite — de la sémiose illimitée, instaure un principe d'indétermination du signifié, qui demeure certes efficace pour tenir compte de la multiplicité de significations qu'il est possible d'admettre pour parvenir, après discussion, à un consensus parmi les membres d'une même communauté, mais qui peut nuire aux possibilités mêmes qu'elle offre sur le plan sémiosique, en autorisant certaines dérives, comme celle que les significations s'équivalent les unes aux autres, au point qu'aucun consensus ou accord, même provisoire, ne soit réellement possible, en cas, par exemple, d'injustice épistémique. C'est que les interactions où les injustices épistémiques sont reconduites impliquent souvent des rapports de pouvoir et de domination, qui ne sont aucunement favorables à la discussion et à la prise en considération des points de vue d'autrui, et surtout de ceux et celles qui sont opprimé.e.s. Si on s'imagine le pire des scénarios, alors il pourrait même y avoir une reconduite perpétuelle des injustices testimoniales basée sur le principe qu'une autre interprétation est toujours possible, et, par conséquent, que d'autres puissent être toujours plus envisageables que celles étant finalement prononcées par des individus ayant littéralement moins de pouvoir épistémique.

Mais, si on tient compte de l'avis d'Eco (1992, 382), alors il est possible de croire que le processus de la sémiose peut quand même donner naissance, à long terme, à des interprétations étant socialement partagées et admises comme étant vraies. Le signifié ne serait donc pas transcendantal, mais devrait être postulé comme un but possible et souhaitable, selon la volonté de la communauté s'en portant garante. De plus, si la difficulté d'identifier une injustice épistémique engendre facilement des erreurs de jugement d'une situation d'interaction, alors il vaut mieux prétendre à une sémiose potentiellement illimitée, afin de pouvoir réactualiser et réviser la situation en cas de problème d'interprétation. Mais, pouvons-nous vraiment prétendre qu'il soit possible de privilégier momentanément un signe dont la signification se comprend en principe à l'infini, et varie incontestablement selon les contextes ?

Les théories herméneutiques, comme celle de Gadamer (1996a; 1996b), offrent quant à elles un cadre adéquat pour la réhabilitation des préjugés et l'émission d'une critique sociale à visée réformiste. D'une part, la compréhension, telle qu'exprimée par Gadamer, permet une certaine réhabilitation des préjugés par le pouvoir de la connaissance, car elle répond du principe que la connaissance doit sans cesse faire autorité, qu'importe les relations de pouvoir qui se tissent entre les individus, dans les champs du savoir humain. Ainsi, cette conception présente l'avantage de nous offrir la possibilité de critiquer les préjugés en vigueur, tout simplement au nom de la connaissance, ainsi que d'adopter une réflexivité propice à la critique de la prétendue objectivité dans les sciences humaines. En ce qui a trait aux situations d'injustices épistémiques, cela nous permettrait de reconnaitre le caractère véridique des témoignages partagés par les victimes, et qui sont, à cause des relations de pouvoir et de domination, généralement délégitimés et sujets à la reconduction d'injustices testimoniales (Fricker 2007), alors qu'elles rendent compte d'une vision parfaitement adéquate de la réalité sociale.

Ceci étant dit, nous savons pertinemment que le monde social se constitue à partir de normes qui régulent l'ensemble de nos conduites sociales, et qui amène les individus à rester empreints de valeurs, de préjugés et de croyances, ce qui peut poser un problème pour les gadamérien.ne.s qui défendraient, coûte que coûte, le pouvoir inéluctable de la connaissance, et de la vérité ontologique émanant des expériences vécues par autrui. Mais, comme le précise Code (2003, 7) par l'invocation des propos de Gadamer (1996a), la possibilité même d'une *tabula rasa* des préjugés, ou d'une lutte contre les préjugés que les individus peuvent porter sur autrui et sur le monde, demeure tout simplement impossible à imaginer. Pour Gadamer (1996a), les préjugés doivent être, au contraire, pris en considération, pour que nous puissions nous questionner, de façon adéquate et juste, sur nos propres manières de concevoir la connaissance que nous cultivons de notre réalité sociale. De plus, d'après les théories du point de vue (i.e *stand-*

point theories), et notamment des travaux de Sandra Harding (1986), un individu postulant une capacité à éliminer l'ensemble des valeurs ou des croyances de
son raisonnement, sans adopter pour autant une posture réflexive adéquate, ne
peut avoir accès à une vision complètement objective de la réalité. Car, dans
l'épistémologie objectiviste qu'elle critique de concert avec Gadamer, quand le
chercheur ou la chercheuse tente de s'émanciper de sa position sociale en adop-
tant un point de vue « de nulle part », il ou elle crée en fait les conditions pour
que ses préjugés, valeurs et croyances soient directement importés dans les
résultats de recherche. Si, qui plus est, le point de vue et les expériences sociales
proviennent d'un individu ayant un statut social de privilégié.e, alors les préjugés, valeurs et croyances étant partagés de la communauté scientifique devien-
nent difficilement délogeables de la culture scientifique dominante, du fait d'être
estimées relativement objectives alors qu'elles ne le sont vraisemblablement pas.
C'est que les épistémologues du point de vue défendent le principe, relativement
similaire à celui de Gadamer (1996a), que tout savoir est produit de façon socialement située, et que l'ensemble des points de vue permet d'avoir une meilleure
compréhension de la réalité sociale. Car, le savoir n'est pas individuel, mais bel
et bien produit collectivement par une communauté capable de représenter cette
diversité des points de vue.

D'autant plus que, pour le cas de l'injustice épistémique, il peut être né-
faste de vouloir mettre une fin à l'existence de ces préjugés, car certains peuvent
incarner, en tant que jugements et qu'intuitions, de véritables sources de connaissance empirique. D'après notamment Nancy Hartsock (1998), pour qui la
production de connaissance est directement liée à la reproduction des rapports
dc domination, la prise en compte des points de vue d'individus marginalisés,
ainsi que des préjugés qu'ils impliquent, est une gageure de la connaissance sur
la réalité sociale qui y est effectivement vécue par l'ensemble des individus. Car,
la vision du monde social promue par les individus en position dominante est
toujours partielle et partiale, et contribue même parfois à la légitimation des
rapports de pouvoir. Il ne s'agit toutefois pas d'affirmer que les points de vue des
dominé.es seraient porteur, intrinsèquement, de savoirs plus véridiques sur le
monde social, mais plutôt d'insister sur la priorisation de leurs points de vue,
puisqu'ils et elles possèdent des expériences de la réalité qui ne sont pas nécessairement vécues par une majorité d'individus. Hartsock et les épistémologues
du point de vue ne font donc aucunement la promotion de l'idée que seulement
les femmes peuvent parler des femmes, les noirs des noirs, etc. Leur but est
uniquement de valoriser les points de vue des individus marginalisés, de manière à bénéficier d'une meilleure connaissance de phénomènes sociaux, tels que
l'injustice épistémique, en vertu du fait qu'ils sont parfois minimisés, invisibili-

sés ou même occultés par la majorité des individus, pour la simple raison que leurs positions sociales privilégiées les amènent à moins vivre ce genre de situations, du moins en tant que victimes. Par la reconnaissance de l'inéluctabilité des préjugés et la défense du primat de la connaissance, la pensée de Gadamer se concilie donc bien avec les théories du point de vue, lesquelles favorisent la reconnaissance de l'expérience véridique étant vécue par les individus marginalisés, ce qui permet, dans l'ensemble, de bien saisir la compréhension étant faite de l'injustice épistémique par les individus marginalisés, qui en sont souvent les victimes.

D'autre part, la conception de la tradition historique requiert de prendre en compte les contextes sociohistoriques dont relèvent les situations d'injustice épistémique, et qui témoignent parfois des conditions sociales dans lesquelles sont les victimes de ces injustices, comme le racisme systémique dont témoignent les situations d'arrestation policière vécues par les afro-américain.e.s. En considérant les situations d'injustice ainsi, cela nous permettrait de relever les rapports d'iniquités étant liés à une distribution inégalitaire des pouvoirs épistémiques, qu'il est important de souligner, au nom de la justice et de l'équité sociale. Donc, la conception gadamérienne de tradition historique permet de rendre compte des dimensions de la vie qui dépassent même le simple cadre de l'interaction, et de pouvoir émettre une critique des sociétés dans laquelle nous évoluons, en repensant certains éléments de cette tradition historique que les individus ont intériorisée pour concevoir les principes de justice, d'égalité et d'équité. Car le projet philosophique de Gadamer est de parvenir à une fusion de l'ensemble de ces horizons interprétatifs, provenant autant de l'expérience vécue par les interlocuteur.rice.s, que de leur compréhension de la tradition historique, dans le but de faire progressivement évoluer les sociétés, en reformant, éventuellement, certains principes, valeurs et croyances, dans le cas hypothétique où elles iraient à l'encontre des déterminations sociohistoriques au travers desquelles les individus expérimentent certaines dimensions de la vie sociale, comme l'injustice épistémique.

Ainsi, la démarche herméneutique de Gadamer exige, finalement, de suspendre nos préjugés, le temps d'interpréter l'expérience que nous avons vécu, et de remettre en question, d'ouvrir et de maintenir ouvertes d'autres possibilités interprétatives, tout en tenant compte de notre propre historicité, en fonction de la tradition à laquelle nous nous référons. Il souligne même la nécessité interprétative de voir le passé dans ses propres termes, donc pas comme un aspect des valeurs et des préjugés de l'interprète, et de se situer dans une autre situation pour le comprendre, tout en restant ouvert.e à développer une conscience critique des préjugés que nous portons éventuellement sur autrui et le monde qui nous entoure. Mais, le plus important est, comme le suggère Code, que :

> Gadamer ouvre une voie d'engagement dans les sciences humaines comme étude de l'expérience et du sens ; où l'expérience est vécue linguistiquement, et le langage, comme producteur de sens ; et où l'expérience est vécue linguistiquement, et où le langage, en tant que producteur de sens, est constitutif du monde que ces sciences cherchent à comprendre (2003, 8, notre traduction).

L'herméneutique offre ainsi une dimension réflexive non négligeable, qui se situe au niveau de l'expérience vécue par l'individu, ainsi que de la tradition défendue par la collectivité, et qui est, en ce sens, extrêmement compatible avec les théories du point de vue, lesquelles sont généralement reconnues pour offrir une vision critique de la vie sociale, et une remise en question des points de vue sur des sujets faisant souvent polémiques, en s'attaquant directement à des problèmes d'ordre systémique, liés bien souvent aux conditions dans lesquelles vivent certaines communautés sociales.

Discussion critique

Autant la sémiotique que l'herméneutique nous permet donc d'analyser les interactions sociales quotidiennes, en offrant des cadres de pensée adéquats pour penser l'ampleur du phénomène. En particulier, elles se focalisent sur les significations et les interprétations énoncées dans le cadre d'une injustice épistémique, et tiennent compte de la réaction des interlocuteur.rice.s qui y sont impliqué.e.s. De plus, ces démarches sont toutes les deux ancrées dans le courant pragmatiste, ce qui nous permettrait alors, par rapport à notre cadre de recherche, de situer l'injustice épistémique au niveau des pratiques, actions et actes de langage posés dans certaines situations, dans le but de nous aider à mieux comprendre la manière dont « les individus structurent leurs rapports, s'attribuent des rôles, jouent leurs images » (Meunier et Peraya 2010, 146).

Cependant, par l'examen approfondi de ces deux démarches au regard de l'injustice épistémique, nous affirmons que notre préférence se porte véritablement sur l'herméneutique, laquelle permet d'adopter une posture réflexive et éthique étant nécessaire, à notre avis, pour mener une analyse approfondie sur les injustices épistémiques. Le principal avantage de l'herméneutique est de pouvoir étudier, en s'attardant sur l'interprétation et la compréhension humaine, nos propres manières d'appréhender et d'expérimenter les choses qui nous entourent, ainsi que de penser la connaissance véridique qui en résulte. Bien que cet exercice de pensée demeure complexe, et requiert une rigueur, souvent exigeante, d'étudier nos expériences et connaissances à la lumière d'éventuels biais et préjugés dont nous ignorons parfois l'existence, elle demeure toutefois nécessaire pour mieux comprendre la manière dont nos préjugés, nos valeurs et croyances les plus profondes s'articulent, et définissent les contours, bien souvent imprécis et abstraits, de nos horizons de pensée passés, actuels et futurs.

Et c'est uniquement en des termes gadamériens que cette (re)lecture de nos horizons interprétatifs soit véritablement possible, par la reconnaissance préexistante d'une tradition se recréant sans cesse en arrière-plan de nos connaissances et de nos savoirs humains. En reprenant l'interprétation de Susan Hekman (2003, 81-109) à propos de la tradition gadamérienne, nous croyons que l'expérience humaine peut créer une confrontation incessante entre une chose nouvelle et une chose traditionnelle, qui se mélangent pour opérer finalement des changements au niveau de cette tradition qui demeure, malgré son apparence stable, en constante évolution. Cela permet donc de considérer que la connaissance humaine, bien qu'elle varie en fonction du contexte sociohistorique dans lequel nous nous situons, ne provient pas à l'origine de nulle part, puisqu'elle est profondément ancrée dans une tradition, une histoire communément partagée par une multitude d'individus, et qui influence, à chaque instant, nos modes d'existence.

Contrairement à ce que certaine.s peuvent croire, la méthode herméneutique gadamérienne permet d'étudier, de façon lucide et concrète, la connaissance humaine directement là où elle émerge, en l'accueillant de manière très ouverte, malgré qu'elle véhicule des préjugés, des jugements et des croyances guidant à chaque instant nos actions humaines. Selon l'interprétation de Linda Alcoff (2003), une philosophe réputée dans le domaine des injustices épistémiques, Gadamer défend une vérité indépendante de l'expérience humaine, mais qui serait, en même temps, immanente au domaine de la réalité sociale, en réussissant à la présenter comme elle est véritablement vécue par les individus. Ainsi, l'herméneutique permet de cadrer épistémique sur une critique éminemment sociale et épistémologique, en vertu du fait de mener un examen méthodique de l'ensemble des préjugés, croyances et valeurs étant reconduites dans les discours véhiculés dans le domaine des sciences naturelles et sociales, ainsi que dans les interactions quotidiennes en société. Malgré ces apports analytiques indéniables, nous pensons tout de même que certains aspects, de nature principalement éthique et politique, ne peuvent s'envisager sans l'appui de d'autres théories, comme celles féministes, pour valoriser par exemple certains points de vue sur d'autres plus privilégié.e.s, au nom certes de la connaissance, mais surtout, dans un profond désir de transformation sociale, afin de changer les normes et les mentalités qui favorisent la reproduction des injustices épistémiques, et du préjudice porté sur des communautés marginalisées. Cela dit, le projet herméneutique de Gadamer, bien qu'il n'a pas été au préalable fondé pour répondre à des visées éthiques et politiques, recèle des pistes de réflexion très pertinentes pour penser une éthique du dialogue, en défendant le désir d'une compréhension commune parmi les interlocuteur.rice.s d'une même situation interactionnelle, par la cultivation d'un profond souci de soi et d'autrui, ce qui peut améliorer la communication entre les diverses communautés sociales, et permettre la recherche d'une meilleure équité épistémique et sociale parmi l'ensemble des individus qui composent nos sociétés contemporaines.

Coline Sénac, M.A., PhD Cand., Faculté des arts,
Université du Québec à Montréal, senac.coline@uqam.ca

Références

Alcoff, Linda. 2003. "Gadamer feminist epistemology." In Code, L. (ed.). *Feminist interpretations of Hans-Georg Gadamer.* University Park: The Pennsylvania State University, 109–133.

Austin, John. 1962. *How to Do Things with Words.* Oxford: Clarendon Press.

Berenstain, Nora. 2016. "Epistemic Exploitation." *Ergo*, 22 (3), 569–590.

Beeby, Laura. 2011. "A Critique of Hermeneutical Injustice." *Proceedings of the Aristotelian Society*, 111, 479–486.

Bencherki, Nicolas et al. 2019. *Authority and Power in Social Interaction: Methods and Analysis.* New York: Routledge.

Byskov, Morten Fibieger. 2021. "What Makes an Epistemic Injustice an 'Injustice'?" *Journal of Social Philosophy*, 51(1), 114–131.

Bourrel, Gérard et Engberink, Agnès Oude. 2018. « En quoi, une théorie sémiopragmatique à partir des théories de Peirce peut-elle renouveler la recherche en sciences humaines et sociales ? » *Cahier de recherche sociologique*, (62), 177–201.

Boutaud, Jean-Jacques. 2005. *Sémiotique et communication.* Paris : L'Harmattan.

Boutaud, Jean-Jacques. et Veron, Éliséo. 2007. *Sémiotique ouverte : Itinéraires sémiotiques en communication.* Paris : Hermes Science Publications.

Code, Lorraine. 2003. *Feminist interpretations of Hans-Georg Gadamer.* University Park: The Pennsylvania State University.

van Dijk, Teun A. (Ed.). 1997. *Discourse as social interaction* (*Discourse Studies: A Multidisciplinary Introduction, Vol. 2*). New York: Sage Publications.

Dilthey, Wilhelm. 1942. *Introduction à l'étude des sciences humaines : essai sur le fondement qu'on pourrait donner à l'étude de la société et de l'histoire.* Paris : Presses universitaires de France.

Dotson, Kristie. 2011. "Tracking Epistemic Violence, Tracking Practices of Silencing." *Hypatia*, 26 (2), 236–257.

Dotson, Kristie. 2018. "Conceptualizing Epistemic Oppression", *Recherches féministes*, 31(2), 9–34.

Eco, Umberto. 1992. *Les limites de l'interprétation.* Paris : Grasset.

Ekman, Paul. 1993. "Facial expression and emotion", *American psychologist*, 48(4): 384–392.

Fleming, Mike. 2003. "Gadamer's Conversation: Does the Other Have a Say?". Dans Code, L. (ed.). *Feminist interpretations of Hans-Georg Gadamer.* University Park: The Pennsylvania State University, 109–133.

Fricker, Miranda. 2007. *Epistemic Injustice: Power and the Ethics of Knowing.* New York: Oxford University Press.

Gadamer, Hans-Georg. 1996a. *Vérité et méthode.* Paris : Éditions Seuil.

Gadamer, Hans-Georg. 1998b. *La philosophie herméneutique.* Paris : Presses Universitaires de France.

Hall, Stuart. 1994. *Codage/Décodage.* Réseaux, 6(68). 27–39.

Harding, Sandra. 1984. *The Science Question in Feminism.* Ithaca: Cornell University Press.

Hartsock, Nancy. 1998. *The Feminist Standpoint Revisited, And Other Essays.* Londres: Routledge Editions.

Hekman, Susan. 2003. "Gadamer's Philosophical Hermeneutics and Feminist Projects". Dans Code, L. (ed.). *Feminist interpretations of Hans-Georg Gadamer.* University Park: The Pennyania State University, 81–109.

Hepburn, Alexa. 2004. "Crying: Notes on Description, Transcription, and Interaction." *Research on Language & Social Interaction* 37 (3): 251–90.

Ipperciel, Donald. 2004. « La pensée de Gadamer est-elle conservatrice ? », *Revue philosophique de Louvain*, Quatrième série, tome 102, 610-629.

Jakobson, Roman. 1967. *Essais de linguistique générale : 1. Les fondations du langage.* Paris : Éditions de Minuit.

Jauss, Robert. 1988. *Pour une herméneutique littéraire.* Paris : Éditions Gallimard.

Kidd., Ian James et al. (éds.) 2017. *The Routledge Handbook of Epistemic Injustice.* New York: Routledge.

Landowski, Éric. 1997. *Présences de l'Autre.* Paris : Presses Universitaires de France.

Lépinard, Éléonore. & Mazouz, Sarah. 2021. *Pour l'intersectionnalité*. Paris: Éditions Anamosa.

Medina, José. 2013. *The Epistemology of Resistance: Gender and Racial Oppression, Epistemic Injustice, and Resistant Imaginations*. New York: Oxford University Press.

Meunier, Jean-Pierre et Peraya, Daniel. 2010. *Introduction aux théories de la communication. Analyse sémio-pragmatique de la communication médiatique*. Bruxelles : De Boeck.

Mills, Charles. 1997. *The Racial Contract*. Ithaca and London: Cornell University Press.

Mills, Charles. 2007. "White Ignorance." In Sullivan S., & Tuana, N. (eds). *Race and Epistemologies of Ignorance*. Albany: State University of New York Press, 11–38.

Odin, Roger. 2000. *De la Fiction*, Bruxelles : De Boeck Université.

Pateman, Carole. 1988. *The Sexual Contract*. Oxford: Polity Press.

Pohlhaus, G. 2020. "Gaslighting and Echoing, or Why Collective Epistemic Resistance is not a 'Witch Hunt.'" *Hypatia*, 35(4), 674–686.

Peirce, Charles Sanders. 1978. *Écrits sur le signe*. Paris : Éditions Seuil.

Proctor, Robert and Schiebinger, Londa (eds.). 2008. *Agnotology: The Making and Unmaking of Ignorance*. Bloomington: Stanford University Press.

Quéré, Louis. 1999. *La sociologie à l'épreuve de l'herméneutique. Essais d'épistémologie des sciences sociales*. Paris : L'Harmattan.

Renault, Emmanuel. 2004. *L'expérience de l'injustice. Reconnaissance et clinique de l'injustice*. Paris : La Découverte.

Ricœur, Paul. 1969. *Le Conflit des Interprétations. Essais d'herméneutique I*. Paris : Éditions Le Seuil.

Ruusuvuori, Johanna. 2007. "Managing Affect: Integration of Empathy and Problem-Solving in Health Care Encounters". *Discourse Studies*. 9 (5), 597–622.

Spivak, Gayatri Chakravorty. 1988. "Can the Subaltern Speak?" In Cary Nelson, Lawrence Grossberg (ed.), *Marxism and the Interpretation of Culture*. Chicago: University of Illinois Press, 271–313.

Vergès, Françoise. 2019. *Un féminisme décolonial*. Paris : Éditions La Fabrique.

ULRICH ARNSWALD (Karlsruhe)

Hans-Georg Gadamers Sprachlichkeit der hermeneutischen Erfahrung im Wechselspiel von Vernunft und Erfahrung, Wissenschaft und/oder soziale Vorstellungen, Tradition(en) und/oder Gemeinschaft am Beispiel von Thomas Morus' *Utopia*

Hans-Georg Gadamer's linguisticity of hermeneutic experience in the interplay of reason and experience, science and/or social imaginaries, tradition(s) and/or community using the example of Thomas More's Utopia

Abstract

Hermeneutics can be understood on the one hand as the art of interpretation, and on the other hand as a medium for dealing with the past, for conveying events, contexts or even writings in new ways of speaking for new recipients. The interpretation of writings, however, places special demands on hermeneutics: it does not take place in a sterile vacuum, but is rather embedded in a social and cultural context that shapes the interpretation or mediation and is an expression of a time, a fashion or a specific requirement of modernity. The question therefore arises as to what role reason and experience, science and/or social ideas, tradition(s) and/or community play in interpretation.

Using Thomas More's masterpiece Utopia *as an example, various resulting interpretative approaches to a concrete writing will be presented. Through the hermeneutic design of a historical horizon in relation to Thomas More's time as well as through the development of a historical awareness of the work, the possibility of an understanding of this world-famous, still controversial writing as well as the efficiency of Gadamer's philosophical hermeneutics will become recognisable.*

Keywords: Hans-Georg Gadamer, Thomas More, Hermeneutics, Utopia

1. Hermeneutik als Wechselspiel von Vernunft und Erfahrung, Wissenschaft und/oder soziale Vorstellungen, Tradition(en) und/oder Gemeinschaft

Hermeneutik kann einerseits als die Kunst der Interpretation verstanden werden, andererseits als Medium um Vergangenheitsaufarbeitung zu leisten, um Ereignisse, Zusammenhänge oder auch Schriften in neuen Sprechweisen für neue Empfänger zu übermitteln. Die Auslegung von Schriften stellt aber besondere

Anforderungen an die Hermeneutik: Sie findet nicht in einem sterilen Vakuum statt, sondern ist vielmehr eingebettet in einen sozialen und kulturellen Kontext, der die Interpretation oder Vermittlung prägt und Ausdruck einer Zeit, einer Mode oder einer spezifischen Anforderung der Moderne ist.

Es stellt sich daher die Frage, welche Rolle Vernunft und Erfahrung, Wissenschaft und/oder soziale Vorstellungen, Tradition(en) und/oder Gemeinschaft bei der Auslegung spielen. Die Komplexität der Hermeneutik, ob wissenschaftlich oder philosophisch, theologisch oder juridisch, bringt daher zwangsläufig unterschiedliche Ansätze und Voraussetzungen für die Kunst der Interpretation mit sich.

Der Weg zum gegenseitigen Verständnis führt über die Enthüllung des jeweiligen impliziten Verständnisses eines Textes, das die Sichtweise des Interpreten bzw. der Interpreten einer Interpretationsschule in seiner bzw. ihrer spezifischen Vernunft und Erfahrung, Wissenschaft und/oder sozialen Vorstellungen, Tradition(en) und/oder Gemeinschaft hebt. Indem wir die Sichtweise des Anderen verstehen, lernen wir, seine Andersartigkeit zuzulassen und gleichzeitig zu erlauben, dass wir selbst in Frage gestellt werden.

Dieses hermeneutische Schema ist auf beide Parteien angewiesen und soll allmählich zur *Horizontverschmelzung* durch Kritik und Austausch führen, was ein zentraler Terminus der philosophischen Hermeneutik Hans-Georg Gadamers[1] ist und auf die Integration verschiedener Sichtweisen im Interesse eines besseren Verständnisses und der Korrektur früherer Missverständnisse und Verzerrungen abzielt.

Anhand von Thomas Morus' Meisterwerk mit dem vollen Titel *Von der besten Staatsverfassung und von der neuen Insel Utopia, ein wahrhaft goldenes Büchlein, genauso wohltuend wie heiter* (Morus 1990), welches die Tradition der teils theoretisch, teils literarisch motivierten Ausarbeitung fiktiver Staatsmodelle prägte und als Eigenname *Utopia* zur Gattungsbezeichnung für politische Fiktionen wurde, sollen beispielhaft verschiedene, sich ergebende interpretatorische Zugänge zu einer konkreten Schrift dargestellt werden.

Durch den hermeneutischen Entwurf eines historischen Horizontes in Bezug auf die Zeit Thomas Morus', der Humanist und englischer Lordkanzler war, ebenso wie durch die Entwicklung eines wirkungsgeschichtlichen Bewusstseins

---

[1] Hans-Georg Gadamer, *Gesammelte Werke 1-10*. Tübingen 1985-1995, 10 Bde., 4579 S.; hier ist vor allem das Opus Magnum *Wahrheit und Methode* (1960) herausgehoben zu benennen, welches die Grundlage der Gadamerschen Hermeneutik ist. In der Werkausgabe handelt es sich um Band 1: Hermeneutik I: *Wahrheit und Methode. Grundzüge einer philosophischen Hermeneutik*, Tübingen (5. durchges. u. erw. Aufl.; Gadamer 1986a).

des Werkes sollen sowohl die Möglichkeit eines Verstehenvollzugs dieser kleinen, nur gut hundertseitigen, weltberühmten, bis heute umstrittenen Schrift, die vor nun über 500 Jahren im Dezember 1516 in Löwen erstmals erschienen ist, als auch die Leistungsfähigkeit der philosophischen Hermeneutik Gadamers erkennbar werden.

2. Thomas Morus' *Utopia* als vielschichtiges Werk des Renaissance-Humanismus

Die Mehrdeutigkeit der *Utopia* Morus' erlaubt eine Vielzahl von Interpretationen, die vielleicht gerade die Attraktivität der Schrift und auch ihre Wirkungsmacht bis heute ausmachen. Es kann letztendlich nicht bewertet werden, inwieweit die Sozialstrukturen des Morus'schen Gemeinwesens vom Autor ernst gemeint waren.

Durch die Mehrschichtigkeit des Werkes wird deutlich, dass sich *Utopia* mit dem Gedankengut der Humanisten beschäftigt, so dass mit einer eindimensionalen Interpretation dem Werk in seiner Komplexität nicht beizukommen ist. Der literarische Charakter unterstreicht, dass Morus sich durchaus bewusst ist, "daß nicht nur der Ernst die Wurzeln der Dinge findet, sondern oft noch leichter, weil spielerischer, die Heiterkeit, die Ironie, der Humor." (Süssmuth 1967, 109f.) *Utopia* ist insofern eine humanistische Studie, in der sich Morus mit seinen humanistischen Freunden über den Charakter der Menschen austauscht und Gedanken macht.

Fest steht bereits hier, dass das Werk nicht die Geschlossenheit einer Einheit hat. Es zerfällt in aneinander gestückelte Teile, die ernst gemeint sein können oder auch ironisch, jedenfalls lässt sich dies oft nicht abschließend klären. Dieses Grundproblem hat einst Hubert Schiel in seiner Einführung zum besagten von ihm übertragenen Werk gut erkannt:

> Das schillernde Bild der 'Utopia' hat es möglich gemacht, daß der Sozialist sowohl wie der Kommunist, der Deist wie der Atheist in Morus einen Vorläufer oder Bannerträger seiner Idee glaubt sehen zu dürfen, während ausgerechnet der Christ bei der Schrift dieses katholischen Heiligen mit mehr oder weniger verlegenem Kopfschütteln sich behelfen muß. (Schiel 1947, 14)

Literarisch ist die humanistische Studie einfallsreich und sehr gekonnt geschrieben. Morus spielt ständig mit seinen Lesern, beispielsweise, wenn er Peter Aegid bittet, gegebenenfalls seine Zusammenfassung der Ausführungen des Reiseberichts des Hyhtlodeus zu korrigieren, oder ihn beauftragt, diesen zukünftig zu fragen, in welchem Teil der neuen Welt die Insel der Utopier liege. Denn ausgerechnet dies zu fragen, hatten die beiden vergessen gehabt:

> Wir haben nämlich gar nicht daran gedacht, ihn zu fragen, und er nicht, uns zu sagen, in welcher Gegend jenes neuen Weltteils denn eigentlich Utopia liegt. (Morus 1990, 11)

Ebenso spektakulär endet der Bericht. In der Schlussszene wird zuerst die Dialogform erneut aufgenommen, ihr schließt sich ein leidenschaftliches Plädoyer des Berichterstatters Hythlodeus an, der zwar anfänglich vorgab neutral zu sein, nun aber leidenschaftlich für das utopische Gemeinwesen des Staates *Utopia* eintritt, um dann schlagartig zu enden, da das Abendessen ansteht. Die fiktive Person Morus' beendet dabei den Dialog mit dem Satz:

> Bis dahin kann ich gewiss nicht allem zustimmen, was er [Hythlodeus] sagte (übrigens ohne allen Zweifel ein höchst gebildeter wie weltkundiger Mann!), indessen gestehe ich doch ohne weiteres, dass es in der Verfassung der Utopier sehr vieles gibt, was ich unseren Staaten eingeführt sehen möchte. (Morus 1990, 147f.)

Mit diesem Ende ist erneut alles offen. Aufgrund des anstehenden Abendessens wird die Bewertung des Berichts der Lebensweise der Utopier einfach vertagt. Zugleich nimmt die fiktive Person Morus den Erzähler Raphael Hythlodeus bei der Hand und führt ihn zurück ins Speisezimmer des Hauses. Ein Vorgang, den man durchaus symbolisch als einen Hinweis verstehen kann, dass der Leser sich vom Autor nach Utopia entführen lassen soll, ohne jedoch *Utopia* zu verfallen, "um [ihn] mit geschärftem Blick in die Realität zurückkehren zu lassen." (Schölderle 2012, 14)

All dies zeigt die literarische Qualität und den Humor des Werkes, das ganz auf die in Latein und Griechisch gebildeten Humanisten abzielt. Morus selbst soll eine Übersetzung des Werkes ins Englische ausdrücklich abgelehnt haben. Sicher ist, dass sich die Schrift an befreundete Humanisten wendet, die in der Lage sind, die Schrift mit ihren literarischen Kniffen und Anspielungen richtig einzuordnen (vgl. Süssmuth 1967, 33).

3. Die unterschiedlichen Interpretationsperspektiven der *Utopia*

Nachfolgend werden die wohl bekanntesten und am meisten verbreiteten Interpretationsperspektiven der Morus'schen *Utopia* möglichst wertfrei *in nuce* zusammengefasst, die dem Leser bereits aufzeigen mögen, wie unterschiedlich dieses Werk rezipiert wurde und immer noch bis heute rezipiert wird.

Diese Auflistung beansprucht keine Vollständigkeit für sich, auch wenn davon auszugehen ist, dass es sich bei diesen Interpretationsperspektiven um die gängigsten handelt:

3.1 *Utopia* als Idealstaat bzw. ideales Gemeinwesen

Die wohl weithin verbreiteste und rudimentärste Interpretationsperspektive der *Utopia* sieht das Werk als Entwurf eines Idealstaates bzw. eines idealen Gemeinwesens an. Diese Lesart glaubt, dass Morus ein mustergültiges Gemeinwesen konzipiert habe (vgl. Voigt 1906, iii; vgl. Höffe 2016, 4-8; vgl. Saage 2015, 216; vgl. Saage 1991, 75; vgl. Saage 1997, 77; vgl. Saage 2006, 13f.; vgl. Schmidl 2016, 35; vgl. Pfetsch 2019, 187; vgl. Kroh 2021, 142; vgl. Elias 1982, 101; 118f.). Gregory Claes verkündet exemplarisch, dass "uns mit Thomas Morus' bahnbrechenden Text *Utopia* ein quasi realistischer Bericht einer bedeutend verbesserten Gesellschaft vorliegt." (Claes 2011, 12)

Der Entwurf der *Utopia* sei zwar noch keine Realität, sondern vielmehr eine Fiktion, wie ein zukünftiges ideales Gemeinwesen aussehen sollte, aber die Idee sei denk- und verfolgbar. Damit ist der Entwurf einer besseren Gesellschaft im Diesseits verankert und zugleich ein Gegenentwurf zu den herrschenden Verhältnissen der vorherrschenden Gesellschaft. Selbst wenn die Idee gegenwärtig noch nicht unmittelbar umsetzbar sei, stelle sie doch eine Vision einer Welt dar, die zukünftig erstrebenswert wäre. *Utopia* ist folglich der Traum einer neuen Ordnung, die alle gesellschaftlichen Lebensbereiche umfasst.

Die Zustimmung aller Gesellschaftsmitglieder wird dabei *a priori* als vorausgesetzt angenommen, da das Idealstaatmodell angeblich so perfekt und erstrebenswert sei, dass jedes Mitglied damit einverstanden sein muss. Damit wird zugleich sichergestellt, dass jeder Entwurf eines Idealstaates immer bereits als Fortschritt angesehen werden kann, den man schon deshalb begrüßen müsse, da die Zustimmung der Gesellschaftsmitglieder für diesen gegeben sei.

3.2 *Utopia* als totalitärer Staat

Die konträre Sichtweise zum Entwurf eines Idealstaates bzw. idealem Gemeinwesen findet sich gleichfalls als eine mögliche Interpretation des fiktiven Inselstaates – nämlich: *Utopia* als Totalitarismus. Diese Interpretationsperspektive sieht die Gefahr eines von außen den Menschen vorgegebenen Idealstaatsmodells, das zu einem Stillstand in der Gesellschaftsentwicklung und zu hermetischer Geschlossenheit der Gemeinschaft und ihrer Gesellschaftsform führt, und dadurch bedingt als Endresultat in einen Totalitarismus verfällt.

Dieses totalitäre Endergebnis sei insofern zwingend, da jede "allumfassende Gemeinschaftlichkeit (…) freilich den latenten Totalitarismus der Utopie ausmacht." (Adam 1988, 137) Insoweit sei in jeder Utopie ihre totalitäre Tendenz automatisch bereits angelegt. Diesen radikalen Ansatz von Utopie arbeitet auch Arno Waschkuhn aus, der diese Form der Gemeinschaft der Gerechten als "Selbstgerechte" beschreibt, die sich selbst genug seien und die gezielt ideologisch-politische Ziele verfolgen,[2] die das eigentliche Ziel der Utopie darstellen:

> Wenn wir einen gemeinsamen Nenner suchen, dann ist Utopia zumeist und in erster Linie eine Gemeinschaft der Gerechten, unbezwinglich und unbesiegbar, aber sich selbst genug. In zweiter Linie aber ist es die Keimzelle der Weltrevolution oder auch Weltreformation bzw. -transformation, die durch symbolisch-beispielhafte Darstellungen heraufbeschworen wird. (Waschkuhn 2003, 4)

Vor dem Hintergrund des Zweiten Weltkriegs begreift Sir Karl Popper Utopien als Gegner offener Gesellschaften, die Schuld an den verheerenden totalitären Entgleisungen des 20. Jahrhunderts gehabt hätten, da diese stets geschlossene Systeme seien, Veränderungen sowie Widerspruch in Gesellschaften unterdrücken würden und nur mit Gewalt durchgesetzt werden könnten: "Wie andere vor mir, so gelangte auch ich zu dem Resultat, daß die Idee einer utopischen sozialen Planung großen Stiles ein Irrlicht ist, das uns in einen Sumpf lockt." (Popper 1987, VIII)

Neben Popper wird eine solche Position u. a. Eric Voegelin (1995), Ralf Dahrendorf (1967), Hans Freyer (1920; 2000), Udo Bermbach (1992) und Joachim Fest (1991; 1992, 22) zugesprochen, die sich alle als Gegner von Utopien hervortaten. Eine Utopie stellt für diese Interpretationsperspektive ein unerreichbares Ideal einer perfekten Gesellschaft dar, welches zur Anwendung von Gewalt und Terror zwingt, da, um erfolgreich umgesetzt werden zu können, dieses nur denkbar sei, wenn jedes Individuum sich unbedingt dem Gesamtziel unterstellt. Ohne Gewalt und Terror ließe sich aber die Gesellschaft nie als Ganzes vollständig erfassen. Dies mache das Totalitäre der Utopie aus.

3.3 *Utopia* als sozialistisch-kommunistische Schrift

Das Endziel von Karl Marx und Friedrich Engels ist der wissenschaftliche Sozialismus, aber beide betrachten die Utopie als einen Schritt auf diesem Weg.[3]

---

[2] Dies wird auch von Elise Boulding hervorgehoben. Vgl. Boulding 2000, 30.
[3] Rosemarie Ahrbeck sieht hingegen bei Morus bereits die Antizipierung des wissenschaftlichen Sozialismus als gegeben an: "Morus antizipiert die Erkenntnisse des wissen-

Während der österreichische Sozialdemokrat Karl Kautsky in Thomas Morus bereits den "Vater des utopistischen Sozialismus" (Kautsky 1907, 320) sah, der ein humanistisches Gegenbild zur Gesellschaft seiner Zeit geschaffen habe, das allerdings nach seinem Dafürhalten noch mit einer "seltsamen Inkonsequenz" (ebd., 240) behaftet war, bezeichnet Engels "neue soziale Systeme" als "von vornherein zur Utopie verdammt" (Engels 1962, 194); womit gemeint war, dass Utopien Vorläufer des wissenschaftlichen Sozialismus mit materialistischer Geschichtsauffassung seien. Sprich: Von der Utopie zur Wissenschaft.

Insoweit stellt Morus' *Utopia* für Marx und Engels nur ein Vorläufer in der Entwicklung des Sozialismus bzw. Kommunismus dar, während für Kautsky die Insel *Utopia* ein Endziel zu sein scheint, auch wenn sie noch unerreichbar sei. Dabei sprach die bekannteste Regel des Inselstaates wohl alle drei Theoretiker gleichermaßen an: Die Abschaffung des Privateigentums. Weiterhin entspricht die Aufhebung der ständischen Ordnung, die klassenlose Gesellschaft, die Abschaffung des Geldes sowie des Wettbewerbs, die in den Mittelpunktstellung der Arbeit, wobei gerade nur so viel gearbeitet wird, wie für den Selbsterhalt nötig ist, sowie der egalitäre Charakter der Gesellschaft, die sich in Einheiten von dreißig Familien zweimal am Tag zur gemeinsamen Mahlzeit versammeln und in Gemeinschaftshäusern leben, dem historisch später im Rahmen der "Kommune"-Idee benannten Lebensmodell der hier propagierten Interpretationsperspektive.

Hieraus entstand wohl in der Folge das bis heute in dieser Auslegung vertretene Bild, dass Morus eine Art Vordenker von Karl Marx und folglich Kommunist gewesen sei. Dabei wird gerne auf die heftige Kritik verwiesen, die der Autor Morus seinem Gast im ersten Buch in den Mund legt: "Wo es noch Privatbesitz gibt, wo alle Menschen alle Werte am Maßstab des Geldes messen, da wird es kaum jemals möglich sein, eine gerechte und glückliche Politik zu treiben." (Morus 1990, 53) Dieser Idee liegt zugrunde, dass ein vernünftiger Staat verpflichtet sei, Verhältnisse zu schaffen, die den Bürgern ein glückliches Leben ermöglichen. Selbstredend muss ein solches Leben auf Gleichheit basieren, denn: "Wo es kein Privateigentum gibt, betreibt man ernsthaft die Interessen der Allgemeinheit." (Morus 1990, 142) Daraus entsteht als Resultat der Interessensberücksichtigung der Allgemeinheit, dass in *Utopia* alle reich sind,

---

schaftlichen Sozialismus, wenn er feststellt, daß erst mit der Beseitigung der ökonomischen Gegensätze die Übereinstimmung von individuellen und gesellschaftlichen Interessen, also eine echte Gemeinschaftsbeziehung aller Bürger, möglich wird." (Ahrbeck 1977, 44f).

obwohl es "keine Armen und keine Bettler" gibt und "obschon keiner etwas besitzt." (ebd.)

Der Marxist Ernst Bloch bezeichnete nicht von ungefähr in seinem Opus magnum *Das Prinzip Hoffnung* Morus' Werk *Utopia* als "das erste neuere Gemälde demokratisch-kommunistischer Wunschträume", dem es gelungen sei, dass "Demokratie im humanen Sinn, im Sinn öffentlicher Freiheit und Toleranz mit Kollektivwirtschaft verbunden" (Bloch 1985, 603) worden sei. Die *Utopia* sei daher, so Bloch, zu einer "Art liberales Gedenk- und Bedenkbuch des Sozialismus und Kommunismus" (ebd.) geworden und in Morus sieht er zugleich einen der "edelsten Vorläufer des Kommunismus" (Bloch 1946, 62-70). In ähnlicher Weise wird er neueren Datums von Gerald Munier als "Urvater des Kommunismus" (Munier 2008, Untertitel) bzw. "Ahnherr" (ebd., 298) bezeichnet.

3.4 *Utopia* als christlich-konservative Schrift unter besonderer Auslegung der der Schrift immanenten heidnisch-humanistischen Perspektive

Eine der umstrittensten Aspekte des Werkes *Utopia* ist bis heute der Umstand, dass die Utopier Heiden sind, denen offenkundig ausgerechnet der von der katholischen Kirche zum Heiligen ernannte Thomas Morus das Wort redet. Viele christliche Interpreten zeigen sich fassungslos darüber, dass ausgerechnet der heilige Thomas dem Heidentum und einem nichtchristlichen Staat zugesprochen haben soll, was sich mit seinem eigenen Leben in keiner Weise in Verbindung bringen lässt (vgl. Brockhaus 1929; vgl. Chambers 1946; vgl. Brie 1941; vgl. Möbus Berlin 1953; vgl. Reynolds 1953; vgl. Berglar 1978). Gerhard Möbus bemüht sich unter diesen Prämissen, die heidnische Schrift in einen Grundriss einer christlichen Lehre vom Politischen umzudeuten und eine Versöhnung zu versuchen (vgl. Möbus 1953, 74).

Bekanntlich ist der katholische Märtyrer und papsttreue Morus hingerichtet worden, weil er gegenüber König Heinrich VIII. den Suprematseid nicht leisten wollte, der eine Distanzierung von der römischen Kirche bedeutet hätte. Daher macht es für diese Interpretationsperspektive keinen Sinn, dass er einen heidnischen Staat mit einem rein vernunftbegründeten Glauben als Ideal sich erträumt haben soll. Es macht den Umstand folglich umso erstaunlicher, dass die Utopier trotz gewisser Parallelen zum Christentum in der Schrift keine Christen, sondern Heiden sind. Allerdings entspringt dies gewissermaßen umso mehr dem Konzept der fernen Insel Utopia als Fiktion, da auf dieser unbekannten Insel kaum Christen hausen konnten, denn dann hätte die Utopier nicht mehr unbekannt sein können.

Der Weltreisende Raphael Hythlodeus, der den Utopiern vom Christentum berichtet habe, behauptet, dass diesen das Christentum gefallen hätte, auch weil er diesen zu berichten wusste: "Christus habe die gemeinschaftliche (kommunistische) Lebensführung seiner Jünger gutgeheißen, und dass diese in den Kreisen der echtesten Christen noch heute üblich sei." (Morus 1990, 128) Darüber hinaus konnte er ihnen von Jesus Christi berichten, dessen Lehre, Sitten und vollbrachten Wunder sowie über den Mut der standhaften christlichen Märtyrer (ebd.), was letztlich dazu führte, dass viele willig zum Christentum übergetreten seien. Merkwürdig ist, dass der christliche Glaube für die Utopier Ähnlichkeit mit ihrem heidnischen Glauben zu haben scheint, der angeblich bei ihnen aber tiefste Wurzeln geschlagen habe – und dies, obwohl viele sich nach nur einem Bericht des Hythlodaeus von diesem unmittelbar lösen und zum Christentum übertreten. Darüber hinaus ist schwer vorstellbar, dass die Utopier, die einem vernunftbegründeten Glauben folgen, nun auf die Offenbarungsreligion des Christentums umschwenken, ohne ansatzweise den fundamentalen Unterschied zu erkennen.

Fest steht, dass Morus in seiner *Utopia* nicht nur bewusst ein heidnisches Volk in den Mittelpunkt seiner Schrift rückt, dessen Staatverfassung als mustergültig gilt und dessen Staatswesen unterstellt wird, tolerant zu sein und einen religiösen Pluralismus zu erlauben, sondern zugleich mit dem Idealstaat *Utopia* den christlichen Glauben an die Erlösung im Jenseits untergräbt, indem eine bereits diesseitige innerweltliche Vollendung des Glücks im Rahmen einer besten Staatsverfassung erzielt werden könne. Das heidnische Volk der Utopier postuliert darüber hinaus ein pragmatisches Scheidungsrecht (vgl. Morus 1990, 108f.), ermöglicht Geistlichen die Ehe (vgl. Morus 1990, 78; 134ff.), lässt sogar Frauen als Priester zu (vgl. Morus 1990, 136) und sieht allgemeine Religionsfreiheit (vgl. Morus 1990, 127ff.) vor. Gewisse religiöse Praktiken sind letztlich für Christen noch irritierender: Etwa die Tatsache, dass sie die Sonne oder den Mond oder die Vorfahren verehren (vgl. Morus 1990, 127) und an "das all-eine Wesen der göttlichen Majestät" (Morus 1990, 138) glauben, den sie als "Mythras" (Morus 1990, 127; 138) bezeichnen.

Insoweit ist es nicht überraschend, dass die katholische Orthodoxie die Schrift seit ihrem Erscheinen als Scherz betrachtet hat, da sie ansonsten, wenn das Werk als ernst aufgefasst würde, an einigen Punkten eine Diskussion über eine Veränderung der religiösen Regeln und Sitten des Christentums führen müsste. Dementsprechend wurde die Schrift als ein Jux verstanden, der mit heidnischen Aspekten nur spielt. Getreu dem Motto:

> Vielleicht hatte Morus sich in der Utopia nur spielerisch eine heidnische 'Brille' aufgesetzt, sei es, weil er das Verhältnis von Heidentum

(Vernunft) und Christentum (Glaube) exemplarisch hatte darstellen wollen (Jaeckel) (die Vernunft der Heiden als Vorstufe des Glaubens, diesem harmonierend, nicht konkurrierend), sei es, weil er hatte sagen wollen: 'seht, wie tolerant und friedlich selbst schon die Heiden sind!' (Ottmann 1996, 336)

3.5 *Utopia* als Gemeinwesen von strenger utilitaristischer Rationalität

Utopia wird weithin mit der Verfassung eines idealen Staates gleichgesetzt. Dieses Konzept eines Musterstaates wird gemäß der Interpretationsperspektive der *Utopia* als Gemeinwesen von strenger utilitaristischer Rationalität, also als ein durch und durch rationales Gemeinwesen auf Lustgewinn abzielendes Gemeinwesen gesteigert, denn in dieser Sichtweise nimmt der Staat zugleich eine allumfassende Rationalität für sich in Anspruch: "Alle Teilbereiche erscheinen als Funktionen eines rationalen Beziehungsgefüges, welches menschlichem Kalkül sein Dasein verdankt" (Kluxen 2003, 41). Für Dietmar Herz ist dies der Kern der Utopie, denn "Morus deutet damit das große Thema seines Buches an, das sich durch alle Bereiche der Erörterung zieht: die Notwendigkeit einer rationalen Gestaltung der Politik und des Lebens – und die Unempfänglichkeit der Politik für einen solchen Rationalismus." (Herz 1999, 55)

Das gesamte Gemeinwesen sei demnach ausschließlich auf utilitaristischer Rationalität gegründet (vgl. Rötzer 1963/64, 357), denn der Staat sei "eine Manifestation der Vernunft" (vgl. Süssmuth 1967, 109), da die "reine ratio (…) im Staat Utopia bis ins Extrem durchkonstruiert" (ebd.) sei und so das Prinzip der Lust als das anzustrebende optimale Resultat angesehen werde, mit welchem *Utopia* den späteren klassischen Utilitarismus vorwegnehme. Die utilitaristische Rationalität sei das dominierende Prinzip an der der Nutzen der Gemeinschaft gemessen würde, was letztlich ausschließlich auf die Generierung allgemeiner Wohlfahrt als ökonomische Zielgröße abstellt. Annemarie Pieper versteht daher die Kernaussage dieser Interpretationsperspektive wie folgt: "Der Slogan vom größten Glück der größten Zahl könnte auch als Leitfaden für die utopische Moral gelten." (Pieper 2016, 91)

Diese Glückseligkeit erreicht aber nur, wer in die staatlichen Gesetze und Regeln *Utopias* einlenkt. Nur innerhalb dieser kann ein glückliches Leben stattfinden, da die Gesetze und Regeln einerseits zur Vernunft führen und andererseits gerade deshalb nicht gegen die Natur der Menschen stehen. Dies sei wahr, da die Tatsachen in *Utopia* dies bestätigen (vgl. Morus 1990, 70). Dinge hingegen, die man selbst als angenehm empfindet oder von denen man sich einbildet, dass diese erstrebenswert seien, dienen nicht der Erreichung der

Glückseligkeit, da sie nicht dem gemäßigten und vernünftigen Leben der Gemeinschaft dienen und jegliches Streben nach Luxusgütern, nach sinnlicher Ausschweifung oder nach Untätigkeit und Faulenzerei unterliegt deshalb der Verachtung der Utopier.

Dementsprechend ist das Sammeln von Gold und Silber verrufen, Perlen und Diamanten sowie andere materielle Gegenstände, mit denen sich nur Kinder schmücken, gelten als verpönt. Wertzuweisung aufgrund von Seltenheit gilt als "Torheit der Menschen" (Morus 1990, 82) und somit als unvernünftig und verachtungswürdig. Allein der Verzicht auf untätige Mitglieder der Gesellschaft, der sich durch den Wegfall der Standespersonen und Edelleute, also des Adels, sowie deren Dienerschaft, des Klerus, der Großgrundbesitzer, der gesunden Bettler und der Tagediebe einstellt, führt dazu, dass die Arbeitszeit täglich auf nur sechs Stunden sinkt. Die dadurch gewonnene Freizeit nutzen die Utopier hauptsächlich zu geistigen Studien, in der sie unübertroffen sind und die nach den Vorgaben *Utopias* das wahre Vergnügen ausmacht (vgl. Morus 1990, 68ff.; 85).

Das rudimentäre utilitaristische Prinzip "vom größten Glück der größten Zahl" zur Maximierung der Wohlfahrt werde z.B. beim Vorrang der Zwangsarbeit vor der Todesstrafe angewandt, die erfolge, da die Gefangenen durch ihre Arbeit mehr als durch ihren Tod der Gemeinschaft nutzen und zugleich als warnendes Beispiel andere abschrecken, ähnliche Taten zu vollbringen. Die Überbleibsel an Straf- und Zwangsarbeit resultieren aus einem letzten Aufbegehren von Subjektivität, der sich dem utopischen Funktionalismus nicht beugen will, ist aber für *Utopia* als Idealstaat nicht maßgeblich (vgl. Kluxen 2003, 48f.). Das Prinzip des Nutzens schlägt sich auch in der in *Utopia* gängigen Praxis der Euthanasie nieder, die aus einer utilitaristischen Betrachtung erfolgt und für diese unter Abwägung der Vor- und Nachteile als Notwendigkeit eingestuft wird, da der Sterbende sonst der Gemeinschaft auf der Kasse liegen würde (vgl. Morus 1990, 106).

Aber auch sonst findet dieses Prinzip des Nutzens allumfassend Anwendung, denn die Utopier verzichten z.B. vollständig und freiwillig auf irgendwelche Laster, denn es "gibt dort nirgends eine Möglichkeit zum Müßiggang, keinen Vorwand zum Faulenzen. Keine Weinschenke, kein Bierhaus, nirgends ein Bordell, keine Gelegenheit zur Verführung, keine Spelunken, kein heimliches Zusammenhocken, sondern überall sieht die Öffentlichkeit dem einzelnen zu und zwingt ihn zu der gewohnten Arbeit und zur Ehrbarkeit beim Vergnügen." (Morus 1990, 80) Stattdessen ist die weitgehende Mobilisierung aller Arbeitsressourcen das oberste Ziel.

Vorgeblich kennen die Utopier keine Einheitsreligion und dennoch findet der Glaubenspluralismus in der Vernunft eine gewisse Grenze, die sich damit eigentlich am Prinzip der utilitaristischen Rationalität orientieren muss. Es wird behauptet, dass die Utopier "sich alle nach und nach (...) von der Mannigfaltigkeit abergläubischer Vorstellungen [losmachen], und statt dessen (...) ihre Anschauungen zu der geschilderten einen Religion [verschmelzen], die alle anderen an Vernünftigkeit (...) übertrifft." (Morus 1990, 127f.)

Alles Geistige im Bereich von Bildung, Erziehung und Wissenschaft gelte als Ausdruck des Rationalen und genieße hohe Wertschätzung bei den Utopiern. Es wird einfach normativ vorausgesetzt, dass "Würfel- und Kartenspiele, Faulenzerei und Ausschweifungen verpönt oder gar unbekannt sind" und "sich die morgendlichen Vorlesungen stets einer großen Zahl von Zuhörern [erfreuen]." (Schölderle 2012, 34) Jegliche Form von Subjektivität wird zu unterbinden versucht. An ihrer Stelle treten "nur Bildung und kontrollierte Lebensführung", die die Vorherrschaft der Vernunft nicht gefährden (vgl. Kluxen 2003, 46). Diese Prämisse wird von den Utopiern nicht infrage gestellt, denn "[d]a die Rationalität der utopischen Gesetze als feststehend betrachtet wird, wird auch das Erziehungskonzept als perfekt angesehen." (Schmidtke 2016, 207)

Vielmehr gehen die Utopier vollkommen unreflektiert davon aus, dass alle Gesetze und Regelungen ihres idealen Gemeinwesens als normativ gesetzt betrachtet werden müssen, da diese als vernünftig, gerecht und damit alternativlos angesehen werden. Daher stellen sie folglich *per se* perfektes Wissen und Wahrheit zugleich dar. Ebenso wird suggeriert, dass die Utopier der modernen Naturwissenschaft nachstreben, deren Erkenntnisse die Befriedigung der natürlichen Bedürfnisse in Form von Produktion und Konsum zum obersten Ziel habe, die mittels der Unterwerfung der Natur erreicht werden sollen. Für technische Erfindungen begabt hätten sie Brutmaschinen für die Hühnerzucht, neue Methoden um Wetterveränderungen zu erfassen, Buchdruckverfahren sowie die Technik der Papierbereitung entwickelt (vgl. Morus 1990, 60f.; 88; 104).

Der Text ist mehr als überreich an normativ gesetzten Vernunftgründen für das Gemeinwesen *Utopias*. Er kann daher diese Interpretationsperspektive hier nicht zur Gänze erörtert werden. Exemplarisch können deshalb nur noch ein paar einzelne Details herausgegriffen werden, um die benannte Interpretationsperspektive noch genauer zu veranschaulichen:

• Die Utopier leben in Siedlungs- und Sozialstrukturen, die streng rational konzipiert sind und auf Funktionalität, auf Homogenität und soziale Kontrolle ausgelegt sind. Insoweit schlägt sich die strenge Rationalität auch in ihrer Stadtplanung und Architektur nieder. Sie sind auf Austauschbarkeit angelegt, so dass Morus selbst schreibt: "Wer eine Stadt kennt, kennt sie alle." (Morus 1990,

62) Zugleich soll die Siedlungsform auch die gesellschaftlichen Beziehungen zum Ausdruck bringen und widerspiegeln (vgl. Bruyn 1996, 61-69).

• Der geometrische Grundriss der Insel Utopia ist ausschließlich zweckmäßig angelegt. Die Tatsache, dass die Küsten *Utopias* "gewissermaßen durch einen Kreisbogen von fünfhundert Meilen Umfang (...) der ganzen Insel die Gestalt des zunehmenden Mondes" (Morus 1990, 58) geben, zeigt bereits, dass es bei dieser künstlich angelegten Insel um maximale Observation und Kontrolle – ähnlich einer später *Panopticon* genannten Anlage – geht und keine Rückzugsräume erwünscht sind. Insoweit ist der Idealstaat auch eine streng rationale Überwachungsgesellschaft.

• Die Insel *Utopia* setzt sich aus 54 gleichförmigen funktionalistischen, dem Grundriss nach fast quadratischen Städten zusammen (vgl. Bruyn 1996, 61-69; vgl. Morus 1990, 59). Jede dieser Städte, "alle geräumig und prächtig, in Sprache, Sitten, Einrichtungen, Gesetzen genau übereinstimmend" (ebd.), ist von der nächsten Stadt einen Tagesmarsch entfernt, der wiederum genau vierundzwanzig Meilen Entfernung entspricht (vgl. ebd.). Die Straßen der Insel sind zweckmäßig angeordnet, d.h., die Straßen nehmen "ebenso auf das Verkehrsbedürfnis wie auf den Windschutz Rücksicht." (Morus 1990, 63) Die Städte sind uniform von jeweils mindestens zwölf Meilen Ackerland umgeben, welches planmäßig zugeteilt wurde. Eine Erweiterung ihres Gebietes wünscht keine Stadt (vgl. Morus 1990, 60).

• Die Städte sind innerhalb ihrer Stadtmauern alle gleich ausgelegt: Die Straßen sind zwischen den Fronten der Häuser stets 20 Fuß breit. Die Wohnhäuser sind in einer langen, den Straßenzug ausmachende Reihe angeordnet, an deren Rückseite sich jeweils ein Garten befindet. Alle zehn Jahre werden die Wohnungen durch Los getauscht, so dass niemand Nachteile und Ungleichheiten befürchten muss (vgl. Morus, 63). Genau in der Mitte der 54 Städte des Inselstaates findet sich die Hauptstadt Amaurotum gelegen, wo sich aus diesem Grund auch der Sitz des Obersten Senats angesiedelt hat. Jeweils drei Vertreter der 54 Städte bilden diesen. Hier werden alle Aspekte des Staates *Utopia* verhandelt, u.a. auch die Verteilung des Wohlstandes sowie die Außenbeziehungen des Staates.

• Alle Haushalte auf dem Lande zählen an Männern und Frauen weniger als vierzig Personen plus zwei an den Haushalt gebundene Ackersklaven. Der Hausvorstand besteht aus Hausvater und Hausmutter, gesetzte reife Personen, die die Großfamilie leiten. Zwanzig Personen gehen aus jedem Haushalt jährlich in die Stadt zurück. Im Gegenzug kommen zwanzig neue Personen, die zwei Jahre vor Ort in der Landwirtschaft ihren Dienst verrichten und von den verbliebenden zwanzig Personen des Vorjahres angeleitet werden. In der Erntezeit werden Bürger aus den Städten aufs Land als Erntehelfer geschickt, um die Ernte einzubringen (vgl. Morus 1990, 60f.).

• Neben der Tätigkeit in der Landwirtschaft, die allen gemein ist, muss jeder Utopier noch ein Handwerk als Beruf erlernen. Grundsätzlich gilt, dass jeder Mann und jede Frau täglich sechs Stunden Arbeit verrichten müssen. Am Vor- wie am Nachmittag jeweils drei Stunden. An den täglich in den Frühstunden stattfindenden öffentlichen Vorlesungen müssen nur diejenigen verpflichtend teilnehmen, die namentlich zum Studium ausgewählt und dafür von der Arbeit freigestellt wurden. Dies sind kaum fünfhundert Personen (vgl. Morus 1990, 66f., 68, 70).

• Die Einheiten von dreißig Familien versammeln sich zweimal täglich zur gemeinsamen Mahlzeit "durch den Schall eherner Posaunen gerufen" (Morus 1990, 76) in den Städten zum Essen. Auf dem Lande werden die gemeinsamen Mahlzeiten in der Großfamilie abgehalten. Jeder Häuserblock in der Stadt hat eine eigene Halle, die u.a. als Speisehalle genutzt wird und jeder dieser Hallen sind immer genau "dreißig Familien zugeteilt, auf jeder Seite fünfzehn, die dort ihre Mahlzeiten einnehmen." (Morus 1990, 75) Vor der Essenszeit gibt es eine moralische Vorlesung, deren Inhalt im Anschluss die Tischältesten in "ehrbare[n], aber nicht etwa trockene[n], sondern recht unterhaltende[n] Reden" (Morus 1990, 78) aufgreifen (vgl. Morus 1990, 75-78).

• Bei den Utopiern wird Prunk in Form von besonderer Kleidung strikt abgelehnt. Seidene Gewänder werden verachtet, Gold als unanständig betrachtet. Die Kleidung ist schlicht und einfach. Mit der Ausnahme der Geschlechter und der Unverheirateten ist die Kleidung einheitlich und gleichartig für alle Lebensalter (vgl. Morus 1990, 66f.; 84f.).

Utopia ist kurzum ein total durchrationalisiertes gesellschaftliches Steuerungssystem, was erstmals als Entwurf die Möglichkeit in der Neuzeit eröffnete, die Gestaltung einer Gesellschaft als Ganzes hypothetisch in die Hand zu nehmen (vgl. Kluxen 2003, 58):

> Das gesamte Konzept Utopias basiert auf dem Glauben an die Kraft der Vernunft. Sie allein, und nicht die Gier nach Macht oder Reichtum, ist in der Lage, einen Ort zu errichten, an dem die Menschen glücklich leben. (Manguel 2017, 14)

Um diesen strengen Staat der Vernunft zu erreichen, muss aber jede individuelle Unvernunft oder Subjektivität ausgeschlossen werden. Alles und jeder muss sich hierfür der Vernunft unterordnen. Folglich steht die Verhaltensteuerung der Einwohner im Mittelpunkt, die sich in ihrer Individualität sowohl der Vorherrschaft des Systems als auch der Gleichförmigkeit seiner Einrichtungen beugen müssen.

3.6 *Utopia* als Satire, Parodie und Spielerei

Die folgende Interpretationsperspektive sieht allein die Wortschöpfungen in Morus' *Utopia* als so aufschlussreich an, dass sich die Frage der Zufälligkeit erübrige. Der ganze Text sei ein Gedankenspiel mit Witz und Geist, den Dietmar Herz als ein "Meisterwerk der Ironie" (Herz 1999, 50) lobt, der sich nur äußerst schwer fassen lasse. Daher ließe sich auch kaum bestreiten, dass Satire und Parodie einen gehörigen Anteil am Erfolg eines Buches haben, dass sich selbst als "*ein wahrhaft goldenes Büchlein, genauso wohltuend wie heiter*" anzupreisen erlaubt. Diese Sichtweise entspricht demnach einer weiteren Interpretationsperspektive der *Utopia*, die die humanistische Satire, Parodie und Spielerei als den eigentlichen Zweck der Schrift ansieht (vgl. Brie 1936/1937; vgl. Ritter 1940; vgl. Doren 1927, 158-205; vgl. Lewis 1954, 165-81; vgl. Kuon 1984).

In der leicht abgeschwächten Form der Interpretation des Werkes gibt es eine Reihe von Interpreten, die zwar konstatieren, dass Satire, Parodie und Ironie zum Werk gehören und seinen Spaß ausmachen, aber es dennoch ebenso klare Botschaften der Kritik im zweiten Buch gebe, die sich gezielt an die Leserschaft richten (vgl. Süssmuth 1967, 35; vgl. Erzgräber 1983, 40; vgl. Münkler 1992, 208). Hans Süssmuth führt dazu aus: "Im Mittelpunkt steht der ludus mit der ratio. Morus weiß, daß nicht nur der Ernst die Wurzeln der Dinge findet, sondern oft noch leichter, weil spielerischer, die Heiterkeit, die Ironie, der Humor." (Süssmuth 1967, 109f.) Angeblich würde der Autor daher dem Leser mit dem Stilmittel der Ironie vielmehr nur in eine alternative Welt führen und "verfolgt damit das Anliegen, diesen mit geschärftem Blick in die Realität zurückkehren zu lassen." (Schölderle 2012, 14) Hans Maier stellt dazu ebenso affirmierend fest: "Die Dialoge transportieren nicht nur Sinn, sondern manchmal auch tiefsinnigen Ulk." (Maier 1982, 49)

Einige kritische Töne seien also ernst gemeint – nämlich immer dann, wenn diese Dinge angeblich Morus wichtig waren: "Mores tiefe Ironie ist die eines Menschen, der die Trivialitäten, die einen großen Teil unserer menschlichen Erfahrung ausmachen, als lächerlich durchschaut, während er seinen Ernst und seine Achtung für die Dinge reserviert, die er für wesentlich hält. Bisweilen wendet er seinen Witz auch auf Dinge, für die er sonst eine aufrichtige Achtung zeigt." (Kristeller 1982, 25) Thomas Schölderle stellt daher zu Recht fest: "Zusammengefasst heißt das: Keine der Figuren der *Utopia* ist eine eindeutige und geschlossene Gestalt. Im Laufe des Dialogs widersprechen sich die Figuren nicht nur gegenseitig, sondern mitunter sogar sich selbst." (Schölderle 2012, 32)

Die ironische Übertreibung im Spiel der *Utopia* beginnt bereits mit einem einleitenden Brief, in dem Morus sich an den Stadtschreiber von Antwerpen Peter Aegid wendet und ihn bittet, sein Gedächtnisprotokoll des gemeinsamen Gesprächs mit Raphael Hythlodeus zu überprüfen und falls nötig zu korrigieren. Für die Berichterstattung aus *Utopia* selbst wird weiterhin besagter Hythlodeus als Gewährsmann und eigentlicher Autor eingeführt. Das gesamte Schauspiel ist, wenn man dieser Interpretationsperspektive folgt, eine humanistische Spielerei, Parodie und Satire, die sich als Schrift ausschließlich an einen ausgewählten Zirkel von hochgebildeten Humanisten ihres Zeitalters wendet, der zwar wesentliche Kritik der Zustände der Zeit untereinander austauscht, aber dessen Austausch zugleich dem Zeitvertreib und der Unterhaltung dienen soll.

Die Schwierigkeit liege daher darin, die ironischen Übertreibungen aufzulösen, geistreich verkehrte Sachverhalte zu erfassen und ihren Aussagewert zu erkennen. Mit diesem anspruchsvollen Rätsel zeige Morus, an welchen Kreis von Lesern sich das Werk richtet und welches der Schlüssel zu seinem Verständnis ist. Heute würde man einen solchen Ansatz wohl *Infotainment* nennen.

3.7 *Utopia* als Fürstenspiegel

Die in einem Fürstenspiegel niedergelegten Grundsätze richtigen Regierens wandten sich seit der frühen Antike bis zur frühen Neuzeit als ermahnende und belehrende Schrift an einen König bzw. Fürst oder dessen Thronfolger. Demnach ist es möglich, Morus' *Utopia* als ein Fürstenspiegcl aufzufassen (vgl. Tremmel 2016; vgl. Herz 1993, 27; vgl. Herz 1999): "*Utopia* wird damit zu einem Kompendium von Ratschlägen für die Gestaltung der Politik eines Landes. Die Rationalität der Politik ist die Klammer, die alle erörterten Bereiche zusammenhält; sie strukturiert die Argumente. *Utopia* wird so zu einer umfassenden Staatslehre." (ebd., 67f.)

Folgende Kriterien sollen für den utopischen Fürstenspiegel gelten:

a. Politische Utopien sind Staatstheorien, die eine fiktive, aber innerweltliche Gesellschaft und ein fiktives, innerweltliches Staatsmodell beschreiben.

b. Der Verfasser erwartet nicht die Umsetzung seiner Utopie in naher Zukunft – sprich: Nicht zu seinen Lebzeiten.

c. Die Utopie selbst ist immer allegorisch oder achron. Dies entspricht dem narrativen Charakter ihrer Gesellschaftskritik. D. h. die Utopie findet nie in der erlebten Gegenwart statt, sondern ist außerhalb der bekannten geographischen und menschlichen Erfahrungswelt.

d. Jede Utopie entwickelt ihre eigene "Wirklichkeit" und dient als Tugend- und Pflichtenlehre eines Herrschers (Fürst) oder dessen Anwärter, um ihm die Grundsätze richtigen Herrschens nahezulegen.

Es gibt eine Reihe von Morus-Interpreten, die dieser Deutung das Wort reden. Exemplarisch kann dies bei Hans Glunz gezeigt werden, der feststellt: "Damit schließt sich die *Utopia* in die Reihe der Fürstenspiegel ein, die mindestens seit dem 12. Jahrhundert eine stehende Literaturgattung waren und seit dem 15. Jahrhundert (Hoccleve) in England eigenartig wiederauflebten, indem im Mäzenverhältnis des Fürsten zum Dichter dieser die geistig-sittliche Beratung des Gönners übernahm." (Glunz 1938, 21)

Morus habe allerdings im Gegensatz zu seinem Freund Erasmus, der in seiner ebenso 1516 erschienen Fürsten-Anleitung mit dem Titel *Institutio Principis Christiani* ausschließlich die Person des Fürsten in den Mittelpunkt gestellt hat, die ganze Gesellschaft zum Gegenstand seiner Schrift gemacht (vgl. Kluxen 2003, 41). Darüber hinaus sei Morus' Ansatz laut Kurt Kluxen äußerst innovativ gewesen, denn "[d]as hatte bisher noch kein Fürstenspiegel in Betracht gezogen, daß die Institutionen den Menschen schaffen, welcher diese Institutionen dann trägt. Das ist der Faden ernsthafter Gedankenarbeit, der die freie Imagination des Zweiten Buches durchzieht." (ebd., 55)

Glunz geht noch weiter, indem er davon spricht was über den engeren Zweck eines Fürstenspiegels hinaus der Sinn der *Utopia* sei – nämlich:

Eigenart, Macht und Dauer des Staates werden getragen und erhalten durch das Ethos des Fürsten und seines Rates, diese nur auf ihr natürliches Dasein hin, als *homines naturales* betrachtet. Der vollkommene Staat setzt die waltende Voraussicht eines gestaltenden Geistes voraus, eines Fürsten, der qua Fürst und Staatsoberhaupt nur seinen Naturanlagen Lauf läßt und so Gutes, einen Staat zum Glücke der Bewohner, bewirkt. Der Staat steht und fällt mit dem Ethos, das ihn beherrscht und dessen Ausdruck er ist. (Glunz 1938, Anm. 2, 23)

Als Utopie gilt demnach eine Idee, die zwar denkbar, aber nicht unmittelbar umzusetzen ist, und die einen Wunschtraum, ein Konzept oder eine Vision einer Welt oder einer Zeit präsentiert, in der eine neue gesellschaftliche, religiöse oder technische Ordnung herrscht. Der Fürstenspiegel *Utopia* soll hierfür als Handreichung an den Herrscher die richtige Anleitung geben. Er war folglich gemäß dieser Interpretationsperspektive dann eine Gebrauchsanweisung zur Weltverbesserung, die sich demnach an den englischen König Heinrich VIII. richtete.

3.8 *Utopia* als "experimentum rationis"

Eine weitere mögliche Lesart der *Utopia* ist die eines "experimentum rationis", also eines Gedankenexperiments. Sicher erscheint für diese Interpretationsperspektive, dass *Utopia* nicht als das umfassende sozialreformerische Werk begriffen werden kann, als dass es vielfach in der Geschichte der Utopieforschung dargestellt wurde und mancherorts immer noch wird. Es handele sich demnach gerade nicht um ein streng utilitaristisch-rationales Gedankenexperiment, sondern ausschließlich um ein Gedankenexperiment, das einen Spielraum zum Debattieren von allen möglichen und denkbaren Staatsentwürfen eröffnen soll (vgl. Jäckel 1955; vgl. Hermand 1981; vgl. Arnswald 2010; vgl. Schölderle 2012, 14; vgl. Schölderle 2016).

Das Werk sei folglich niemals als anzustrebendes Ideal zu verstehen gewesen. Zugleich aber sei es nicht einfach nur als eine intellektuelle Spielerei anzusehen, denn zu ernst sei der Hintergrund, vor dem dieses fiktive Gedankenexperiment stattfindet, zu beißend die Kritik an den Zuständen der Gegenwart, als dass es keine Konsequenzen zeitigen könnte. Von der Spielerei mit der wahren Bedeutung der Eigennamen bis zu den ironischen Relativierungen oder gar der inneren Inkonsistenz seiner Ausführungen weise vieles darauf hin, dass der Autor Morus seine Leser zu einer kritischen Hinterfragung seines angeblich idealen Gesellschaftsentwurfs ebenso wie zur kritischen Hinterfragung der gesellschaftlichen Realität der damaligen Zeit bewegen wollte. Der offene Ausgang der Unterhaltung zwischen Morus und Hythlodeus sei gleichfalls ein Beleg hierfür. Warum solle das Gespräch sonst offen enden, wenn doch alle Probleme und Übel beseitigt wären?

Morus will dem vorherrschenden Diskurs seiner Zeit eine Gegenposition gegenüberstellen, die er mittels eines detaillierten entgegengesetzten Gesellschaftsentwurfs stark macht. Ähnlich einer fiktiven Anti-Ideologie zur bestehenden realen Ideologie soll diese den Leser in eine Außenperspektive versetzen, die es ihm erlaubt, sich unvoreingenommen neuen Gedanken zu stellen. Es wird nichts darüber ausgesagt, ob Morus den von ihm als Diskussionsgrundlage entworfenen Gesellschaftsentwurf befürwortet oder nicht. Auch wenn dieser Entwurf selbst einen Absolutheitsanspruch enthält, sagt dies ebenso nichts darüber aus, ob der Autor diesen auch teilt. Dies alles deutet darauf hin, dass es dem Autor der *Utopia* vermutlich ausschließlich darum geht, einen Freiraum zu schaffen, in dem das Pro und Contra bestimmter Ideen abstrakt intellektuell diskutiert und abgewogen werden kann.

Die Insel *Utopia* ist somit eine gezielte Provokation, die eine Infragestellung der realen, gesellschaftlichen Wirklichkeit zum Ziel hat. Die Ironie und Satire sollen die Ambivalenz des Textes unterstreichen, so dass dieser als Gedankenexperiment vom Leser hinterfragt werden muss. Das Oszillieren zwischen vermeintlichen Reformmodell und Ironie ist dementsprechend vom Autor gewünscht (vgl. ebd., 72).

Statt weiterhin gedankenlos den *Status quo* als gottgegeben anzusehen, sollen die Leser sich zur radikalen Erkenntnis der miserablen und dringend verbesserungswürdigen politischen und gesellschaftlichen Verhältnisse Europas des begonnenen 16. Jahrhunderts durchringen. Der fiktionale Entwurf der Insel *Utopia* stellt keine Rezeptur eines mustergültigen Staatswesens dar. Daher geht es letztlich primär um ein lehrreiches und anregendes Gedankenspiel mit dem didaktischen Ziel, den Möglichkeitssinn der Leserschaft anzuregen und zum Entwurf von neuen möglichen Staatsverfassungen und alternativen Gesellschaftsentwürfen aufzufordern (vgl. Barnouw 1985, 31).

4. Die hermeneutische Herausforderung der Schrift *Utopia*

Die zusammengefassten, stark voneinander abweichenden Interpretationsperspektiven des Klassikers *Utopia* belegen, dass jede Interpretation sich in einem Spannungsverhältnis von zwei Extremen bewegt – nämlich "zwischen der Vorstellung, daß der Plan einer besseren Gesellschaft, der darin entwickelt wird, den gleichen Grad der Wirklichkeitsbezogenheit hatte wie etwa Marx' *Kommunistisches Manifest* und der entgegengesetzten Auffassung, daß dieser Plan nichts als ein merry jest, ein fröhlicher Scherz ohne jeden Wirklichkeitsbezug, war." (Elias 1982, 118)

Diese extreme Spannbreite möglicher unterschiedlicher Auslegungen des Werkes zeigt auf, wie sehr ein Text auf zusätzliche prozessurale Aufarbeitung angewiesen sein kann. Die Gadamersche Hermeneutik ermöglicht entweder ein gemeinsames Werksverständnis durch Verständigung oder zumindest einen inhaltlichen Austausch über unterschiedliche, konkurrierenden Werksverständnisse. Die philosophische Disziplin der Hermeneutik kann Ereignisse, Zusammenhänge oder auch Textstellen in neuen Sprechweisen übermitteln helfen und so versuchen, die unterschiedlichen Auslegungen in einem Dialog zueinander in Verbindung zu setzen.

Die jeweilige Interpretationsperspektive ist offenkundig eingebettet in einen sozialen und kulturellen Kontext, der die Interpretation oder Vermittlung prägt und Ausdruck einer Zeit, einer Mode oder einer spezifischen Anforderung einer Ideologie bzw. einer vorherrschenden Theorie ist. Wenn Norbert Elias daher fordert, dass es "[e]ine ausgewogenere und differenziertere Diagnose (…) als Bezugsrahmen eines Prozeßmodells [bedarf] (ebd.), lässt sich darauf verweisen, dass der hermeneutische Dialog im Sinne der Philosophie Hans-Georg Gadamers genau einen solchen Bezugsrahmen zum Aushandeln der verschiedenen Interpretationsperspektiven anbietet.

Bei dem Klassiker *Utopia* wird von Anfang an in doppelter Weise auf die Hermeneutik verwiesen: Denn neben dem notwendigen hermeneutischen Dialog im Nachgang zur Diskussion der unterschiedlichen und konkurrierenden Interpretationsperspektiven verweist Morus' *Utopia* intern bereits auf eine Art offen dargelegten hermeneutischen Dialog zwischen den Protagonisten in der Schrift. Schließlich stellt die Schrift gerade nicht auf eine Realisierung ab, sondern vielmehr ist sie eine Diskussion über die herrschenden Übel ihrer Zeit, so dass das Ende des Gesprächs in der Schrift bewusst offen und unbestimmt bleibt, und der dort begonnene Dialog der in der Schrift benannten Akteure von den Lesern aufgegriffen werden und auf diese übergehen soll. Insoweit gibt es kein Zweifel, dass die Schrift in doppelter Hinsicht als ein philosophisches Gespräch geplant und entworfen wurde.

Umso weniger macht eine Aussage von Gerald Munier Sinn, die hermeneutische Herausforderung erst gar nicht anzunehmen und die verschiedenen Interpretationsperspektiven so zu belassen wie sie sind. Munier urteilt wie folgt: "Ob dies ein sonderlich fruchtbares Unterfangen ist, muss bezweifelt werden, denn die Interpretationen werden damit lediglich in Schubladen sortiert und am Resultat ändert die ohnehin nichts: Die *Utopia* hat eine Wirkungsgeschichte sowohl im sozialistischen Lager, als auch bei Humanisten und Katholiken entfaltet, egal welche eigenen Absichten Morus mit der Schrift verfolgt haben mag und ob diese dezidiert praktisch-politischer Natur, gar sozialrevolutionär oder nur humorvoll-satirisch waren." (Munier 2008, 142f.)

Dies kann und ist aber gerade nicht der Sinn der *Utopia* sein; also der Schrift, die im Gesprächsdialog bewusst das Ende offen lässt und so die Fortführung des Gesprächs an die Leser delegiert. Gerade da sich dies so eindeutig darstellt, konterkariert die präemptive Resignation Muniers das eigentliche Anliegen der gesamten Schrift *Utopia*. Es ist vielmehr so, dass es der Wunsch des Autors Morus ist, dass sich das Resultat der verschiedenen Interpretationsperspektiven der *Utopia*-Rezipienten durch den werkimmanenten Modus des Gesprächs auflösen und zu neuen Perspektiven verschwimmen lasse – und damit gerade nicht dauerhaft "in Schubladen sortiert" wird, wie es Munier voreilig mit wenig Neugier auf andere Perspektiven abtut.

Wenn überhaupt, müssten selbst dann die anderen konkurrierenden Interpretationsperspektiven Anlass für jede einzelne sein, ihre eigene Überzeugungskraft durch gute Argumente noch weiter zu stärken und das Gegenüber durch noch trefflichere Überlegungen zu überzeugen. Darüber hinaus aber sollte die Bereitschaft zur Auseinandersetzung auch im aufgeklärten Eigeninteresse bestehen, denn jeder Vertreter einer Interpretationsperspektive kann nicht nur durch das Gegenüber seine eigene Position kritisch hinterfragen, sondern ebenso durch die andere Interpretationsperspektive eigene Erkenntnisgewinne erzielen. Und selbst wenn diese Erkenntnisgewinne nicht unbedingt in der Übernahme der anderen Interpretationsperspektive enden, aber so erzeugen sie doch zumindest ein besseres Verständnis, wie und warum das Gegenüber zu dieser Perspektive gekommen ist.

Der Weg zum gegenseitigen Verständnis, der immer auch die eigene Infragestellung umfasst, führt daher über die Offenlegung des jeweiligen eigenen Textverständnisses vor dem eigenen Erfahrungshintergrund. Die jeweilige Sichtweise des Interpreten in seiner spezifischen Vernunft und Erfahrung, Wissenschaft und/oder sozialen Vorstellungen, Tradition(en) und/oder Gemeinschaft soll dabei möglichst nachvollzogen werden, denn nur im Zur-Sprache-Kommen des Sachverhaltes kann sich die Integration unterschiedlicher Ansichten im Hinblick auf ein besseres Verständnis und eine Korrektur früherer Missverständnisse oder Verzerrungen vollziehen.

Es ist nicht von ungefähr ein herausgehobenes Charaktermerkmal des Genres der Utopie, die bekanntlich erst mit Morus' Werk *Utopia* aufkam, dass diese dem Leser aufgrund der diskursiven Struktur abverlangt, dass das in den Raum gestellte Modell einer alternativen Gesellschaft hinterfragt wird, indem der Leser selbstreflexiv tätig wird.

5. Der Bezugsrahmen des hermeneutischen Dialogs für den Diskurs der konkurrierenden Auslegungsmöglichkeiten

In gewisser Hinsicht ist Thomas Morus tatsächlich immer noch ein Fremder (vgl. Herz 1999, 7), nämlich im Hinblick darauf, dass wir immer noch nicht abschließend sagen können, wie ernst er es mit dem von ihm vorgeschlagenen und als Gesellschaftsalternative eingebrachten Sozialstrukturen gemeint hat – selbst dann, wenn wir gewisse Indizien haben. Wer genau hinschaut, erkennt, dass dies wohl nicht von ungefähr das entscheidende Rädchen der *Utopia*-Rezeption ist, welches das *Perpetuum mobile* immer neuer Interpretationsansätze und -auslegungen sowie ständiger Diskussionen in Gang hält. Auch hier tut sich eine Parallele zur Gadamerschen Hermeneutik auf, dessen hermeneutisches

Gespräch gleichfalls nie endet und immer wieder neu angestoßen werden kann bzw. muss (vgl. Gadamer 1986a, 318).

Insoweit ist es also im Sinne des Autors Thomas Morus, wenn der Diskurs der konkurrierenden Auslegungsmöglichkeiten nicht endet, was wiederum bedeutet, dass eine intensive Auseinandersetzung mit den einzelnen Perspektiven, deren spezifischen Vernunft und Erfahrung, Wissenschaft und/oder sozialen Vorstellungen, Tradition(en) und/oder Gemeinschaft erfolgen soll. Selbst wenn die Auseinandersetzung manchen an eine Art "Selbstfindung oder dem sich dem Sich-selbst-Verstehen ganzer Generationen" erinnert, weil "fast jeder" letztlich "in der Utopia das gefunden [hat], was er selbst suchte" (Göller 1990, 115), wäre dies nicht nachträglich. Auch die Selbstfindung des Einzelnen oder einer Generation in und/oder durch die Schrift ist ein wünschenswertes Anliegen, was den Absichten des Autors kaum abträglich gewesen wäre.

Eingangs war festgestellt worden, dass Hermeneutik einerseits als die Kunst der Interpretation verstanden werden kann, andererseits als Medium um Vergangenheitsaufarbeitung zu leisten. Beides findet sich in der *Utopia* wieder: Beispielsweise verlangt die Auslegung der *Utopia* als Satire, Parodie und Spielerei die Beherrschung der Kunst der Interpretation, um überhaupt z.B. die humanistischen Spielereien mit den verschiedenen Namensbedeutungen erkennen zu können, die sich über Umwege aus dem Griechischen oder Lateinischen ableiten, was im Übrigen auch von keiner der konkurrierenden Interpretationsperspektiven infrage gestellt wird, auch wenn diese andere Schwerpunkte setzen.

Andererseits bedarf es aber auch der Vergangenheitsaufarbeitung, z.B. dann, wenn die Anhänger der *Utopia* als christlich-konservative Schrift unter besonderer Auslegung der der Schrift immanenten heidnisch-humanistischen Perspektive ansetzen, diese mit der christlichen Religion in Einklang zu bringen. Dies setzt stillschweigend voraus, dass sie mit der historischen Praxis der katholischen Kirche hinreichend vertraut sind, so dass diese auch ausbuchstabiert werden kann. Oder wenn die Verfechter der Interpretationsperspektive der *Utopia* als totalitärer Staat den vermeintlichen Idealstaat *Utopia* mit Totalitarismus der Vergangenheit vergleichen, wie z.B. den verheerenden totalitären Entgleisungen des 20. Jahrhunderts, bedarf dies durchaus einer gewissen historischen Kenntnis und Verständnis der Vergangenheit, denn sonst ließe sich eine solche These weder aufstellen noch mit Quellen unterlegen.

Gleichfalls muss der soziale und kulturelle Kontext einer Schrift geprüft werden. Man muss auf die jeweilige Zeit eingehen, indem die Schrift entstand und nachzeichnen, auf welche kulturellen und sozialen Praktiken der Autor Morus konkret Bezug nimmt. Norbert Elias unterstreicht diese Notwendigkeit am Beispiel des Dialogs in der *Utopia* mit Hilfe einer rhetorischen Frage: "Wie kann man z.B. wissen, warum Thomas Morus für seine Utopie die Form eines Dialogs wählte, wenn man keine recht klare Kenntnis von der besonderen Funktion besitzt, die die literarische Form des Dialogs in der Gesellschaft des Tudor-Staates besaß." (Elias 1982, 105f.) Die literarische Form des Dialogs war durch antike Vorläufer bereits den Zeitgenossen Morus' bekannt und verhalf diesen, kritische Äußerungen so zu platzieren, dass man diese ihnen nicht unmittelbar in Hinblick auf die Zensur zuschreiben konnte (vgl. ebd., 131).

Ohne Bezug auf Morus' Zeit z.B. kaum die Rolle der Frau in der Schrift *Utopia* erklärbar. Obwohl angeblich *Utopia* eine klassenlose Gesellschaft sei, spielen Frauen in dieser Gesellschaft immer noch eine untergeordnete Rolle, was sich schon daran ablesen lässt, dass die Männer ihre Frauen züchtigen (vgl. Morus 1990, 109), was kaum Ausdruck von Gleichberechtigung sein kann. Zugleich aber arbeiten die Frauen Seite an Seite mit den Männern im Ackerbau (vgl. Morus 1990, 66) und ziehen sogar mit diesen in die Kriege (vgl. Morus 1990, 115). Die Widersprüche der angeblich klassenlosen Gesellschaft *Utopia* sind folglich nicht unerheblich. Dies mag in der werkimmanenten Logik ein deutlicher und erkennbarer Widerspruch sein, der sich aber aus Kenntnis der Zeit Morus' insofern nachvollziehen lässt, dass die wahre Gleichberechtigung der Frau wohl aufgrund seiner eigenen täglichen Lebenspraxis selbst die Imagination des Autors noch überstieg.

Ein hermeneutisches Verständnis für die Zeit und die Entstehungsgeschichte des Werkes, den Sitten und Gebräuchen in dieser Zeit zu erlangen, ist also unerlässlich. Man muss zugleich um die sozialen Praktiken Bescheid wissen, wie z.B. Kritik vorgetragen wurde, welche Ausdrucksformen und Medien zur Verfügung standen, welche Hürden wie z.B. Zensur existierten etc. etc. Durch den hermeneutischen Entwurf eines historischen Horizontes in Bezug auf die Zeit Thomas Morus' ebenso wie durch die Entwicklung eines wirkungsgeschichtlichen Bewusstseins des Werkes soll die Möglichkeit eines Verstehensvollzugs eröffnet werden. Hans Ulrich Seeber erfasst diesen Punkt:

Erstens sind die entstehungsgeschichtlichen Zusammenhänge zwischen der jeweiligen Utopie und der zeitgenössischen Wirklichkeit, die sie radikal kritisiert (More, Utopia), genau zu untersuchen. Zweitens ist – sofern Zeitkritik überhaupt explizit vorkommt – zu fragen, welche literarisch ausgebildeten Formen des Tadels, der Kritik und der Aggression (Satire, Groteske, Komödie, Polemik, Argumentation, selektive Beschreibung, etc.) von der literarischen Utopie im Einzelfall mediatisiert wurden. Bei implizierter Zeitkritik wird die kritische Spannung in den Kopf des (zeitgenössischen) Lesers verlegt, der sein soziales Wissen an der Norm des ausschließlich dargestellten utopischen Systems mißt. (Seeber 1983, 14)

Es stellt sich darüber hinaus in einer hermeneutischen Gesprächsausei-
nandersetzung auch die Frage, welche Rolle Vernunft und Erfahrung, Wissenschaft und/oder soziale Vorstellungen, Tradition(en) und/oder Gemeinschaft bei
der jeweiligen Auslegung spielen. Im Kontext der benannten Interpretationsperspektiven müsste man z.B. mehr über die streng rationale Vernunft wissen und
hinterfragen, ob diese wirklich so vernünftig ist, wie die Anhänger dieser Auslegung angeben und meinen. Hier könnten sich Widersprüche zwischen dem
vermeintlichen Resultat der Vernunft und der tatsächlichen Erfahrung dieses
Vernunftprimats in der Praxis des Inselstaates auftun, die es zu erörtern gilt.

Führt z.B. die stumpfsinnige Gleichheit, die den Utopiern in der Lebenspraxis modellhaft vorgegeben ist, wirklich zu mehr Nutzen? Oder ist dies nur
eine Chimäre, weil die Gleichheit und absolute Unterordnung letztlich zu Eintö-
nigkeit, mangelnde Kreativität, zu weniger Neugierde und damit auch zu weniger Innovation sowie weniger Verantwortungsbereitschaft der Utopier führt?
Ihre Erfindungen sowie ihre Affinität zu den Naturwissenschaften wirken doch
auf den zweiten Blick recht altbacken (u.a. Hühnerbrutmaschine, Wetterprogno-
semethoden, Buchdruckerkunst und Papierbereitung) und lassen zumindest die
hypothetische Frage aufwerfen, was denn daran so innovativ sein soll, dass sich
daraus ergebe, dass die Utopier "merkwürdig begabt für technische Erfindungen" (Morus 1990, 104) seien.

In der Gesellschaft gibt es darüber hinaus keine Anreize für den Einzelnen, mehr zu tun, als das unter Kontrolle und Zwang von ihm von der Gemeinschaft abverlangte. Es ist der Preis der Vernunft, dass jeglicher private Rück-
zugsraum verschwinden muss und alles, aber auch alles kontrolliert wird. Der
Mensch wird somit tendenziell zu einer Art Maschine, der ständig einen ihm
von außen vorgegeben Tagesablauf abzuspulen hat. Verliert eventuell am Ende
nicht das Leben durch eine solche Diktatur der Vernunft und des Utilitarismus
seinen Sinn?

Selbst die ideologische bzw. wissenschaftliche Auslegung in Form der
Utopia als sozialistisch-kommunistische Schrift ist nicht unangreifbar bzw.
unhinterfragbar. Es müsste ausbuchstabiert werden, inwieweit die Vorstellungen
der kommunistischen und sozialistischen Theorien sich wirklich in *Utopia* widerspiegeln oder ob dieser Inselstaat nicht eine andere Art von Gemeinschaft ist,
die z.B. mehr mit dem Ansatz des Heidentums korrespondiert als mit einer
kommunistischen oder sozialistischen Kommune. Auch ist nicht wirklich das
Eigentum und das monetäre System ganz abgeschafft, wie die Autoren der besagten Interpretationsrichtung voreilig zu insinuieren versuchen. Ein Blick auf
den Außenhandel mit anderen Ländern und das Kriegswesen macht überdeut-

lich, dass hier definitiv nicht von einer kommunistischen oder sozialistischen Internationale die Rede sein kann. Solidarität ist *a priori* erst einmal nur auf das eigene Staatswesen beschränkt (vgl. Morus 1990, 81f.; 104f.; 115-27).

Zugleich müsste man sich aber auch mit dem Verständnis der besagten Anhänger der sozialistisch-kommunistischen Interpretationsperspektive und mit ihren eigenen Ideologien und Theorien auseinandersetzen, sowohl um zu sehen, ob hier wirklich in Blick auf das Utopie-Konzept Kommunismus und Sozialismus weitgehend einheitlich verstanden werden können als auch um nachzuzeichnen, ob sich die ideologischen Konstrukte des Sozialismus und Kommunismus dann wiederum mit dem korrespondierenden Konzept des Inselstaates in Einklang bringen lassen. Hier können sich auf dem zweiten Blick Widersprüche auftun, denn auch der Inselstaat kennt eine Hierarchie und Klasse, wenn auch eine sehr schlanke. Durch gewisse Vorgaben, die u.a. auf den Gründer König Utopos zurückgeführt werden (vgl. Morus 1990, 129) oder durch z.B. das vorgegebene Religionskonzept (vgl. Morus 1990, 127ff.), was genau genommen auch bestenfalls nur für eine Art Halbheidentum qualifiziert, kommen noch wesentlich mehr Schwierigkeiten zum Vorschein, als man auf den ersten Blick wahrzunehmen in der Lage sein mag.

Jedenfalls ist der gesamte Text von einer Komplexität, so dass er in einem hermeneutischen Dialog der konkurrierenden Auslegungen in großem Umfang und zumal inhaltlich recht detailliert, auf verschiedenen Ebenen und unter Berücksichtigung verschiedener zeitlicher Epochen aufzuarbeiten ist. Gerade weil Utopia von so vielen verschiedenen Interpretationsperspektiven in Anspruch genommen wird, ist keine eindeutige Einordnung möglich. Dieser beschwerliche Weg zu einem denkbaren gegenseitigen Verständnis bzw. Austausch führt im Falle *Utopias* über die Enthüllung des jeweiligen impliziten Textverständnisses und seiner jeweiligen Kontextualisierung, indem im Dialog die jeweilige Sichtweise den anderen Interpretationsperspektiven ihre spezifische Vernunft und Erfahrung, ihre Vorstellungen, Traditionen und sozialen Konventionen offenbaren muss.

6. Die Bedeutung der Hermeneutik für Textinterpretationen am Beispiel der *Utopia*

In *Wahrheit und Methode* betont Gadamer die Bedeutung des hermeneutischen Dialogs, um zu einer Verständigung mit dem Anderen zu kommen. Dadurch erhalten wir einen Ansatz, mit dem wir einen Text oder ein Ereignis verstehen können, wobei das Verstehen nie endgültig sein kann. Durch den Austausch unterschiedlicher Ansichten und Perspektiven, unterschiedlicher

Lebensformen und unterschiedlicher Weltbilder können wir unser eigenes Verständnis und Wissen aber umfangreich bereichern.

Von dem immensen Beitrag, den Gadamer zur Philosophie und zum Denken des zwanzigsten Jahrhunderts geleistet hat, könnte sich seine wichtigste Einsicht als ein begriffliches Schema erweisen, das es uns ermöglicht, sowohl exegetische Konflikte als auch das Aufeinanderprallen verschiedener Lebensformen und Weltansichten durch das Explizieren durch Vernunft und Erfahrung, Wissenschaft und/oder soziale Vorstellungen, Tradition(en) und/oder Gemeinschaft zu überwinden. Gadamer entwickelt ein Schema, das auf jene Bereiche der Philosophie anwendbar ist, in denen die Bedeutung mehrdeutig bleibt, d.h. auf jene Bereiche, die sich einer Systematisierung widersetzen.

Dies ist sicherlich der Fall, wenn wir über verschiedene Lebensformen, Sprachspiele, Weltansichten oder die Interpretation von Texten sprechen. Hier gewinnen wir nur dann Verständnis, wenn wir auf unseren ererbten Hintergrund zurückgreifen. Indem wir unsere eigene Sprache, unsere eigene Lebensform verwenden, können wir Schwierigkeiten überwinden und das Sprachspiel so lange erweitern, bis wir die Aussage des anderen und dessen Sprachspiel verstehen. Für Gadamer bilden wir durch die Sprache einen Horizont zu anderen Sprachen, "die eben nicht einfach Gegenstand der Erforschung, des Sichauskennens und Bescheidwissens" (Gadamer 1986a, 445) sind. Damit drücken wir bereits ein gewisses Maß an Offenheit gegenüber diesen anderen und/oder neuen Welten aus.

Durch die Geschichte der Gesellschaft und der Kultur, der wir angehören, erben wir bestimmte Parameter der Interpretation, oder, wenn man so will, einen bestimmten Hintergrund. Der Gadamersche hermeneutische Ansatz verlangt jedoch nicht nur, dass wir die Geschichte oder das Wissen der Vergangenheit verstehen, sondern dass wir uns der Begegnung mit dem Anderen stellen und mit dessen Einstellung zu Vernunft und Erfahrung, Wissenschaft und/oder soziale Vorstellungen, Tradition(en) und/oder Gemeinschaft auseinandersetzen. Ziel dieses Prozesses ist es nicht, den anderen zu kontrollieren, sondern in der einen oder anderen Form zu einer gemeinsamen Übereinkunft zu gelangen, eine gemeinsame Grundlage für die weitere Neudefinition der eigenen Ziele zu entwickeln und zu weiterem Verständnis und Wissen zu gelangen. Georgia Warnke weist explizit darauf hin, dass es charakteristisch für echte Gespräche ist, "dass alle Teilnehmer über ihre anfänglichen Positionen hinaus zu einem Konsens geführt werden, der differenzierter und artikulierter ist als die getrennten Ansichten, mit denen die Gesprächspartner begonnen haben." (Warnke 1987, 169 [Übersetzung vom Autor])

Hermeneutisches Verstehen ist parteiabhängig. Als solches ist es immer an die Subjektivität des Menschen gebunden und kann daher nicht zu einem "objektiven Wissen" im epistemischen Sinne führen. Für Gadamer macht es daher keinen Sinn, an ein Konzept von "objektiver Erkenntnis" zu glauben, da objektive Erkenntnis weder in menschlichen Angelegenheiten noch in der Wissenschaft erreicht werden kann. "Objektive Erkenntnis" ist folglich im menschlichen Leben und Alltag nicht wahrheitsfunktional, denn "*[s]prachliche Form und überlieferter Inhalt lassen sich in der hermeneutischen Erfahrung nicht trennen.*" (Gadamer 1986a, 445)

Was aber bringt Gadamer dazu, nicht an "objektives Wissen" zu glauben? Es gibt zwei Hauptargumentationsstränge: Einerseits würde ein solches "objektives Wissen" die Bedeutung der Kultur in unserem Leben nicht ausreichend berücksichtigen. Kultur mache Dinge undefinierbar, sie sei eine immer neue Quelle für Kreativität, Inspiration und Innovation. Andererseits müsse ein solches "objektives Wissen" auf der Möglichkeit beruhen, dass menschliches Wissen und menschliche Erfahrung in einem generationenübergreifenden Transfer von einem Menschen auf einen anderen übertragen werden könnten, was aber – davon ist auszugehen – unmöglich ist. Da unser Leben endlich ist, können wir Wissen und Erfahrung nur in unserer eigenen Lebenszeit sammeln. Daher ist das, was wir als Wissen betrachten, nach Gadamer immer mit einer gewissen Kontingenz verbunden, was er deutlich unterstreicht: "In Wahrheit gehört die Geschichte nicht uns, sondern wir gehören ihr." (Gadamer 1986a, 281)

7. Das Zur-Sprache-kommen des Sachverhaltes als Erleben

An dieser Stelle wird ein weiteres Thema Gadamers relevant: Das bereits kurz erwähnte Thema der Erfahrung. Gadamer versteht das Zur-Sprache-kommen des Sachverhaltes durch den Gesprächspartner als ein Erleben, was Sprache zum hermeneutischen Medium von Erfahrung werden lässt. Sprache ist die Vollzugsweise hermeneutischer Erfahrung. Gadamer stimmt mit Humboldt darin überein, dass die Sprache eines jeden Individuums auch eine "Weltansicht" darstellt. Folglich kann der Ausdruck des Sachverhaltes in der Sprache nur partiell sein, da die gesamten "Weltansichten" nicht in der Sprache erfasst werden können (vgl. Gadamer 1986a, 442-60, 445ff.).

Erst wenn wir die richtigen Worte finden, um die Erfahrung auszudrücken, erkennen wir, so Gadamer, die Erfahrung als das, was sie ist. Das liegt daran, dass das Erleben ein sprachlich geprägter Prozess ist und das Finden der passenden Formulierung Teil unserer Erfahrung ausmacht. Für Gadamer liegt die Erfahrung darin, die richtigen Worte zu finden, da wir erst dann die Erfahrung des Sachverhaltes als solche erkennen können: "Etwas ist für uns ein Gespräch gewesen, was etwas in uns hinterlassen hat." (Gadamer 1986b, 211)

Wenn wir das Finden der richtigen Worte zugleich als das Finden eines neuen Sachverhaltes verstehen, dann ist offensichtlich, dass beides, Zur-Sprache-kommen wie das Erlebnis des Sachverhaltes, in Übereinstimmung sind, denn dann hat die Inanspruchnahme durch das Gesagte "nicht nur ihre eigene Wahrheit *in sich*, sondern auch eine eigene Wahrheit *für uns*." (Gadamer 1986a, 445)

Es sind die Sprache und ihre Artikulation, die unsere Lebensformen formen, indem sie weitere Reaktionen auslösen, denn den im lebendigen Vollzug des Sprechens und den damit einhergehenden Sprachspielen spiegelt sich unsere Sprache, unser eigenes Handeln und das Handeln der anderen wider. Jede Lebensform ist an einen gemeinschaftlichen Aspekt der Sprache gebunden. Dieser gemeinschaftliche Aspekt der Sprache macht uns bewusst, dass wir Teil einer Tradition sind, Mitglieder einer Sprachgemeinschaft. Diese Sprachansicht ist zugleich eine Weltansicht (vgl. Gadamer 1986a, 446).

Darüber hinaus folgt eine Gemeinschaft bestimmten Regeln und Gebräuchen sowie bestimmten Gewohnheiten und Regelmäßigkeiten, die sowohl unsere Sprachspiele als auch unsere Lebensformen prägen und führt dazu, dass wir als Mitglieder einer Sprachgemeinschaft zu der Erkenntnis gelangen, dass die Tradition unserer Gemeinschaft unsere Sprache und unser Handeln vom ersten Tag an, an dem wir auf die Welt kamen, uns geprägt hat. Genau dies, was wir beim Eintritt in die Welt und beim Erlernen einer Sprache erben, versteht Gadamer als eine ererbte Menge von Vorurteilen, die wir passiv aufnehmen, da sie Teil der ererbten Tradition sind, die wir unseren Hintergrund nennen. Wir erben Vorurteile durch Kultur. Den größten Teil der Kultur erben wir auf passive Weise, indem wir in eine bestimmte Gesellschaft hineingeboren werden. Wir sind insofern Teil einer Tradition, als wir eine Reihe von Vorurteilen geerbt haben, die uns in diese Tradition einbetten (vgl. Gadamer 1986a, 281ff.).

Es folgt jedoch für das hermeneutische Verstehen, "dass wir nicht auf die Prämissen unserer Tradition beschränkt sind, sondern sie in den Begegnungen und Diskussionen, die wir mit ihnen führen, ständig revidieren. In der Konfrontation mit anderen Kulturen, mit anderen Vorurteilen und auch mit den Folgerungen, die andere aus unseren eigenen Traditionen ziehen, lernen wir, sowohl unsere Annahmen als auch unsere Vorstellungen von Vernunft zu reflektieren und sie im Sinne einer besseren Darstellung zu ändern." (Warnke 1987, 170 [Übersetzung vom Autor]) Gadamer hat damit ein begriffliches Schema oder ein Werkzeug geliefert hat, das uns hilft, den Teilen der Philosophie, die für uns unklar bleiben, einen Sinn zu geben.

Es macht Sinn, dass Hans-Georg Gadamer darauf Wert legt, wie wir einen Gesprächspartner behandeln und wie wir in einem Dialog vorgehen. Ich nenne nur Stichworte: die Anerkennung der Ansicht des anderen als ein ernsthafter Wahrheitsanspruch, der zuerst einmal als richtig vorausgesetzt werden muss. Auf diese Weise kann die eigene Sichtweise vom anderen in Frage gestellt werden und Argumente, die gegen die eigene Sichtweise sprechen, können freiwillig akzeptiert werden. Das heißt aber nicht, dass wir automatisch blindlings dem folgen, was der andere selbst tut oder von uns fordert (vgl. Gadamer 1986a, 367). Ein anderer Fall ist, wenn Gadamer problematisiert, dass jeder Gesprächspartner "guten Willen" haben, zuhören und anerkennen müsse, was der andere zu sagen hat (vgl. Gadamer 1986c, 343).

Diese Voraussetzungen für den hermeneutischen Dialog sind auf die Tatsache zurückzuführen, dass die Gadamersche Hermeneutik auf die Anwendung eines hermeneutischen Schemas angewiesen ist, bei der sowohl der Fragende als auch der Antwortende Teil der Situation und damit auch an der Anwendung des hermeneutischen Schemas beteiligt sind. Es ist daher wesentlich, dass besondere Erkenntnisse Auswirkungen auf das eigene Sein haben (vgl. Gadamer 1986a, 317).

Der maßgebliche Vergleichspunkt ist, dass sowohl der fragende als auch der antwortende Dialogpartner in dieselbe Situation involviert sind, wie z.B. in die Interpretation der *Utopia*, da davon das Verstehen der Anwendung des allgemeinen Schemas in der besonderen Situation abhängt und auch das Verstehen somit das eigene Sein beeinflusst. Der Weg zum gegenseitigen Verstehen führt über die Enthüllung unseres impliziten Verständnisses, das den Blick auf den anderen in unserer Lebensform und Kultur verbirgt. Indem wir den anderen zu verstehen versuchen, lernen wir, seine Andersartigkeit zuzulassen und uns gleichzeitig von ihm infrage stellen zu lassen.

Das hermeneutische Schema ist somit doppelt parteiabhängig und sollte uns schließlich zur *Horizontverschmelzung* führen (vgl. Gadamer 1986a, 311), was ein Gadamerscher Begriff für die Integration unterschiedlicher Ansichten im Hinblick auf ein besseres Verständnis und eine Korrektur früherer Missverständnisse oder Verzerrungen ist. Das Ergebnis wird auch dann noch lange weit von jeglicher Perfektion sein, denn vielmehr handelt es sich um einen fortlaufenden Prozess hin zu einem wirklichen Verständnis des Anderen, der eher langsam und nur unter Schwierigkeiten erreicht werden kann. Bei der Überwindung unterschiedlicher Verständniskontexte müssen wir die Meinungen, Ansichten und Überzeugungen anderer berücksichtigen, wenn wir mit ihnen auf gleicher Augenhöhe über einen Sachverhalt diskutieren.

Wir profitieren in vielerlei Hinsicht von solchen Bemühungen. Selbst wenn wir unseren Standpunkt letztlich nicht ändern, können wir doch aus den Einwänden, Gegenbeispielen und Überlegungen des anderen lernen. Wir können sogar unsere Position stärken, indem wir unseren eigenen Standpunkt verbessern und ihn gegen Kritik immunisieren. Wir können auch die Position des anderen in unsere Sichtweise einbeziehen. Es spielt keine Rolle, ob wir die Kritik annehmen oder nicht. In jedem Fall werden wir viel besser über den anderen und seinen Standpunkt informiert sein.

Unabhängig davon, was diese Kritik für unseren ursprünglichen Standpunkt bedeutet, werden wir unsere eigene Sichtweise weiterentwickeln und sie wird nicht mehr die sein, mit der wir begonnen haben. Und da dies bei allen an diesem Prozess Beteiligten der Fall sein wird, ist das Ergebnis pareto-optimal und damit erstrebenswert.

8. Konklusion

Die *Horizontverschmelzung* verschiedener Interpretationsperspektiven (vgl. Gadamer 1986a, 311), die der Rolle der Vernunft und Erfahrung, Wissenschaft und/oder soziale Vorstellungen, Tradition(en) und/oder Gemeinschaft Rechnung trägt, geht einher mit der Erweiterung unserer Sprachkompetenz durch immer neue Sprachspiele. Die Generierung immer neuer Sprachspiele ist eine Kernkompetenz des Menschen, die es uns ermöglicht, Übergänge zwischen zwei Sprachspielen und damit auch zwei divergenten Interpretationsperspektiven zu schaffen. Dadurch bringen wir spracherweiternd neue Arten von Sprache, neue Sprachspiele hervor und vergessen dadurch andere, die dann obsolet werden.

Für Gadamer sind es auch die Sprachspiele, mit denen die Gesprächspartner in das Gespräch mit dem Anderen geführt werden und sich der Be- und Hinterfragung durch den anderen öffnen. Dies ist für Gadamer deshalb der Fall, "da vielmehr das Spiel es ist, das spielt, indem es die Spieler in sich einbezieht und so selber das eigentliche *subjectum* der Spielbewegung wird." (Gadamer 1986a, 493) Jede Veränderung ist dabei das Ergebnis der Verschiebung menschlicher Horizonte. Horizonte entwickeln sich und ein Horizont beschreibt die Welt eines Menschen, und muss als solcher stets in Bewegung sein. Wie Gadamer anmerkt: "Ein Horizont ist ja keine starre Grenze, sondern etwas, das mitwandert und zum weiteren Vordringen einlädt." (Gadamer 1986a, 250)

Man könnte hinzufügen, dass somit die Sprachspiele zugleich unmittelbar die Veränderung der Horizonte der einzelnen Menschen wiedergeben. Darüber hinaus hat Gadamers Konzept der "Horizonte" eine Art "innere" Bewegung, die für uns wesentlich ist, wenn wir versuchen, das Problem der Verzerrungen im

Verstehen und in der Kommunikation nachzuvollziehen, da es so etwas wie einen "stabilen" Horizont nicht geben kann.

Wir müssen daher die Gadamersche Hermeneutik als Erweiterung der Diskussion über unterschiedliche Lebensformen, unterschiedliche Sprachspiele und die konkurrierenden Interpretationsperspektiven anwenden, um zu einem Verständnis des Anderen, seiner Weltsicht und seiner Auslegung einer Schrift zu gelangen. Niemand hat dies eleganter ausgedrückt als Georgia Warnke: "In dem Maße, in dem Individuen und Kulturen dieses Verständnis der Anderen und ihrer Unterschiede in ihr eigenes Selbstverständnis integrieren, in dem Maße also, in dem sie von den Anderen lernen und eine breitere, differenziertere Sichtweise einnehmen, können sie Sensibilität, Feinsinnigkeit und Unterscheidungsvermögen erwerben." (Warnke 1987, 174 [Übersetzung vom Autor])

Das Problem der *Utopia* ist auch dann nicht abschließend gelöst. Selbst dann nicht, wenn es gelingen sollte, zu einer *Horizontverschmelzung* und damit zu einer Übereinstimmung zu kommen (vgl. Gadamer 1986a, 311), da der Dialog immer ein über jedes Subjekt und seine Lebenszeit hinausgehender und damit unendlicher ist. Das hermeneutische Problem gipfelt nämlich darin, "daß die Überlieferung als dieselbe dennoch je anders verstanden werden muß" (Gadamer 1986a, 317), so dass ein unendlicher Rekurs notwendig ist. Es gilt deshalb auch dann immer noch:

Utopia und kein Ende.

Dr. Ulrich Arnswald, Institut für Kulturforschung, Heidelberg
arnswald[at]ulrich-arnswald.de

References

Adam, Armin. 1988. "De Optimo reip.[ublicae] statu, deque nova insula Utopia." In *Lexikon der philosophischen Werke*, herausgegeben von Franco Volpi und Julian Nida-Rümelin, 136-38. Stuttgart: Kröner.

Ahrbeck, Rosemarie. 1977. *Morus – Campanella – Bacon. Frühe Utopisten*. Leipzig; Jena; Berlin: Urania-Verlag.

Arnswald, Ulrich. 2010. "Zum Utopie-Begriff und seiner Bedeutung in der Politischen Philosophie". In *Thomas Morus' Utopia und das Genre der Utopie in der Politischen Philosophie*, herausgegeben von Ulrich Arnswald und Hans-Peter Schütt. 1-35. Karlsruhe: KIT Scientific Publishing.

Barnouw, Dagmar. 1985. *Die versuchte Realität oder von der Möglichkeit, glücklichere Welten zu denken.* Utopischer Diskurs von Thomas Morus zur feministischen Science Fiction. Meitingen: Corian-Verlag Heinrich Wimmer.

Berglar, Peter. 1978. *Die Stunde des Thomas Morus.* Einer gegen die Macht. Olten; Freiburg i.Br.: Walter.

Bermbach, Udo. 1992. "Die Utopie ist tot – es lebe die Utopie!" In *Hat die politische Utopie eine Zukunft?*, herausgegeben von Richard Saage. 142-51. Darmstadt: Wissenschaftliche Buchgesellschaft.

Bloch, Ernst. 1946. *Freiheit und Ordnung.* Abriß der Sozial-Utopien. New York: Aurora-Verlag.

Bloch, Ernst. 1985. *Das Prinzip Hoffnung.* In fünf Teilen. Kapitel 33-42. 3 Bd., Bd. 2. Frankfurt a.M.: Suhrkamp.

Boulding, Elise. 2000. *Cultures of Peace.* The Hidden Side of History. With a Foreword by Federico Mayor. New York: Syracuse University Press

Brie, Friedrich. 1936/37. "Thomas Morus der Heitere." *Englische Studien* 71 (1): 27-57.

Brie, Friedrich. 1941. "Machtpolitik und Krieg in der Utopia des Thomas Morus" *Historisches Jahrbuch* 61: 116-37.

Brockhaus, Heinrich. 1929. *Die Utopia-Schrift des Thomas Morus.* Leipzig: B.G. Teubner.

Bruyn, Gerd de. 1996. *Die Diktatur der Philanthropen.* Entwicklung der Stadtplanung aus dem utopischen Denken. Braunschweig; Wiesbaden: Friedr. Vieweg & Sohn.

Chambers, Raymond W. 1946. *Thomas More.* Ein Staatsmann Heinrichs des Achten. Deutsch von Wolfgang Rüttenauer. München; Kempten: Kösel.

Claes, Gregory. 2011. *Ideale Welten.* Die Geschichte der Utopie. Aus dem Englischen von Raymond Hinrichs und Andreas Model. Stuttgart: Theiss.

Dahrendorf, Ralf. 1967. *Pfade aus Utopia.* Arbeiten zur Theorie und Methode der Soziologie. München: Piper.

Doren, Alfred. 1927. "Wünschträume und Wunschzeiten" *Vorträge der Bibliothek Warburg* 4: 158-205.

Elias, Norbert. 1982. "Thomas Morus' Staatskritik. Mit Überlegungen zur Bestimmung des Begriffs Utopie" In: *Utopieforschung.* Interdisziplinäre Studien zur neuzeitlichen Utopie, herausgegeben von Wilhelm Voßkamp. 3 Bd., Bd. 2. 101-50. Stuttgart: Metzler.

Engels, Friedrich. 1962. "Die Entwicklung des Sozialismus von der Utopie zur Wissenschaft.", in: *Karl Marx: Werke.* Band 19. 189-228. Berlin: Dietz.

Erzgräber, Willi. 1983. "Thomas Morus: *Utopia*" In *Literarische Utopien von Morus bis zur Gegenwart*, herausgegeben von Klaus Leo Berghahn und Hans Ulrich Seeber. 25-43. Königstein/Ts.: Athenäum.

Fest, Joachim. 1991. *Der zerstörte Traum.* Vom Ende des utopischen Zeitalters. Berlin: Siedler.

Fest, Joachim. 1992. "Leben ohne Utopie" In: *Hat die politische Utopie eine Zukunft?*, herausgegeben von Richard Saage, 15-26. Darmstadt: Wissenschaftliche Buchgesellschaft.

Freyer, Hans. 1920. "Das Problem der Utopie." *Deutsche Rundschau* 183: 321-45.

Freyer, Hans. 2000. *Die Politische Insel*. Eine Geschichte der Utopien von Platon bis zur Gegenwart. Herausgegeben von Elfriede Üner. Wien; Leipzig: (2., unver. Aufl.) Karolinger.

Gadamer, Hans-Georg. 1986a. *Wahrheit und Methode*. Grundzüge einer philosophischen Hermeneutik. Tübingen: (5. durchges. u. erw. Aufl.) Mohr Siebeck.

Gadamer, Hans-Georg. 1986b. "Die Unfähigkeit zum Gespräch", in: Hans-Georg Gadamer, *Gesammelte Werke*. Bd. 2. 207-15. Tübingen: Mohr Siebeck.

Gadamer, Hans-Georg. 1986c. "Text und Interpretation", in: Hans-Georg Gadamer, *Gesammelte Werke, Bd. 2*, 330-60. Tübingen: Mohr Siebeck.

Glunz, Hans. 1938. *Shakespeare und Morus*, Bochum-Langendreer: Heinrich Pöppinghaus.

Göller, Karl Heinz. 1990. "Die Utopia Thomas Mores", In *Hauptwerke der Literatur*. Vortragsreihe der Universität Regensburg, herausgegeben von Hans Bungert. 97-120. Regensburg: Mittelbayerische Druck.- und Verlags-Gesellschaft.

Hermand, Jost. 1981. *Orte. Irgendwo*. Formen des utopischen Denkens. Königstein/Ts.: Athenäum.

Herz, Dietmar. 1993. "Zwei Wahrheiten. Zur Interpretation von Thomas Morus' Utopia", *Der Staat* 32 (1): 1-28.

Herz, Dietmar. 1999. *Thomas Morus zur Einführung*. Unter Mitarbeit von Veronika Weinberger. Hamburg: Junius.

Höffe, Otfried. 2016. "Einführung" In: *Politische Utopien der Neuzeit. Thomas Morus, Tommaso Campanella, Francis Bacon*, herausgegeben von Otfried Höffe. 1-18. Berlin; Boston: Walter de Gruyter.

Jäckel, Eberhard. 1955. *Experimentum rationis*. Christentum und Heidentum in der "Utopia" des Thomas Morus. Freiburg i.Br.: (Philosophische Fakultät: Inaugural-Dissertation) Albert-Ludwigs-Universität Freiburg.

Kautsky, Karl. 1907. *Thomas More und seine Utopie*. Stuttgart: (2., durchges. Aufl.) Verlag J.H.W. Dietz Nachf.

Kluxen, Kurt. 2003. "Thomas Morus und seine ‚Utopia' als Wegbereiter moderner Sozialanalyse", in: Kurt Kluxen, *England in Europa*. Studien zur britischen Geschichte und zur politischen Ideengeschichte der Neuzeit. 38-59. Berlin: Duncker & Humblot.

Kristeller, Paul Oskar. 1982. "Thomas Morus als Humanist", in: Paul Oskar Kristeller und Hans Maier, *Thomas Morus als Humanist*. Zwei Essays. 9-37. Bamberg: H. Kaiser.

Kroh, Jens. 2021. "Thomas Morus, Utopia" In: *Schlüsselwerke der Kulturwissenschaften*, herausgegeben von Claus Leggewie, Dariuš Zifonun, Anne Lang, Marcel Siepmann und Johanna Hoppen. 142-44. Bielefeld 2021: transcript.

Kuon, Peter. 1984. *Utopischer Entwurf und fiktionale Vermittlung*. Studien zum Gattungswandel der literarischen Utopie zwischen Humanismus und Frühaufklärung. Tübingen: Verlag Science & Fiction.

Lewis, Clive S. 1954. *English Literature in Sixteenth Century, Excluding Drama*. Oxford: Clarendon Press.

Maier, Hans. 1982. "Der Humanist und der Ernstfall. Thomas Morus 1478-1978", in: Paul Oskar Kristeller und Hans Maiers, *Thomas Morus als Humanist*. Zwei Essays. 39-58. Bamberg: H. Kaiser.

Manguel, Alberto. 2017. "Thomas Morus (1478-1535) Utopia. Löwen, Dezember 1516", in Alberto Manguel, *Sehnsucht Utopie*. Eine Reise durch fünf Jahrhunderte. Aus dem Französischen von Amelie Thoma. 13-15. Bozen; Wien: Folio Verlag.

Möbus, Gerhard. 1953. *Die Politik des Heiligen*. Geist und Gesetz der Utopia des Thomas Morus. Berlin: Morus-Verlag.

Morus, Thomas. 1990. *Utopia*. Übersetzt von Gerhard Ritter. Nachwort von Eberhard Jäckel. Stuttgart: Philipp Reclam Jun.

Münkler, Herfried. 1992. "Das Ende des Utopiemonopols und die Zukunft des Utopischen" In *Hat die politische Utopie eine Zukunft?* Herausgegeben von Richard Saage. 207-14. Darmstadt: Wissenschaftliche Buchgesellschaft.

Munier, Gerald. 2008. *Thomas More*. Urvater des Kommunismus und katholischer Heiliger. Hamburg: VSA-Verlag.

Ottmann, Henning. 1996. "Der Geist der Moderne. Sekten und Humanismus bei Eric Voegelin" *Zeitschrift für Politik* 43 (3): 333-38.

Pfetsch, Frank. 2019. *Theoretiker der Politik*. Von Platon bis Habermas. Baden-Baden: (3., akt. Aufl.) Nomos.

Popper, Karl R. 1987. *Das Elend des Historizismus*. Tübingen: J.C.B. Mohr (Paul Siebeck).

Pieper, Annemarie. 2016. "Die Moral der Utopier" In: *Politische Utopien der Neuzeit*. Thomas Morus, Tommaso Campanella, Francis Bacon, herausgegeben von Otfried Höffe. 77-92. Berlin; Boston: Walter de Gruyter.

Reynolds, Ernest Edwin. 1953. *Saint Thomas More*. London: Burns Oates.

Ritter, Gerhard. 1940. *Machtstaat und Utopie*: Vom Streit um die Dämonie der Macht seit Machiavelli und Morus. München; Berlin: Verlag von R. Oldenbourg.

Rötzer, Hans Gerd. 1963/64. "Utopie und Gegenutopie" *Stimmen der Zeit* 174: 356-65.

Saage, Richard. 1991. *Politische Utopien der Neuzeit*. Darmstadt: Wissenschaftliche Buchgesellschaft.

Saage, Richard. 1997. *Utopieforschung*. Eine Bilanz, Darmstadt: Wissenschaftliche Buchgesellschaft.

Saage, Richard. 2006. "Thomas Morus", in: Richard Saage, *Utopisches Denken im historischen Prozess*. Materialien zur Utopieforschung. 7-14. Berlin; Münster: LIT.

Saage, Richard. 2015. "Das Erbe des Thomas Morus. Zur Gegenwart des klassischen Utopiebegriffs" *Neue Politische Literatur* 61: 213-28.

Schiel, Hubert. 1947. "Zur Einführung", in: Thomas More, *Des Heiligen Thomas Morus Utopia, das ist Nirgendland oder von der besten Staatsform*. Übertragen und eingeleitet von Hubert Schiel. 5-29. Köln: Pick.

Schmidl, Johannes. 2016. *Bauplan für eine Insel*. 500 Jahre Utopia. Wien: Sonderzahl.

Schmidtke, Oliver. 2016. *Ideal und Ironie der Gesellschaft*. Die 'Utopia' des Thomas Morus. Frankfurt a.M.: Campus.

Schölderle, Thomas. 2012. *Geschichte der Utopie*. Eine Einführung. Köln; Weimar; Wien: Böhlau.

Schölderle, Thomas. 2016. "Zwischen Reform und Satire. Vernunft als experimentelle Fundament in Morus' *Utopia*" In: *Politische Utopien der Neuzeit*. Thomas Morus, Tommaso Campanella, Francis Bacon, herausgegeben von Otfried Höffe. 57-75. Berlin; Boston: Walter de Gruyter.

Seeber, Hans Ulrich. 1983. "Zur Geschichte des Utopiebegriffs." In *Literarische Utopien von Morus bis zur Gegenwart*, herausgegeben von Hans Ulrich Seeber und Klaus Berghahn. 7-23. Königstein/Ts.: Athenäum.

Süssmuth, Hans. 1967. *Studien zur Utopia des Thomas Morus*. Ein Beitrag zur Geistesgeschichte des 16. Jahrhunderts. Münster/Westfalen: Aschendorffsche Verlagsbuchhandlung.

Tremmel, Jörg. 2016. "Thomas Morus: Der Philosoph als Fürstendiener oder Staatsmann? In *Politische Utopien der Neuzeit*. Thomas Morus, Tommaso Campanella, Francis Bacon, herausgegeben von Otfried Höffe. 43-56. Berlin; Boston: Walter de Gruyter.

Voegelin, Eric. 1995. "Die spielerische Grausamkeit der Humanisten." Eric Voegelins Studien zu Niccolò Machiavelli und Thomas Morus. Aus dem Englischen übersetzt und mit einem Vorwort von Dietmar Herz. Nachwort von Peter J. Opitz. München: Fink.

Voigt, Andreas. 1906. *Die sozialen Utopien*. Fünf Vorträge. Leipzig: G. J. Göschen'sche Verlagshandlung.

Warnke, Georgia. 1987. *Gadamer*: Hermeneutics, Tradition and Reason. Stanford: Stanford University Press.

BENJAMIN HUTCHENS (Newark, NJ)

Gadamer's Gorgias: The Imperative of Self-Refutation

Abstract

Gadamer has written several powerful studies of Platonic dialectic. His emphasis on shared understanding, the fusing of horizons and other hermeneutic notions are partially drawn from a study of Plato's elenctic dialogues. However, Socrates in Gorgias makes a claim about the imperative of self-refutation that not only complicates our understanding of Socratic method, but Gadamer's reading of it as well.

This article is meant to explore just how the imperative of self-refutation causes difficulty for Gadamer's understanding of dialectic, especially his distinction between authentic and inauthentic dialectic. After considering the nature of 'refutation', this article will examine whether Gadamer's notions of shared understanding, the 'facts of the matter', and self-understanding help us to resolve this problem. It shall be concluded that the teacher must take any refutations of his/her own views seriously, but has no special obligation to refute (introspectively) any of their own views, even those beliefs, theories, principles or criteria that enable him to guide the argument.

Keywords: Hans-Georg Gadamer, Gorgias, refutation, shared understanding, introspection

---

There is a truly perplexing passage in Plato's Gorgias. Socrates asks:

> And what kind of man am I? One of those who would be pleased to be refuted (ἐλεγχθέντων) if I say anything untrue; one who, however, wouldn't' be any less pleased to be refuted (ἐλεγχθέντων) than to refute. For I count being refuted (ἐλεγξάντων) a greater good, insofar as it is a greater good for oneself to be delivered from the worst thing there is than to deliver someone else from it. I don't suppose there's anything quite so bad for a person as having false belief about the things we're discussing right now. (Gorgias 458a-b)

What is one to make of this? Are there other passages of Plato's work that explicitly bring to mind Socrates' desire to be refuted? Are we to understand that the elenchtic method involves discussion for the purpose of introspective self-refutation? Is this a special obligation for the secondary interlocutor, the teacher? What would a teacher need to do to satisfy this obligation? Wouldn't any teacher-led discussion in which the teacher paused to refute his/her own presuppositions be eristical in practice? Wouldn't such a discussion come to center on the teacher's own beliefs and not on those he/she is ("maieutically'") trying to give birth from the mind of the student? When Socrates gives birth to a notion from the mind of the primary interlocutor, in what sense is that notion Socrates' own, no matter how much he molds and refines it? Given the vital importance of refuting a refutable belief, then isn't there something akin to an imperative to seek out and refute such beliefs, if possible? Can the 'Socratic method' aim at self-refutation, in whole or in part?

Self-Refutation and the 'Paradox' of Socrates

To understand the significance of the passage, let us consider how it affects our perception of Socrates the man as well as his "method". First, we might note that this is one of those novel occasions when Socrates declares who he thinks he is. We might follow Vlastos when he writes:

> Moments of self-revelation like these are rare in the dialogues. Socrates is not a character out of Chekhov, introspecting moodily on a public stage. He is a man whose face is a mask, whose every word is deliberate, and who seems calculated to conceal more than to reveal. One gets so used to this artful exterior that one is left unprepared for moments like these and is apt to discount them as irony (Vlastos 1995, 10).

We are here at the very crux of Socrates as paradox, the Socrates who "preaches a gospel" in philosophizing for the health of the soul, as Vlastos so movingly described, and the questioner, the demoralizing smasher of personal idols. It is occasioned by an emphasis on the dubious notion that "virtue is knowledge", which for Vlastos means that there is no virtue without knowledge, such that Socrates "makes you feel that the failure to sustain a thesis or find a definition is not just an intellectual defeat, but a moral disaster" (Vlastos 1995, 8). But it also means that anyone who has this knowledge would necessarily respond to the exigencies of life with perfect virtue. In any event, this evangelistic Socrates teaches that only the soul is "worth saving" and knowledge is the only way to do so. But the paradox becomes evident when we see the other Socrates, who often does not act like an evangelist. We come to the Socrates who refutes: "you say A, and he shows you that A implies B, and B implies C, and then he asks, 'But didn't you say D before? And doesn't C contradict D? And there he leaves you with our shipwrecked argument, without so much as telling you what part of it, if any, might yet be salvaged" (Vlastos 1995, 9).

How does self-refutation figure in this paradox? At a glance, the preaching of Socrates seems to imply it. One might think that self-refutation is an important way to cleanse the soul by means of the elimination of false beliefs represented as knowledge. And the "moral disaster" of not being able to sustain a thesis in dialogue must imply that one was not resolute in refuting that thesis by means of self-examination. But elenchtic dialogue is clearly the vehicle for the purpose of this preaching. Socrates is not declaiming in the streets, but speaking quietly with people. The iconoclastic Socrates asks questions in such a way that his primary interlocutors (Gorgias, Polus, Callicles) shatter (or are meant to shatter) their own arguments, leaving them to sit forlorn in the wreckage of their own theoretical orientation. Or at least they would if they understood what had befallen them. Yet, it should be clear that the primary interlocutors do not meet this fate as a result of self-refutation, but rather with the active involvement of Socrates. They are not bereft because Socrates has incidentally helped them in their effort to refute their own theses. And besides, the imperative of self-refutation is not binding solely on the primary interlocutor, but on Socrates himself, the "sort of guy" who would prefer to be refuted than to refute. We might be clear that the primary interlocutor is not shipwrecked because Socrates, the secondary interlocutor, has sought to refute his own theses. On the contrary, it is the primary interlocutor's thesis that has not sustained demolition, while Socrates' own position has not even been considered for such a fate. Anyone who speaks with Socrates about weighty matters is likely to succumb to his questioning, falling into a moral disaster that Socrates himself—the masked man whose 'method' conceals rather than reveals— never seems to experience. Such moral disasters arc for those whom Socrates helps, but Socrates is not able to help because he answers to any imperative to self-refutation. Thus, in respect of establishing cosmic harmony by means of truth, of the common good through the virtue that is knowledge, of fostering knowledge through dialectics for the purpose of cleansing the soul, self-refutation might play some part because a poorly supported thesis promotes disharmony, personal pleasure and empowerment at the expense of truth and "the good"; but it appears to play no role in the dialectic that serves as the means for doing so.

Does Socrates have sufficient knowledge to be able to answer to the imperative of self-refutation? What is meant here is not that he would have knowledge of this or that subject area—justice, courage, or the price of beans— but knowledge of dialectics itself. Does Socrates know that he wants to know, which is only partly addressed by the Socratic maxim that one knows only that one knows (is wise about) nothing. At Gorgias 453b he openly professes: "You should know that I'm convinced I'm one of those people who in a discussion with someone else really want to have knowledge of the subject the discussion's about." We might notice that Socrates is insisting that Gorgias "should know" something. But what he should know is merely that Socrates is *persuaded* that he wants knowledge, but not that he knows he wants it. He can only profess to have persuaded himself that he wants knowledge, though what role knowing plays in this persuasion is unclear. This assertion of self-persuasion is not dialectical, the internal dialectic of examining and potentially refuting the claim, an "expression of impersonal allegiance to the logos", but rhetorical (Wardy 1996, 64). The problem may be with the assertion that it would give Socrates "pleasure" to be refuted, which does not sit well with the notion of a selfless devotion to the truth (Benardete 1991, 25). "Pleasure" in the original quote cannot be discussed as merely rhetorical, as that would raise the issue of what motivates Socrates to pursue truth and accept refutation. And yet to accept that Socrates is justified by reasons to take such pleasure is not in accord with his overall unremitting pursuit of truth.

While we are still on the subject of Socrates the thinking man, we might also consider those important places in dialogue where he does not seem at all like the "sort of guy" who prefers self-refutation. What do we make of Socrates' strict adherence to the thesis that "one should never do wrong to others, even when they have caused harm" at Crito 49d-e. Here he declares he has "held it for a long time and still hold it now, but if you think otherwise, tell me now" but if Crito assents to it, then the dialogue can proceed as planned. Notice that this is a minor crux in the argument: the secondary interlocutor asserts a position in considering the belief of the primary interlocutor; if the primary assents to it, then together they can continue to discuss the belief of the primary interlocutor; but if the primary dissents from it, then the secondary interlocutor will have a chance to examine it, potentially refuting it, then somehow fruitfully return to the original course of dialogue about the thesis of the primary interlocutor. As is commonplace in the dialogues, the primary interlocutor assents to the position, so it is never examined, never submitted to the process of refutation. It is as if Socrates dangles the prospect of refuting his own position before Crito, knowing full well he is unlikely to reach for it.

Second, let us turn to the question of his method. One might maintain that Socrates has a set body of logical and dialogical functions used from situation to situation, as some traditional interpreters have (e.g. Vlastos 1995, Irwin 1995, 18-19); or one might adhere to any number of views to the effect that Socrates' activity differs by situation with primary interlocutors, such as Teloh's Phaedrus principle (Teloh 1986 and 2007, 60). In fact, it is now not unheard of for scholars to question whether 'elenchus' is even uniquely Socratic, as in the collection edited by Scott [2002, see especially the essays by Lesher (19-36) and Ausland (36-61)]. One need take no stand on the issue of whether Socrates has "a method" to see how self-refutation causes difficulty. How might one support the role of self-refutation in Socrates' method? If adhering to false beliefs causes disharmony etc. then refutation of such beliefs is good because it promotes harmony by cleansing the soul etc. So, one ought to strive to refute one's own beliefs. However, as we have seen, neither the primary nor the secondary interlocutor actively strives to refute his/her own beliefs. If we wonder how the former is stripped of a belief and how the latter played a role in doing so, we are effectively put off with claims about 'the elenchus', or the merging of subjectivities into a single dialectic for the purpose of a dialogical pursuit of truth, or some such. In other words, we focus on the theses and beliefs proposed, examined and demolished within the dialogue, as if they were subjected to an impersonal force of the dialectic of reason. We can find no place for the very personal process of self-refutation in the work of this impersonal force.

The Uniqueness of Gorgias

Given a certain grasp of the elenchtic method, one might think that the imperative of self-refutation is present throughout Plato's dialogues. Yet, one would be hard pressed to find mention of it even in those places where Socrates pauses to discuss dialectics itself. One might also imagine that it is at least implied in the many analysis of the soul, self-understanding, teaching and learning, wisdom and temperance and the like. There would be disappointment here as well. One might be forced to integrate the imperative into the subject matter, all the while wondering why, if it is so important for dialectics, it is not more explicit.

It must be acknowledged from the outset, however, that the imperative is made explicit only in Gorgias, which is something puzzling. Gorgias is one of several dialogues devoted to oratory or rhetoric, dialectics versus eristics, philosophy distinguished from sophistry. At the center of such issues is the figure of Gorgias himself, and the respects in which he is either rhetorician and sophist, or both (Tusi 2020). So why isn't the imperative more explicit in Phaedrus, Phaedo, Protagoras, Charmides, or for that matter a range of dialogues from Republic I, where refutation is at work, to Sophist, where refutation is a theme? For example, there is no sign of the imperative in the lengthy discussion of dialectic at 277-278 in Phaedrus; and although Socrates does retract his claim to knowledge of love at 257, this is not clearly the result of answering to the imperative. In Protagoras (350), Socrates affirms a position Protagoras forces him to retract, but there is little sign that Socrates examines the claim in the light of the imperative. Even though Socrates says that "I don't want you to think that my motive in talking with you is anything else than to take a good hard look at things that continually perplex me" (348c), he seems to be using the dialogue as an opportunity to dissolve a perplexity, even though refutation befalls him in ways for which he was not prepared.

And when Charmides suspects that Socrates is merely trying to refute him, not addressing the real question at issue (166c-d), Socrates replies that he is impartial in the use of reasons when he refutes theses and beliefs that turn up in dialogue. Claiming to have a "fear of unconsciously thinking I know something when I do not", he claims to be examining Charmides' belief for his own sake primarily, as if he wanted to make sure that the position he was refuting was not one he himself held dear without realizing it. He claims to be doing this secondarily for his friends and for the common good of most people. But even here Socrates is prevaricating: he is eliminating Charmides' belief from consideration, not any particular belief of his own. Charitably, we might accept that Socrates is refuting others' beliefs so as to cleanse his own soul of its contaminant, but whatever theses and beliefs led him to do so and assisted him in doing so remain unchallenged.

In Phaedo, Socrates makes a claim about what Cebes would do hypothetically if one of his beliefs were challenged. We are left with a sense that this is how Socrates understands his own procedure. Socrates insists that one should ignore anyone who attacks one's claim and instead consider whether the consequences are contradictory. And it may be necessary to propose another "hypothesis" in order to determine the relation between the original claim and its consequences. In other words, rather than getting lost in the morass of a claim and its many possible consequences in response to an objection, one should control the fate of the claim by proposing what Socrates calls a "higher" hypothesis to settle the matter. This is, he insists, what a philosopher should do (101d-e). Notice that in the process of examining and weighing claims and consequences, there is no mention of refutation. And even though one is sticking to one's guns and not being distracted by objections, it is not implied that one is answering to the imperative of self-refutation.

A wider glance at Gorgias (and Euthydemus) might be helpful to sort out what is at issue with the presence of the imperative in certain dialogical situations. Perhaps what is most unique about Gorgias is Socrates' claim to have expertise in the art of living (*politikē*), the craft dealing directly with the good of the soul itself. It is famously divided into legislation, which fosters the health of the soul as gymnastics does the health of the body, and justice, which sustains it, much as medicine does for the body. Socrates at 521d claims that, in being alone in his care for the good of other citizens, he is the sole expert in the art of living. Our question here is whether self-refutation plays any role in this process. Does the process of self-legislation for the good of the soul involve it? Does the process of fostering justice in and for the soul imply it? Is Socrates as legislator and justiciar of the soul the "sort of guy" who prefers to be refuted rather than to refute?

To address these questions, we could not do better than to look at the context of the quote. We are told that we ought to submit ourselves to a discussion as a patient does to a doctor (475e), which takes us to the role of the subject at hand in the dialogue. At 453, Socrates states that, in a discussion, he wants to "have knowledge of the subject the discussion's about". He suspects that Polus means something in particular by the role of persuasion in sophistical discussion, yet holds back: "And why, when I have my suspicions, do I ask you and refrain from expressing them myself?" and answers the questions himself: "It's not you I am after, it's our discussion, to have it proceed in such a way as to make the thing we're talking about most clear to us" (453c). He returns to this claim shortly in a clearer way: "I'm asking questions so that we can conduct an orderly discussion. It's not you I'm after; it's to prevent our getting in the habit of second-guessing and snatching each other's assumptions away ahead of time. It's to allow you to work out your assumption in any way you want to" (454c). It is worth pausing over this claim. In being focused on the discussion as such, in trying to get the right kind of dialogue, each interlocutor should beware of hastily assuming what the other might say and rejecting their claim proleptically on the basis of a spurious grasp of its assumptions. And then Socrates states that the point is to help the other person, the non-teacher if one likes, to work out their own assumptions. There is no sign of any effort at self-refutation. Shortly thereafter, however, his interlocutor Polus accuses Socrates of being pig-headed, refusing to acknowledge when he has been implicitly refuted, when "even a child could refute you". To this, Socrates playfully exclaims that he could be grateful to the child or anyone else who could rid him of the nonsense Polus claims to find in his approach. Refute me!, Socrates challenges (470c). But of course, Socrates is demanding that Polus refute him by working through the assumptions of Polus own position! When Polus offers a rather tepid argument involving the sort of testimony offered in a law court in order to refute Socrates, Socrates responds that he disagrees with everything Polus says and so does not feel refuted. Interestingly, in offering the kind of refutation he finds satisfactory, he claims that when discussing an important subject, it is shameful not have knowledge of it (472d, and see Cain 2008, 214-218). It would appear that someone in the discussion should be ashamed, since they have a rather heated exchange of "You're refuted. No, I'm not, you are" soon thereafter (473a-d). In the chaos of eristic dialogue, it can be unclear whether anyone has been refuted, since the conditions of refutation are not established by agreement.

Success in dialectic, in the overall sweep of the dialogue, means that a claim one desires to be true withstands the concerted assault of refutation. One can find this claim to success in the concluding remarks of Gorgias. The reference to "worse thing there is" in the leading quote above indicates the greatest injustice, namely not paying one's due for the harm one has done, which provides the context for the quote. In fact, in the conclusion of Gorgias Socrates claims that this is one of the few claims made in the discussion to "survive" refutation (527b). The dialogical context for this claim is worth quoting. After claiming that he and Callicles are not very talented in their deliberations over weighty matters, Socrates claims:

> For it's a shameful thing for us, being in the condition we appear to be in at present—when we never think the same about the same subjects, the most important ones at that—to sound off as though we're somebodies. That's how far behind in education we've fallen. (527e)

Being poorly educated, he says, we shamefully fail to find common ground, fail to think the same things about the same subjects, so cannot see the truth of the matter. Socrates believes that one of the core tenets of Socratism provides support for the imperative of self-refutation: *not submitting an important belief to the scrutiny that could refute it is akin to not paying one's due for the harm one has done.* One should "pay one's due" by submitting one's own belief to self-refutation (Sermamoglou-Soulmaidi 2017, 277-301). Why? Because of the harm one has done? But what harm has one done? Holding a belief that has not survived the elenchtic process? Is one causing harm to others by holding a belief that has not yet passed dialogic muster? Socrates alludes to a certain symmetry between the tenet and the practice, but it remains unclear what harm one has done, such that one should pay a debt by striving to refute one's own belief. It may be that we are not addressing eristics in any or all dialogue, but only the shortcomings of sophistical teaching itself. In round terms, the sophist causes harm by placing false beliefs and expectations into the minds of gullible "students". The harm they do to the student, and to truth itself, is "worse" than the harm the student experiences. But what is worst of all is that the sophist shamelessly acknowledges no debt owed for the harm that has been done by misguided teaching. If only the sophist imposed the imperative of self-refutation upon themselves! Unfortunately, if the imperative is limited solely to sophistry, it would be of little interest to us. But if it has wider application to dialectics generally, then we return to wondering why it is not explicit in other

Platonic discussions of dialectic and implicit in the broader philosophical analysis mentioned earlier.

Curiously, something of the same happens in Euthydemus. After struggling with the brothers Euthydemus and Dionysodorus throughout a lengthy dialogue, Socrates maintains not only that they are mistaken, but also that the way he is proven right illustrates something about dialectics itself. In challenging the brothers' sophistical notion that nothing one believes can be (shown to be) false, Socrates suggests that such a notion is incompatible with the imperative to refute refutable beliefs, including one's own. At 286d, it is suggested that if it is impossible to speak or even think what is false, then there is no such thing as a false opinion, and so no ignorance at all! Indeed, the sophists even challenge Socrates to refute this notion, though he rightly wonders whether any such refutation is possible if there are no false beliefs (or even ignorant people!). Thus, Euthydemus insists that there is no such thing as refutation either. Compounding this error, Dionysodorus claims to have shown up in order to teach the notion that there are no false beliefs, when it is unclear that there are any ignorant people in need of teaching, or any counter-claims in need of refutation. When Socrates ensnares him in the implicit contradiction, the sophist can only respond with silence. Later, when Socrates summarizes one of Euthydemus' s notions of knowledge, Euthydemus claims that Socrates is "refuted out of his own mouth" (293d-e). In other words, when Socrates is offering a clearer formulation of his interlocutor's claim, the other person thinks that Socrates has somehow refuted his own view. Even later, at 295, Socrates strikes the head squarely by stating incredulously that, *although he is happy to be refuted*, the sophists' teaching leads him to the idea that everyone has knowledge all the time. On this score, once Socrates concedes that if one has knowledge, it is knowledge of something, and one has it by means of the soul, Dionysodorus and Socrates come to verbal blows, with the former claiming that the latter refuses to answer a question he understands but does not want to see refuted, while the latter does not want to answer the question without clarifying what is meant or intended by it. At the end of the dialogue, when asked what he thought of the brothers' skills in dialectic, Socrates states that even the common people impressed by such techniques ought to feel ashamed to defend them and use them to refute other positions (303d). Left unchallenged, such wise men feel no need to explain themselves, since their beliefs cannot be false. "Keeping clear of risk and conflict", sophists at once refuse to expose their own positions to refutation whilst insisting that they can refute any argument against their own (305d).

Ultimately, another core tenet of Socrates, that one is wise only insofar as one knows nothing, survives refutation even as Socrates uses it to challenge the sophists contradictory notion that there are no false beliefs. Along the way, he alludes to the imperative of self-refutation, though nowhere near as clearly as in Gorgias. His interlocutors in Euthydemus are rather unskilled, even oafish, conversationalists, and so he has a challenge he did not quite have in Gorgias: on the one hand, the sophists here are too dim-witted to understand how they might benefit in helping Socrates to refute his own position, and on the other, the sophists seem to think that Socrates is actually refuting his own position when he is merely summarizing their position for the purpose of refuting it!

Gorgias (and Euthydemus, to a smaller extent) provides us with an intriguing problem, and little in the way of a solution to it. it is unlike other dialogues in that Socrates seems to acknowledge the imperative to self-refutation as important with dialectics within the context of *politikē,* an art of living involving dialogue. What is intriguing is that, where Socrates discusses the nature of dialectics itself, especially in respect of some moment or movement of dialogue, he does not even allude to this imperative. We may be left with a sense that self-refutation has no place in dialectics, since this moment in Gorgias is so exceptional. Or we may suspect that the imperative is not only commensurate with dialectics, even if Socrates makes little or nothing of it, but even necessary for it to achieve its goals. How we respond may depend on what we take refutation to mean.

The Shame in Refutation

Perhaps nowhere does Plato address the matter of 'refutation' more clearly than in Sophist. In particular, he understands it to mean a "cleansing", specifically a cleansing of false knowledge (230) and empty beliefs (231b). In fact, we are meant to understand that admonition is necessary in this process in order to cleanse the recalcitrant soul of beliefs that interfere with the process of learning (231d). Plato's Sophist thus provides us with a lead for understanding refutation in terms of admonition (and with it shaming), cleansing and learning.

What is meant by 'refutation' here? Are we to understand that refuting something just means finding fault with it, discovering it to be wanting in some respect, politely exposing its inadequacy? Perhaps that is the way Socrates often gently lets someone down. But ἐλεγξάντων has nothing nice about it. ἐλέγχω has the sense of disgracing something, shaming it. Shame is explicitly important in Gorgias, especially in the dialogue with Polus. We might do well to notice that, for Socrates, there is a distinction between two kinds of shame: shamefulness, which carries with it a sense of inhibition or internal constraint on motivation and volition, and being ashamed, the negative feeling that overcomes an interlocutor in the moment they realize they are profoundly mistaken about a claim (Cain: 2008, 218). We may be meant to think that a sense of shame impels an interlocutor to make claims responsibly and a sense of being ashamed reminds them of the consequences of not doing so.

For my part, there is something unnecessarily excessive in the notion that refutation is a kind of shaming. There is a fascinating moment in Euthydemus in which one of the sophists, Dionysodorus, exclaims that when good men "speak ill" of bad things, there is the potential for abusing the one who holds bad things dear. But Socrates replies that ruining or destroying a person is a condition of making them good, so a good teacher can strongly admonish someone so long as they are striving to make them good. And Ctesippus adds something important to what Socrates is saying: contradiction is not a form of abuse (284d-285d). We are meant to make a connection between the often harsh effort to refute a belief and the non-abusive attitude one has towards the person who holds it. As we have heard Socrates say in Gorgias, "It's not you I am after" (453c), but something else.

Refutation, I tender to surmise, has the *qualitative strength of a shaming*: one strives to refute a false belief with the same intensity that one admonishes what is disgraceful. Socrates, then, is not merely recognizing an imperative to refute any idea that is inadequate for a task, but to submit his own beliefs to a process of refutation with the very force of conviction one has when admonishing the shameful. He might be "ironic" about the wisdom of the "wise" men from whom he seeks wisdom. He might be "ironic" about his own desire to learn from those who can only teach him by means of error. But he cannot be at all "ironic" about the imperative to refute his own false beliefs if he should do so with the intensity of condemning what is disgraceful.

And in what sense can Socrates be pleased to be refuted if refutation has the force of shaming? Does this suggest that being refuted results in learning something, such that one is pleased to learn it even if it was painful to be shamed for having believed otherwise? There is clearly a problem with the notion of pleasure in the conversation with Callicles (Jenks 2007, 204-207), but we are addressing the problem of whether the pleasure of being refuted and the shame of being refuted can be compresent in Socrates' participation in the dialogue. At a stretch, one might find some trace of self-refutation in some of Socrates' efforts to "examine" himself. But if self-refutation would have the force of shaming, one is unlikely to find a situation in which he is willing to undergo such humiliation. For example, if a primary interlocutor affirms a thesis or belief by which they live, then according to Vlastos some part of his or her life has been "indicted or discredited". Seeing that refutation has the force of shaming, he asserts that

> You get into the argument when you realize that this is the price you have to pay for it—that in the course of it your ego may experience the unpleasant sensation of a bloody nose—takes courage. To search for moral truth that may prove your own life wrong takes humility that is not afraid of humiliation. (Vlastos 1995, 17-18)

Of course, readers often see how primary interlocutors react to this threat: by being ignorant of it, or feigning ignorance so as not to have to "deal" with it, or hurtful accusations and threats leveled back at Socrates himself. Callicles might threaten to give Socrates a bloody nose (Gorgias 486c, also 508d), but is Socrates' ego willing to take a punch to the nose, as it were? Better yet, is he willing to deal himself that blow, courageously striving to refute his own beliefs with the very force of shaming, often with humiliating results? If, on the off chance that Socrates actually submitted himself in the way that he often casually insists he would, would he acknowledge shamefully and humiliatingly that his life would have been wrong in some important respect, a moral disaster? This would clearly have gigantic ramifications for his own life, and consequently, for his status as secondary interlocutor. Who would Socrates be if he had succeeded in humbling himself? How could he teach others how to discover truth within themselves if he himself had lived in moral disaster for so long?

Perhaps it would be possible to invert this: if we were to say that Socrates is even more entitled to guide dialectically in the way that he does because he had shamefully submitted himself to acknowledging his moral disaster, then what are we to make of the textual Socrates, the secondary interlocutor who has done no such thing? By what right does he "teach" without having undergone what he demands all primary interlocutors undergo?

Gadamer on the Internalization of Dialectic

Perhaps the primary characteristic of Gadamer's approach to dialectics in dialogue is the urgency of the pursuit of truth and the necessity of being unrelenting in its pursuit. He insists that Plato understands phronesis to be necessary for true dialectic, that is to say, to the practice of "holding undisconcertingly to what lies before the eyes as right, and in not allowing anything to convince one that it is not" (Gadamer 1986, 52, 54 and 41, see also Gadamer 1980, 11). In spite of the emphasis on reaching consensus by work done on the basis of shared understanding, Gadamer never loses this sense that there is urgency in dialogue.

Can Gadamer help us grapple with the imperative to self-refutation? Some commentators suggest he can, though without developing the argument. For example, Kevin Decker writes:

> It is the case that one of the products of dialogue is an increasing sense of self-knowledge; overcoming mere opinion in ourselves through the realization of its inferior status can be seen as the meta-level goal of any inquiry. (Decker 2000, 13)

This claim is made in the context of a discussion of the priority of the question and a standard of truth, but is not developed. Catherine Zuckert has also directly addressed the notion of self-refutation: "If one is really to learn anything from a text or a person and so to expand one's own horizon, one has to be open to the possibility that the other view is correct and one's own is wrong" (Zuckert 1996, 90). This assertion takes place at the confluence of claims about hermeneutics and interpersonal dialogue, but it does not develop any special understanding of refutation in internal dialogue.

For the Gadamer of *Truth and Method*, the status of the question and the nature of openness to questioning determine the value of dialectic in any conversation. With sophistry in particular and perhaps rhetoric in general in mind, Gadamer makes a simple distinction between authentic and inauthentic dialogue, the former determined by the proper role of dialectic within it, the latter the lack (or perversion) of it. In inauthentic dialogue, each interlocutor seeks only to prove oneself 'right', does not seek insight, proposes questions that run no risk of not being answered, and overall does not want to know because he or she does not know that they do not know. But Gadamer is insistent that the problem is not with poor participation in dialogue alone, but with the lack of proper questioning. If an interlocutor thinks their claims are already justified, then they cannot even ask the right questions. In that sense, it is more difficult to ask the questions proper to dialectic than to answer the proper question once it has been posed. At the incipience of dialectic in a conversation, asking a question brings something into the open, at which point the answer is not settled. When the question is open, the answer is undetermined. Before justification is found, the dialectic is sustained in indeterminacy. But this indeterminacy dissolves when a question reveals a specific, material opposition between "this or that". This material opposition becomes even more determinate when counterinstances are proposed, weighed, and found to be inadequate (Gadamer 1989, 362-4). Gadamer has provided an intriguing description of the development of the form of dialectic, from the indeterminacy of the asking, the determinacy of the question when answers are proposed, to the further specificity once an answer is settled.

However, this provides only the framework of dialectic. In his much earlier *Plato's Dialectical Ethics*, Gadamer offers a more detailed analysis of dialectic in respect of the subject of discussion and the roles of the interlocutors. Inauthentic dialogue here is understood in terms of a degenerate form of speech, which is a form of dialogue without dialectic. If the primary interlocutor professes to understand Socrates when he contradicts him, without addressing the contradiction, he or she is thereby "protected" from that contradiction. One is pushing the other person away in order to be unreachable oneself (Gadamer 1991, 37-8). Clearly, in such an instance one has not fostered the conditions of a shared understanding.

In order to develop his notion of authentic dialogue, Gadamer compares the development of shared understanding and "scientific conversation". Each is largely shaped in response to the "facts of the matter" as proposed and worked through in dialogue. Each interlocutor must be open to the assistance of the other to help one to gain access to the facts of the matter. Gadamer insists that the interlocutors must share an "antecedent understanding"' about "things", claims about them and what qualifies as "a reason". But in conversation generally, this is not merely the result of proposing reasons that provide access to the fact of the matter, as in scientific inquiry. It is mainly determined by whether the other person's agreement or disagreement is sought.

> For if it is possible to contradict it, one's claim is refuted; but at the same time, each contradiction contains a new insight and thus a pointer to a correct account. The substantive productivity of conversation consists in its letting such contradictions indicate the direction of its search. (Gadamer 1991, 39)

If one does not do this, then inauthentic dialogue ensues. Gadamer understands this inauthenticity as being the result of a certain exclusion within the conversation: Socrates can exclude the other, the other can exclude themselves, and, most interestingly, Socrates can exclude himself from it. If the primary interlocutor faces Socrates' challenge with the claim that the contradiction is owed to a difference of assumptions (without discussing them), then the conversation ceases to be a "process of coming to a shared understanding about the facts of the matter" (Gadamer 1991, 40). There is the same result if Socrates contradicts the primary interlocutor's claim without being able to account for this contradiction. In that case, Socrates has excluded himself from the conversation by constantly professing to understand the other's assumptions without accounting for the contradictions of his own position. Before we proceed to the situation in which Socrates excludes himself, we ought to take note of the consequences of Gadamer's notion of shared understanding. Since the interlocutors share a common "reason", as is necessary for the fact of the matter to be accessible, the other interlocutor is "in no way different from any other person, or better, he is needed only in the ways in which he is precisely not different from others". In other words, anyone with whom Socrates is conversing dialectically could be replaced by most anyone else. The other is a strictly formal self: an abstract self defined by its ability to ask questions properly, refer to "reason" to justify claims, etc.

Such a claim is especially interesting as we turn to the situation in which Socrates excludes himself from the conversation.

> So it is the structure of this idea of coming to an understanding which explains why I am able, *even without speaking to another person*, to press forward, in a process of scientific, reason-giving disclosing and appropriating, and to arrive at the real logos. For thought that is not expressed is also speech, except that *the other person with whom I speak is in this case myself.* But the only reason why this is possible is that even in a real conversation, *the other person is not needed for anything other than what I can do for myself:* to return to an explication that has been given and to test it *against my understanding* of the facts of the matter. (Gadamer 1991, 41, italics added)

This is a shocking claim in the context of Socratic dialectics. Gadamer continues with the observation that "confronting oneself freely with contradiction" requires that one overcome one's own tendencies, much as one must overcome the tendencies of an interlocutor. Whether one is engaging with an other person or with oneself, one must "attend only to the substantive intention of what is said and not to what the speech expresses". If "conversing" with oneself, one confronts one's own logos while disregarding it as one's own. Just as the other person is actually just a formal self in the light of reason's access to the matter at hand, so is one's own self merely a formal self in the same way. Not only is one other person transposable with any other, but an other is transposable with oneself, so long as all such selves are formal in the required way. Gadamer makes the same claim about teaching: as long as the subject at hand is teachable, then any formal self could teach it and any formal self could learn it. He writes:

> Thus the teachability of knowledge follows from the scientific logos' claim to address the facts of the matter in their necessity by showing how they follow from reasons.

> This function of the other person within the tendency of conversation toward coming to a substantive understanding constitutes the very essence of the dialectical. For a dialectical contradiction of a thesis is not simply a

contrary thesis which someone opposes to the stated opinion as his (or her) opinion. A dialectical contradiction is not present when one opinion is opposed by another; instead, it is constituted precisely when one and the same faculty of reason has to grant validity to both the opinion and the counter-opinion. It is not a contradiction in the dialectical sense when another person speaks against something, but only when *a thing* speaking against it, *whether it is another person or myself who has stated this*. (Gadamer 1991, 44, second italics added)

Consequently, if we return to the matter of Socrates excluding himself from a "real conversation" by internalizing the dialectic, it would seem that a proper dialectical contradiction is not found between opinions, but between a thesis and a thing, whether the interlocutor's questioning and answering assists in its disclosure, or this is performed within the self in the disclosure of a claim and one's grasp of the logos.

"Strong Logos" in the Work of Refutation

Gadamer's work on dialectic is especially strong in offering *external* descriptions of the origin and work of refutation in dialogue, as is well known. But for those looking for an *internal* evaluation of the refutation, what it is that is originating and functioning in this way, there is considerably less with which to work. In respect of the external description, Gadamer puts it best in *Plato's Dialectic Ethics*: "Socrates' logical traps are not meant to be the manipulations of a virtuoso technician which are simply applied where they promise success; instead, they are living forms of a process of seeking shared understanding which always has the facts of the matter themselves before it and which *finds its criterion solely in it success in developing its capacity to see these facts*" (Gadamer 1991, 58, italics added). "Shared understanding" and "facts of the matter" are familiar enough, but the "criterion" for assessing the success of understanding in grasping such facts is likely less so.

In order to elucidate the role of criteria of refutation in dialogue, we need to move forward from this point to understand the overall purpose of dialectic in working toward the unitary purpose of the good as well as work back to a pre-understanding of this good. As we shall see, refutation in Gadamer is largely a matter of working out criteria for testing the relationship between a claim that is subjected to the work of shared understanding. In this respect, Gadamer thinks of himself as challenging a traditional prejudice about dialogue. We may think that an "I" is set over against a 'Thou", as if they are distinct entities that collide in dialogue. But in order to make this distinction at all, a common understanding and even a common "accord" is first necessary for there to be any such dialogical situation in the first place (Gadamer 1976, 7-8). There is good reason to believe that Gadamer regards this as a commonly shared pre-understanding of "the good" itself. There is shared understanding between the interlocutors, but the justification of any claim between them is only possible on the basis of a pre-understanding. Each interlocutor can only participate in a common process of "coming to an understanding" if there is already acknowledgement that the explication of a shared understanding between them is possible (Gadamer 1991, 63-64).

The matter of testing is very important here. In *Truth and Method*, we find Gadamer mentioning an "art of testing" in questioning in which the interlocutor tries to bring out the real strength of the logos, not merely to poke holes in its weak points. The art of testing is an art of such strengthening (Gadamer 1989, 367). He devotes considerably more attention to this matter in his earlier studies of Plato. As he says there, one is always testing one's explicit understanding of oneself and one's world against what one takes as a rational grounding. The search for a grounding of such understanding comes in the form of a testing by both interlocutors: together they are "testing the logos to see whether it is refutable". Testing, he avers, sets up something "in the middle", accessible to both, with neither interlocutor having any personal stake in it. Yet, each of the interlocutors experiences the testing and its results as a work of understanding itself. It has consequences for his or her self-understanding (Gadamer 1991, 64-65). The very "justification" of the person professing the claim is at stake, since the task of the work of dialectic is to liberate the person from their ignorance (Gadamer 1991, 53-54, and 57). After all, when logos is proposed in a dialogue, its distinct claim to being an item of knowledge is tested.

In discussing "inauthentic" dialogue and the degenerate speech involved in it, Gadamer takes note of an important difference between refutations. For Gadamer, refutation functions differently in authentic dialectic and in the degenerate forms of speech that contrast with it. In sophistry, it would seem, the teacher makes a certain claim to knowledge, and in doing so, a "disposition over the strongest logos". Exactly how we can characterize the "strength" of the logos deserves mention.

> This "strength" is due to the impossibility of the logos's coming to grief, the impossibility of contradicting it. In this sense, every logos that wants to be knowledge has to be strong, and to the extent that it is irrefutable, it is strong. "Strength," looked at in this way, is simply an expression of the adequacy to the facts of the matter of what is said. In this way, strength is not something that is striven for for its own sake; rather it is a side effect of the striving to make what one says adequate to the facts of the matter. (Gadamer 1991, 46).

This is how the "strength" of a claim under consideration can be justified. Gadamer continues.

> But it can also be separated from the idea of adequacy to the facts of the matter, and its being stronger can be striven for in the interests of ascendency over other people. *This* way of aiming at the stronger logos is characterized by the fact that its goal is, by using possibilities that are inherent in discourse itself, to make any randomly chosen logos (even a logos that is substantively weaker, that is, one that is not adequate to the facts of the matter) into a stronger one and thus to fulfill the (otherwise unfulfillable) claim always to have the stronger logos. (Gadamer 1991, 46-7).

Gadamer is not merely making the familiar claim that the sophist aims to win arguments, to make the weaker argument seem stronger etc. The teaching sophist claims to have the strongest logos at hand and is thereby able to justify most any claim submitted to scrutiny. Why? Because of a difference in the functioning of the criterion of strength. In authentic dialogue, strength will be striven for, for its own sake, in the way that Socrates attempts, according to Gadamer. But when the strength of the logos is merely a side effect of the striving for justification and is an instrument of self-empowerment, the criterion of "strength" functions differently.

There is another equally important difference in the work of justification in authentic and inauthentic dialogue. If the (sophistical) interlocutor turns out to lack knowledge in a certain instance, if what they claim to be irrefutable is refuted,

> then what happens is not that a more correct explication of the facts of the matter is developed from the substantive content of the refutation and from the logos that was initially put forward. Instead, *the place of the refuted logos is filled with a new one that is oriented toward the refuting argument, and only toward it.* Thus, each logos, when it is refuted, is *entirely dropped and replaced with a new one* that seems to be *strong enough* to stand up against this refutation in particular. Thus each logos is chosen only for the sake of its being stronger. It is meant to be definitive and not to open up a substantive discussion. So if it is refuted, it is not retained, but *disappears entirely*, without regard to whether what it said exhibited something of the facts of the matter in question or not. (Gadamer 1991, 47-48, italics added)

We might notice the behavior of the *logos* throughout this process. Once a claim is refuted, a new claim is made that is meant to withstand the argument that refuted the first claim. The interlocutor who proposed the refuted belief and now pushes a second is simply trying to get a belief, any belief, through the filter of refutation. What should have happened, according to Gadamer, is that something ought to have been learned from the refutation that would help understand the facts of the matter. The original claim should have been posited as definitive and should have helped foster a substantive discussion. Rather than simply following through on lessons learned by refutation, the interlocutor simply switches loyalty, dropping the claim that was originally put forth and now proposing another. It is as if the whole point of the dialogue is to finally get a claim through the process of refutation, presumably for the purpose of being proven "right".

Refutation and Dialectic as a "Way of Being"

Dialectic, it should be clear by now, is an exercise in seeking "true" justification, that is to say, justification for the claims one makes, not merely justification that proves one right; but beyond this, it is justification of one's way of being. Such dialectic, whether in subjective thought or interpersonal dialogue, consists in the giving and receiving of justification for beliefs, and for the believer in believing them (Gadamer 1986, 38-39). Like Vlastos, Gadamer understands that Plato's Socrates is a philosopher fully committed to truth as a way of being, to dialectics as an art of living, in the terms Socrates proposes in Gorgias.

Self-understanding obviously will play a role in such justification. Socrates discloses to his primary interlocutors that they lack understanding *of* something, and do not know *that* they lack *this* understanding, and so lack *self-*understanding. Conversely, there is self-understanding in the respect that there is understanding, and a knowledge that this is understood. Gadamer writes:

> Plato gives self-understanding a more general meaning: wherever the concern is knowledge that cannot be acquired by any learning, but instead only through examination of oneself and of the knowledge on believes one has, we are dealing with dialectic. Only in dialogue—*with oneself or with others*—can on get beyond the mere prejudices of prevailing conventions. And only the person who is really guided by such pre-knowledge of the good will be able to hold to it unerringly. (Gadamer 1986, 43, italics added).

We might notice again the notion that there can be dialogue with oneself alone, so long as one is examining one's beliefs and knowledge, with the additional benefit of being able to step outside of mere conventions. This understanding is not merely some grasp of conscious activity, but a "mode of the event of being", a relation in which the process of understanding is more important than its *relata*, the one who understands and that which is understood. This process is one in which the substantial self involves something very like a loss of self, in which it is "taken up into a higher determination" in the play of understanding, the game that dialogue is. In this scenario, understanding of this or that is part of a process of overall self-understanding, not in the sense that the self comes to "realize" itself more by means of understanding, but in the narrower sense that, in understanding some subject matter, the self "happens". There is enrichment in and of the happening that the self is, without the self becoming a possession that is ever more possessed as understanding grows (Gadamer 1976, 50-51, 54-55 and 57).

The question here is whether refutation plays a role in dialectics as a way of being, whether understanding that amounts to self-understanding is arrived at on a journey in which refutation plays a role. If there is a lack of understanding, then it is not known that understanding is lacked. But if there is knowledge that understanding is lacked, is that the result of elenchtic work, of refutation, specifically refutation of some belief in which one's way of being is implicated? Does the "happening" of the self involve self-refutation, the refutation of a sense of selfhood drawn from not knowing that one does not understanding oneself in a truthful respect? Perhaps the convolution of questions of this kind signals the complexity of the self-understanding of a self that is "happening", or rather, the "happening" of self-understanding that is taken to be the self.

Ultimately, the paramount question issue is this: does Gadamer think that dialectics can be an internal matter involving self-understanding without any external interlocutor? Does he think that the self can, in its work of understanding and its way of being, examine and refute a belief, without the influence of any external interlocutor. The Gadamer of *Plato's Dialectical Ethics* certainly thinks so, though the Gadamer of "Socratic knowing and not knowing" is less forthright. Even the Gadamer of *Truth and Method* may defend such an internal dialectic 'hermeneutically', so long as there is a stress on texts, and the notions such texts convey, and the tradition in which such texts convey such notions; but in terms of his representation of Socratic dialogue as such, he is more reticent about the possibility, as it is in such dialogue that "shared understanding", the "fusion of horizons" and other Gadamerian concepts help us to unpack interpersonal matters. Dialectic, as an art of life in which one's way of being is as much formed as it is at issue, involves the internal dynamic of proposing, examining and if necessary, refuting beliefs in a work of understanding in which the happening of the self is implicated. This may involve texts, their content, and their tradition, or it may simply involve introspection that treats one's belief as if it were "like" a text, with content, and even with a tradition.

Conclusion

Does Gadamer help us to understand the original problem? Which Gadamer? The Gadamer of *Plato's Dialectical Ethics*, who may be silent about the imperative of self-refutation, but at least acknowledges that there can be an internal dialectic structured much like an interpersonal one? Or the Gadamer of *Truth and Method*, who contrasts Socratic dialogue with hermeneutics, noting however that they are equally though differently dialectical. In this case, dialogue and reading texts in a tradition are equally game-like, though there is little suggestion that such gaming could be akin to an internal dialectic. The point is not that the development of a mature hermeneutic theory enables Gadamer to reject his more youthful admission that an internal dialectic (of self-refutation) is possible; on the contrary, internal dialectic, mediated by the text, has been raised up into a hermeneutic context. At first, all dialectic is interpersonal, unless one has an inner "dialogue" with oneself about some "fact of the matter". But later, dialectic is hermeneutic, so that whether one is speaking with others or with oneself, the relation is akin to reading a text.

Although Gadamer makes much of other Socratic dialogues and little of Gorgias, there are interesting points of correspondence. For example, when he emphasizes the importance of persistence in inquiry and the clarification of claims, this is supported not only in Protagoras and Phaedo, but also Gorgias (e.g., 453c). In his discussion of the role of non-knowledge and the discovery of facts of the matter that become benchmarks of dialogue, we find this not only in Charmides but also Gorgias (e.g., 472d and 527e). And surely no dialogue better illustrates the degenerate speech of inauthentic dialogue than Euthydemus (see for example, 293d-e). One could only wish that, given the matter of self-refutation, this engagement was a bit more explicit.

What we need from Gadamer is a solution to the problem posed by Gorgias 458-a-b. Given the other-directed nature of Socratic dialectics, specifically the practice of guiding the primary interlocutor through their own beliefs, can the secondary interlocutor strive to refute their own beliefs? Indeed, is there an imperative to do so, since the pursuit of truth, the elimination of false beliefs, and the acquisition of knowledge seem to imply it? In other words, refutation is not simply something that "happens" in dialogue, exigently emerging on occasion, but something that the secondary interlocutor, who is guiding the dialogue with questioning, should willfully strive to do.

Gadamer's "later" work on dialogue and dialectic provides us with a unique external description of interpersonal relations. It emphasizes the role of understanding, specifically, on the one hand, the shared understanding out of which proper dialectic emerges and on the other hand, the pre-understanding of the good—the good at which the inquiry aims—that impels each interlocutor into the dialogue in the first place. The possibility of refutation can be found in the former in terms of the nature of the facts of the matter at stake in that dialogue, and in the latter in terms of the criteria for testing claims proposed in the dialogue. One might conceive of a myriad of ways understanding might benefit from refutation, but little of this is made explicit in Gadamer's work.

We might also take note that the distinction between authentic dialogue (in which understanding figures correctly in dialectic) and inauthentic dialogue (which has little or no dialectic) offers little more help. In particular we can see this in the fate of the refuted claim. In inauthentic dialogue, the secondary interlocutor can propose an irrefutable claim that proves to be refutable. He or she then drops the claim and strives to propose another claim that would satisfy the criteria that found the first claim wanting. This tells us little about self-refutation, since the secondary interlocutor, with a false sense of mastery of dialogue, refuses to acknowledge refutation. Even in authentic dialogue, where the secondary interlocutor presses on to find out the truth behind the criteria that enabled a claim to be refuted, we learn nothing about whether there is an imperative to refute one's belief, only loosely what to do once it has been.

We are also faced with the question whether the self-refutation of the secondary interlocutor requires the presence of the primary interlocutor at all. Once the "early" Gadamer proposes the notion of formal selfhood, such that it is not the specific, empirical "other" but a formal other that ideally participates in the dialogue, then not only can one "self" be replaced with another, but the "other" can be transposed into the "self". Consequently, it seems that dialectic can take place in the absence of the other's presence altogether. So long as it has the same formal structure as an interpersonal dialogue, there is no reason why there cannot be a dialectic internal to the formal self of the secondary dialectic. This has little place in Gadamer's "later", hermeneutic work, where emphasis is placed on conversation and interpretation.

Where Gadamer's work is helpful on the subject of self-refutation is in its development of the importance of criteria for testing claims. Sadly, we can see *that* there are such criteria and to some extent how such criteria "behave" in the course of dialogue, not what those criteria are and how they are modified. One might think that such criteria would stimulate the work of refutation, but the connection remains somewhat unclear. It is evident that such criteria are implicated in the work of accessing the facts of the matter, but whether some claim can be refuted precisely because criteria adequate to the task of refuting it are developed, is left open. This is doubly troubling since the very "justification" of the self is at stake. Gadamer occasionally asserts that refutation is at work in the play of justification of a belief, and indeed the believer; but nowhere does he show what refutation consists in. Generally speaking, we learn much about the dialectical framework of dialogue and the role of shared understanding, and somewhat less about the nature of the self in respect of its self-understanding. However, whether there is an imperative to self-*refutation* in the former and *self*-refutation in the latter remains open to further inquiry.

Dr. Benjamin Hutchens, Rutgers, The State University of New Jersey,
Newark NJ, hcb24[at]newark.rutgers.edu

References

Benardete, Seth. 1991. *The Rhetoric of Morality and Philosophy: Plato's Gorgias and Phaedrus.* Chicago: University of Chicago.

Cain, R. Benson. 2008. "Shame and Ambiguity in Plato's Gorgias." *Philosophy and Rhetoric*, vol. 41., no. 3: 212-237.

Decker, Kevin. 2000. "The limits of radical openness: Gadamer on Socratic dialectic and Plato's idea of the good." *Symposium,* IV: 5-32.

Gadamer, Hans-Georg. 1976a. 'The universality of the hermeneutic problem" in idem. *Philosophical Hermeneutics.* Translated by David E. Linge, editor. Berkeley: University of California Press, 3-17.

Gadamer, Hans-Georg. 1976b. "On the problem of self-understanding" in idem. *Philosophical Hermeneutics.* Translated by David E. Linge, editor. Berkeley: University of California Press, 44-58.

Gadamer, Hans-Georg. 1980. "*Logos* and *Ergon* in Plato's Lysis" in idem. *Dialogue and Dialectic: Eight hermeneutical studies on Plato.* Translated by P. Christopher Smith. New Haven: Yale University Press, 1-21.

Gadamer, Hans-Georg. 1986. 'Socratic knowing and not-knowing' in idem. *The Idea of the Good in Platonic-Aristotelian Philosophy.* Translated by P. Christopher Smith. New Haven: Yale University Press, 33-63.

Gadamer, Hans-Georg. 1989. *Truth and Method.* Second revised edition. Joel Weinsheimer and D.G. Marshall, trans. New York: Crossroad Press.

Gadamer, Hans-Georg. 1991. *Plato's Dialectical Ethics: Phenomenological interpretations relating to the Philebus.* Robert M. Wallace, trans. New Haven: Yale University Press.

Irwin, Terence. 1995. *Plato's Ethics.* Oxford: Oxford University Press.

Jenks, Roy. 2007. "The Sounds of Silence: Rhetoric and dialectic in the refutation of Callicles in Plato's Gorgias." *Philosophy and Rhetoric.* vol. 40, no. 2: 201-215.

Plato. 1997. *Complete Works.* John. M. Cooper, editor. Indianapolis: Hackett Publishing.

Sermamoglou-Soulmaidi, Georgia. 2017. "The refutation of Polus in Plato's Gorgias revisited." *Apeiron* (50) 3: 277-310.

Scott, Gary Alan. 2002. *Does Socrates have a method? Rethinking the Elenchus in Plato's Dialogues and Beyond.* University Park: Pennsylvania State University Press.

Teloh, Henry. 1986. *Socratic Education in Plato's Early Dialogues.* Notre Dame, IN: University of Notre Dame.

Teloh, Henry. 2007. 'Rhetoric, refutation and what Socrates believes in Plato's *Gorgias"* in *Proceedings of the Boston Area Colloquium in Ancient Philosophy*, 23: 57-77.

Tusi, Jacqueline. 2020. "Between rhetoric and sophistry: the puzzling case of Plato's Gorgias" in *apeiron* 53(1): 59-80.

Vlastos, Gregory. 1995. *Studies in Greek Philosophy. Volume II: Socrates, Plato and their tradition.* Daniel. W. Graham, editor. Princeton: Princeton University Press.

Wardy, Robert. 1996. *The Birth of Rhetoric: Gorgias, Plato and their Successors.* London: Routledge.

Zuckert, Catherine. 1996. *Postmodern Platos: Nietzsche, Heidegger, Gadamer, Strauss, Derrida.* Chicago: University of Chicago Press.

Zuckert, Catherine. 2010. "Why Socrates and Thrasymachus become friends." *Philosophy and Rhetoric*, vol. 43, No. 2: 163-172.